AF540876

NATURAL ECOSYSTEM AND CLIMATE CHANGE

ENV BOOKS SERIES

NATURAL ECOSYSTEM AND CLIMATE CHANGE

Editors

Dr. Pawan Kumar 'Bharti'

Vice President (Executive)
Society for Environment, Health, Awareness of Nutrition & Toxicology (SEHAT)
1775, Sohan Ganj, Near Clock Tower, Delhi-7, India
E-mail: *gurupawanbharti@rediffmail.com*

Dr. Khwairakpam Gajananda

Associate Professor
Addis Ababa University
Addis Ababa, Ethiopia

DISCOVERY PUBLISHING HOUSE PVT. LTD.
NEW DELHI-110 002

Published by:

Tilak Wasan

DISCOVERY PUBLISHING HOUSE PVT. LTD.

4383/4B, Ansari Road, Darya Ganj

New Delhi-110 002 (India)

Phone : +91-11-23279245, 43596064-65

Fax : +91-11-23253475

E-mail : discoverypublishinghouse@gmail.com

sales@discoverypublishinggroup.com

web : www.discoverypublishinggroup.com

First Edition: **2015**

ISBN: 978-93-5056-745-6

Natural Ecosystem and Climate Change

Printed at:

Infinity Imaging Systems

Delhi

ENV Books Series, India

Calls lengthy and error free chapters for further volumes of books on various environmental issues. (Send your manuscripts to envbooks@gmail.com)

Founding Editor **(*Editor-in-Chief*)**

Dr. Pawan Kumar 'Bharti'

Society for Environment, Health, Awareness of Nutrition & Toxicology (SEHAT-India)
1775, Sohanganj, Near Clock Tower, Delhi-7, India
E-mail:*gurupawanbharti@rediffmail.com*

Other Titles by Editor-in-Chief:

1. **Advances in Biotechnology and Ecological Sciences (2013)**
   Bharti, P.K., Chauhan, A. and Ray, J. (eds.)
   (ISBN: 978-93-5056-358-8).
2. **Advances in Agriculture and Ecology (2013)**
   Bharti, P.K.; Chauhan, A. and Ezeaku Peter Ikemefuna (eds.)
   (ISBN: 978-93-5056-362-5).
3. **Agriculture and Environmental Biotechnology (2014)**
   Bharti, P.K. and Chauhan, A. (eds.)
   (ISBN: 978-93-5056-479-0).
4. **Agriculture Ecology and Environment (2014)**
   Bharti, P.K. and Olubukola O. Babalola (eds.)
   (ISBN: 978-93-5056-480-6).
5. **Agro-forestry and Climate Change (2014)**
   Bharti, Pawan K. and Singh, Narayan (eds.)
   (ISBN: 978-93-5056-514-8).
6. **Aquaculture and Fisheries Environment (2014)**
   Gupta, S.K. and Pawan K. Bharti (eds.)
   (ISBN: 978-93-5056-408-0).
7. **Aquatic Biodiversity and Pollution (2013)**
   Bharti, P.K.; Chauhan, A. and Kaoud, H.A.H. (eds.)
   (ISBN: 978-93-5056-359-5).

8. **Aquatic Ecology and Biotechnology (2014)**
Bharti, P.K. and Zaki, M.S.A. (eds.)
(ISBN: 978-93-5056-451-6).

9. **Aquatic Environment and Toxicology (2013)**
Bharti, Pawan K. (ed.)
(ISBN: 978-93-5056-236-9).

10. **Biodiversity, Biotechnology & Environmental Conservation (2015)**
Bharti, P.K. and Bhandari, G. (eds.)
(ISBN: 978-93-5056-750-0).

11. **Biodiversity of Aquatic Ecosystem: *Significance, Threat and Conservation* (2013)**
Bharti, P.K. and Kaoud, H.A.H. (eds.)
(ISBN: 978-93-5056-297-0).

12. **Clean Technologies and Environmental Protection (2015)**
Chauhan, A.; Sharma, S. and Bharti, P.K. (eds.)
(ISBN: 978-93-5056-731-9).

13. **Climate Change and Agriculture (2012)**
Bharti, P.K. and Chauhan, Avnish (eds.)
(ISBN: 978-93-5056-148-5).

14. **Climate Change and Biodiversity (2013)**
Bharti, P.K. and Chauhan, Avnish (eds.)
(ISBN: 978-93-5056-360-1).

15. **Conservation and Cultivation of Medicinal Plants (2015)**
Bharti, P.K. and Singh Narayan (eds.)
(ISBN: 978-93-5056-740-1).

16. **Eco-toxicology and Eco-technology (2013)**
Bharti, P.K. and Zaki, M. (eds.)
(ISBN: 978-93-5056-313-7).

17. **Environmental Biotechnology and Application (2013)**
Bharti, P.K. and Chauhan, Avnish (eds.)
(ISBN: 978-93-5056-262-8).

18. **Environmental Conservation and Biotechnology (2014)**
Chauhan, A. and P.K. Bharti (eds.)
(ISBN: 978-93-5056-512-4).

19. **Environmental Health and Problems (2013)**
Bharti, P.K. and Gajananda, Kh. (eds.)
(ISBN: 978-93-5056-263-5).

20. **Environmental Pollution and Biodiversity (2012)**
Bharti, P.K.; Chauhan, Avnish and Kumar, P. (eds.)
(ISBN: 978-93-5056-149-2).

21. **Fisheries and Toxicology (2014)**
Zaki, M.S.A.; Bharti, P.K. and Chauhan, A. (eds.)
(ISBN: 978-93-5056-452-3).

22. **Fish Habitat and Aquaculture (2015)**
Bharti, P.K.; Gupta Kr. Sanjay (eds.)
(ISBN: 978-93-5056-744-9).

23. **Freshwater Ecosystem and Xenobiotics (2013)**
Bharti, P.K.; Zaki, M. and Chauhan, A. (eds.)
(ISBN: 978-93-5056-299-4).

24. **Limnology and Aquatic Science (2015)**
Sharma, S. and Bharti, P.K. (eds.)
(ISBN: 978-93-5056-735-7).

25. **Medicinal Plants:** ***Distribution, Utilization and Significance*** **(2015)**
Sharma, P.; Bharti, P.K. and Narayan Singh (eds.)
(ISBN: 978-93-5056-734-0).

26. **Microbial Applications and Environment (2014)**
Bharti, Pawan K. (ed.)
(ISBN: 978-93-5056-515-5).

27. **Microbial Ecology and Habitat (2014)**
Bharti, Pawan K. (ed.)
(ISBN: 978-93-5056-514-8).

28. **Prakriti me Aushadhi (*in Hindi*) (2012)**
Singh, J.R.; Bharti, P.K. and Bharti, B.
(ISBN: 978-93-5056-200-0).

29. **Seed Technology, Plant Growth and Cropping System (2015)**
Tyagi, P.K. and Bharti, P.K. (eds.)
(ISBN: 978-93-5056-738-8).

30. **Soil Contamination and Conservation (2015)**
Ezeaku, P.I. and Bharti, P.K. (eds.)
(ISBN: 978-93-5056-737-1).

31. **Soil Quality and Contamination (2013)**
Bharti, P.K. and Chauhan, Avnish (eds.)
(ISBN: 978-93-5056-361-8).

32. **Waste Disposal and Management (2015)**
Bharti, P.K.; Tabassum, B. and Bajaj, P. (eds.)
(ISBN: 978-93-5056-729-6).

33. **Water Resources and Agriculture (2014)**
Bharti, P.K. and Ezeaku Peter Ikemefuna (eds.)
(ISBN: 978-93-5056-481-3).

Preface

An ecosystem is an interdependent system of plants, animals, and microorganisms interacting with one another and with their physical environment. An ecosystem can be as large as the Mojave Desert or as small as a local small pond. Ecosystems provide food, goods, medicines, and many other products to people. They also play a vital role in nutrient cycling, water purification and climate moderation on the Earth.

The world's climate is changing, and it will continue to change throughout the 21st century and beyond. Rising temperatures, new precipitation patterns and other changes are already affecting many aspects of human society and the natural world. Climate change is transforming ecosystems on an extraordinary scale, at an extraordinary pace. As each species responds to its changing environment, its interactions with the physical world and the organisms around it change too. This triggers a cascade of impacts throughout the entire ecosystem. These impacts can include expansion of species into new areas, intermingling of formerly non-overlapping species and even species extinctions.

Climate change is happening on a global level, but the impacts on ecosystems are often local and vary from place to place. Climate change will affect nature's ecosystems and the habitats that support life—from oceans to grasslands to forests. Changes are expected to alter the makeup and functioning of ecosystems, as well as some of the critical benefits that ecosystems provide to people. Climate change can threaten ecosystems that have already been weakened by other human activities such as pollution, development, and overharvesting. This fact sheet describes some of the ways that climate change affects ecosystems.

This book updates the subject matter, illustrations and problems to incorporate new concepts and issues related to natural ecosystem, biodiversity, ecology, environmental pollution and global climate change.

Thanks are due to contributors from different institutions and publisher for their interest in this book. I hope this book will provide a multi-disciplinary forum to explore emerging areas in the field of natural ecosystem, biodiversity, ecology, environmental pollution, global warming and global climate change.

–Editors

(envbooks@gmail.com)

Contents

	Preface	
Chapter 1:	Agroforestry for Climate Change Mitigation and Livelihood Security **Alok Kumar Patra**	1-20
Chapter 2:	Global Warming and Microorganisms **Garima Arya** and **Purshotam Kaushik**	21-30
Chapter 3:	Environmental Impacts of Hydropower Projects in Upper Satluj Basin **Kesar Chand, Jagdish Chandra Kuniyal** and **Dev Dutt Sharma**	31-50
Chapter 4:	Role of Human Being in Changing Global Environment and its Impact on Human Health **Monika Khanna** and **Roma Khanna**	51-56
Chapter 5:	Effect of Climate Change on Pesticide Use **Osadebe, Vivian Ogechiand Echezona, Bonaventure C.**	57-70
Chapter 6:	The Contribution of Ruminant Animals to Climate Change and its Mitigation Strategies **Oyeagu Chika E., Akpa Martins O,** and **Ani Augustine O.**	71-86
Chapter 7:	Management Strategies for Rodents within Different Ecosystems **Abd El-Aleem Saad Soliman Desoky**	87-167
Chapter 8:	Climate Change: *An Overview* **Shobhit Rawat**	168-178
	Index	179-183

Pages: 1-20

NATURAL ECOSYSTEM AND CLIMATE CHANGE

Edited by: Dr. Pawan Kumar 'Bharti'; Dr. Khwairakpam Gajananda

ISBN: 978-93-5056-745-6

Edition: 2015

Published by: Discovery Publishing House Pvt. Ltd., New Delhi (India)

CHAPTER - 1

Agroforestry for Climate Change Mitigation and Livelihood Security

Alok Kumar Patra

ABSTRACT

The demographic pressure has significantly reduced the agricultural lands and forest areas during the last few decades, and the requirement of basic needs seems to be inadequately met through the existing land use system. Farming community is also facing challenges due to climate change and environmental degradation, and is trying all means to increase the land productivity. Agroforestry, a combination of agriculture and forestry, has been developed as a science to help farmers increase the productivity, profitability and sustainability of production on their land by combining the best attributes of forestry and agriculture. Today, agroforestry has established itself as a viable approach of integrated land management system not only for meeting the deficits of food, fruit, fodder, firewood and timber but also for ecological considerations like soil conservation, biodiversity preservation, watershed protection, wasteland management, carbon sequestration and mitigation of

Associate Professor (Agronomy), All India Coordinated Research Project on Integrated Farming Systems, Orissa University of Agriculture and Technology, Bhubaneswar - 751 003, Odisha, (India).

climate change effects. With the modern day crisis of shortage of agricultural and forest land, agroforestry is well positioned to provide a perfect balance and a solution.

INTRODUCTION

Feeding the world's population is one of the most pressing challenges facing humanity in the twenty-first century. Food and Agriculture Organization of the United Nations estimates that 925 million people in the world are food insecure, representing around one in six of the world's population. It is also estimated that food production will need to expand by 70 percent at the global level and to double in developing countries to achieve the food and nutritional security. This goal is made ever harder by the increasing impacts of climate change, including extreme weather events.

Man's association with forest is much older than with agriculture. First man was a food gatherer and hunter in forests. Then he learnt the art of domesticating plants and animals. Man's desire to live in a community created settled agriculture. But growth of human and livestock population necessitated acquisition of more and more forest land for cultivation. So the origin of agroforestry practices, *i.e.* growing trees and shrubs with food and fruit crops and grasses is traditional and very old (Tejwani, 2008). Forests as well as trees on farms are a direct source of food and cash income for more than a billion of the world's poorest people. More than 50 million people in India alone depend directly on forests for subsistence. Trees are an integral part of the agricultural systems of many small-scale farmers, providing both cash and subsistence benefits (FAO, 2011).

Now the existence of life is in danger due to pollution, climate change, disease, loss of biodiversity, *etc*. Under all these circumstances agroforestry has shown that besides sustainable agriculture it can also help promote a better environment. Agroforestry has been recognized as a land-use system which is capable of yielding both food and wood and at the same time conserving and rehabilitating the ecosystems. It has two major roles to play, the productive role and the service or protective role (Patra, 2013a). Trees have the dominant role to play in all agroforestry systems for sustainable agriculture and environmental protection.

DEFINITIONS OF AGROFORESTRY

The general concept of agroforestry is to integrate trees and agriculture so as to create a more diversified landscape, while providing the producers with environmental and economic benefits. This relatively young science known as agroforestry was brought from the realm of indigenous knowledge into the forefront of agricultural research and was promoted widely as a sustainability-enhancing practice that combines the best attributes of forestry and agriculture (Bene, 1977).

Several definitions of agroforestry have been suggested since its conceptualization as a land use approach in 1977. In the early 1980s International Council for Research in Agroforestry (ICRAF), Nairobi, Kenya defined agroforestry as "a collective name for land-use systems and technologies where woody perennials (trees, shrubs, palms, bamboos, *etc.*) are deliberately used on the same land management units as agricultural crops and/or animals, in some form of spatial arrangement or temporal sequence". This definition gained wider acceptance and it was used till the mid 1990s. Then in 1996 ICRAF redefined agroforestry as "a dynamic, ecologically based natural resource management system that, through the integration of trees on farms and in the agricultural landscape, diversifies and sustains production for increased social, economic and environmental benefits for land-users at all levels".

The four key characteristics - intentional, intensive, interactive and integrated - are the essence of agroforestry which distinguish it from other agricultural or forestry practices. Thus, a land use practice to be called as agroforestry must satisfy all of these four criteria. Additionally, there are three attributes - productivity, sustainability and adoptability - which, theoretically, all agroforestry systems possess (Nair, 2008).

BENEFITS FROM AGROFORESTRY

Agroforestry is the system of developing agricultural land in combination with forestry technologies. Through this system, land with shrubs and trees are used to grow crop and livestock to encourage health, profitability, productivity, diversity and sustainability. There are numerous benefits to agroforestry as it encourages the adaptation of natural ecological processes within the commercial system. It helps farmers in terms of controlling land degradation, sheltering crop and livestock, improving their landscape and enhancing wildlife habitat while making the most out of commercial opportunities. All that can be done through sustainable agroforestry without the use of complicated machinery and man-made technologies that can be expensive and also have the potential to produce unnecessary waste. Benefits from agroforestry can be grouped under three broad categories; environmental, economic or social benefits.

Environmental Benefits

1. Reduction of pressure on natural forests.
2. More efficient recycling of nutrients by deep rooted trees on the site.
3. Better protection of ecological systems.
4. Reduction of surface run-off, nutrient leaching and soil erosion through impeding effect of tree roots and stems on these processes.
5. Improvement of microclimate, such as lowering of soil surface temperature and reduction of evaporation of soil moisture through a combination of mulching and shading.

6. Increment in soil nutrients through addition and decomposition of litter fall.
7. Improvement of soil structure through the constant addition of organic matter from decomposed litter.

Economic Benefits

1. Increment in an outputs of food, fuel wood, fodder, fertilizer and timber.
2. Reduction in incidence of total crop failure, which is common to single cropping or monoculture systems.
3. Increase in levels of farm income due to improved and sustained productivity.

Social Benefits

1. Improvement in rural living standards from sustained employment and higher income.
2. Improvement in nutrition and health due to increased quality and diversity of food outputs.
3. Stabilization and improvement of communities through elimination of the need to shift sites of farm activities.

NEED OF AGROFORESTRY

Agroforestry, in true sense, has been realized as a need of the day. It does not confine to the regional, geographical or agroclimatic boundaries. Agroforestry concept has got a universal application. Though several factors may contribute to the agroforestry interventions throughout the world these factors are basically interdependent.

Decreasing Land Resources

Owing to increase in population of human and cattle, there is increasing demand of food as well as fodder. However, the land resources are decreasing due to various reasons like conversion of agricultural lands to wastelands as a result of erosion, salinization and water logging; and infra-structural developments. There is slight scope to increase food production by increasing the area under cultivation. A management system therefore, needs to be devised that is capable of producing food from marginal agricultural land and is also capable of maintaining and improving quality of producing environment. The shrinking of land per capita, huge demand supply gap of various kind of woods, food products as well as fodders are making agroforestry viable and alternative land use option.

Limiting Carrying Capacity of the Land

The carrying capacity of the arid and semi-arid regions is overstressed. The consequence is destruction of environment leading to desertification.

Agroforestry interventions hold the key to check soil erosion and leaching loss of nutrients and to improve the soil productivity through biological nitrogen fixation, organic matter addition and efficient nutrient cycling.

Overgrazing

The main reasons of overgrazing are increase in livestock population, increase in size of the herd and decrease in pasture availability. This problem is acute in arid and semi-arid regions. Integrating cultivation of fodder tree species with suitable grasses in the wastelands would address the problem of overgrazing and thus check the desertification effectively.

Soil Erosion

Soil is the most precious natural non-renewable resource. Soil erosion is the major cause of land degradation and loss of productivity. Erosion control has always started with tree and grass planting. Tree roots bind the soil and their leaves break the force of wind and rain on soil. Trees fight soil erosion, conserve rainwater and reduce water runoff. Trees also absorb dangerous chemicals and other pollutants that have entered the soil (Young, 2005). Trees can either store harmful pollutants or actually change the pollutant into less harmful forms. Trees filter sewage and farm chemicals and reduce the effects of animal wastes. Thus, agroforestry practices are most suited for sustainability.

Overexploitation of Land Resource

Heavy fertilization coupled with high irrigation frequencies leads to soil loss, nutrient loss and degradation of land whereas in forest cover land upgradation is a continuous process, it restores soil and moisture conservation and there is a gain from all angles. Taking good points from forest and agriculture, agroforestry concept itself becomes a profitable profession.

Fuel Wood Crisis

There is a global crisis of energy and man is striving hard to find out some alternative source of energy. Fuel wood is one of the established sources to meet energy requirement. About 90% people in the developing countries depend upon wood as source of fuel. But in these regions deforestation is five times more than afforestation. If this continues a time may come when there will be sufficient food but not the fuel to cook. So the only solution is to promote agroforestry.

Depletion of Forest

Forest area is decreasing alarmingly due to demographic pressure and infrastructural developments causing thereby environmental pollution, ecological imbalance, global warming and climate change. Afforestation is costly and involves a long gestation period. There is also scarcity of land for creating new forests. Thus, an individual farmer cannot develop a new forest. But if both agriculture and forest are integrated (i.g. agroforestry) then farmers can very easily adopt it as there will be no reduction in agricultural output. Besides, all the utilities of forest will be available.

SCOPE OF AGROFORESTRY IN INDIA

1. Forest cover in the country is 67.71 million ha, constituting 20.60% of its total geographical area against the ideal coverage of 33.33%. Out of this, very dense forest (>70% canopy density) constitutes 5.44 million ha (1.66%), moderately dense forest (40-70% canopy density) 33.26 million ha (10.12%) and open forest (<40% canopy density) constitutes 28.99 million ha (8.82%). The forest cover in the hilly districts is only 35.85% compared with the desired 66.66% area. Thus to bridge the gap between desired and available forest coverage in the country, agroforestry is the best intervention.
2. Areas presently not available for arable cropping can be put to agroforestry practices. According to the estimation of National Wasteland Development Board, 123 million hectare area of land is lying as wasteland in India. The extent of degraded forests in the country is more than 40 million ha. Besides, about 50 million ha area is degraded due to mining activity (Gautam and Narayan, 1988). These areas can be reclaimed by adoption of suitable agroforestry practices.
3. Large area is available in the form of farm boundaries and field bunds, where also agroforestry systems can be adopted.
4. Since land holding is becoming smaller and smaller due to demographic pressure, forest area in the vicinity of the thickly populated villages is diminishing with increasing human demands for fuel, fodder, small timber and other minor products met from the forest. Thus, by adopting agroforestry in the community lands near the villages, the pressure on natural forest could be greatly reduced.
5. The agroforestry plot remains usually productive for the farmer and generates continuous revenue, which is not feasible in arable land. Agroforestry also allows for the diversification of farm activities and makes better use of environmental resources.
6. About 87% of the annually harvested wood in India is used as firewood. In addition, at present in rural India 60-80 million tonnes of dry cow dung is utilized as fuel, equivalent to 300-400 million tonnes of freshly collected manure. Thus, there is a vast scope to meet the acute shortage of fuelwood through agroforestry.
7. The grazing lands in almost all parts of the country have to support animals beyond their carrying capacity. Repeated grazing by animals hardly leaves any vegetational element to survive unless specially

protected. Inclusion of fodder tree species with suitable grasses in the agroforestry system will check overgrazing.

8. Agroforestry provides employment with relatively less investment and that too for unskilled rural community. It has a tremendous potential for rural employment generation due to great diversity of products from homegarden which provides opportunities for development of small scale rural industries and creation of off-farm employment and marketing opportunities.

DIFFERENT AGROFORESTRY SYSTEMS IN INDIA

Based on the nature of components, agroforestry systems can be broadly classified into agrisilvicultural (agricultural crops + trees), silvipastoral (trees + forage crops), agrisilvipastoral (agricultural crops + trees + forage crops) and other systems like aquaforestry, mushroom in mixed tree species and apiculture with trees. A few common agroforestry systems practiced in our country are given below.

Multispecies Tree Gardens

This system consists of a mixture of tree plantations of conventional forest species and other commercial perennial tree crops, especially tree species, lending a managed mixed forest appearance. As opposed to homegardens which surround individual houses, these tree gardens are usually away from houses, and are typically found on community owned lands surrounding villages with dense clusters of houses. The multispecies, multilayer dense plant associations are with no organized planting arrangements. The major groups of components are different woody components of varying forms and growth habits. Perennial woody fruit trees are also included in the system. Herbaceous plants are usually absent; but the shade tolerant ones are sometimes present. The major function of this system is production of food, fodder and wood products. This agroforestry practice is adaptable to areas with fertile soils, with good availability of labour, and high human population pressure. Important woody species planted in this system are *Acacia catechu, Phoenix dactifera, Artocarpus* spp, *Acacia mangium, Acacia auriculiformis, Gmelina arborea, Mangifera indica, Syzygium aromaticum, etc.*

Alley Cropping

Alley cropping or hedgerow intercropping is a management-intensive agroforestry practice in which perennial, preferably leguminous trees or shrubs are grown simultaneously with an arable crop. The trees, managed as hedgerows, are grown in wide rows and the crop is planted in the interspace or 'alley' between the tree rows. The trees are pruned regularly during the cropping phase and allowed to grow freely to shade the inter-rows when there are no crops. Alley cropping retains the basic restorative attributes of the bush fallow through nutrient recycling, fertility regeneration and weeds suppression and combines these with arable cropping so that all processes occur concurrently on the same land, allowing the farmer to crop the land for an extended period. Right kind of tree species is to be planted at right spacing, with proper management to reduce competition between trees and agricultural crops for nutrients, moisture and light (Patra, 2013c).

Benefits from alley cropping

1. An important benefit of alley cropping is the addition of large amounts of organic materials from the prunings as mulch or green manure which can have favourable effects on soil physical and chemical properties, on microbiological activity and hence on soil productivity. This ultimately improves crop performance in alleys (Mohapatra and Patra, 2011).
2. There is a reduction in the use of chemical fertilizers which decreases environmental pollution and maintains soil health.
3. There is an overall improvement in the physical nature of the soil environment. The addition of mulch lowers soil temperatures, reduces evaporation, and improves soil fauna activity and soil structure resulting in better infiltration, reduced runoff and improved water use efficiency.
4. The tree rows on sloping land, act as a physical barrier to soil and water movement, resulting in significant reductions in erosion losses. The presence of prunings applied as mulch in the alleys also controls soil erosion.
5. Alley cropping provides additional products such as forage, firewood or stakes when a multipurpose tree is used as the hedgerow.
6. During the fallow period shading of the interspaces reduces weed growth, while in the cropping phase, the mulch inhibits germination and establishment of weeds.

The suitable species for hedgerow planting are *Cassia siamea*, *Leucaena leucocephala*, *Glyricidia sepium*, *Calliandra calothyrsus*, *Sesbania sesban*, *Acacia mangium*, *Gmelina arborea*, *Albizia* spp., *Cajanus* spp., *Chamaecytisus* spp., *Desmodium* spp., *Erythrina* spp., *Flemingia* spp., *Inga* spp. and *Tephrosia* spp.

Multipurpose Trees and Shrubs on Field Bunds

In this system, trees are scattered haphazardly or according to some systematic patterns on bunds, terraces or plot/field boundaries, crop lands, pastures and rangelands. Multipurpose trees like *Acacia nilotica*, *Acacia albida*, *Casuarina equisetifolia*, *Azadirachta indica*, *Acacia senegal*, *Cocos nucifera*, *Leucaena leucocephala* and *Acacia mangium* are planted on field bunds and boundaries (Patra, *et. al.*, 2011).

Benefits:

1. Farmers consider such trees not to be competitive against food crops.

2. Trees provide shade for livestock during intense heat of the long dry season.
3. The trees diversify farmers' products and increase crop production and the duration of cropping season without fertilizer use.
4. The system reduces soil erosion due to high wind velocity or rain water runoff.
5. Sale of non-timber products, such as charcoal, firewood, tree borne oil and fruits significantly increases income.

Crop Combinations with Plantation Crops

On large estates plantation crops such as tea, coffee, cashew, oil palm, rubber, cocoa and coconuts are grown in monoculture but on small-holdings, these are often grown as intercrops. The reasons why intercropping in these perennial tree crops is possible or even desirable are:

1. There are large spaces between tree crops during the early stages of growth.
2. The intercrops reduce soil erosion between widely spaced tree crops, especially during the early tree growth stages.
3. Roots of some tree intercrop combinations complement each other.
4. Shade tolerance of understorey crops such as arrowroot, pine apple, turmeric, ginger, *Aloe vera* etc. favours growth under some plantation crops.
5. Complementary use of light; *e.g.*, up to 8 years and after about 25 years, coconuts allow a considerable amount of light to reach the intercrops. On the other hand, while oil palm has a high light requirement that is available in the upperstorey, cocoa in the understorey requires considerable shade, except at flowering stage.
6. Intercropping during early growth period of tree crops is economically viable while waiting for harvest of long maturity tree crops.
7. Some intercrops are compatible because of differing labour calendars.
8. Some tree crops require an intercrop to serve as a nurse crop during the early growth period. For instance, newly transplanted coffee seedlings benefit from the shade cast by taller intercrops, such as maize.

Agroforestry for Fuelwood Production

In this system, fuelwood species are planted in or around agricultural lands. Tree species commonly used as fuel wood are *Acacia nilotica, Albizia lebbeck, Casuarina equisetifolia, Prosopis juliflora, Cassia siamea, Eucalyptus tereticornis, etc.*

Shelterbelts

A shelterbelt is a wide strip of vegetation consisting of several rows of trees that slows wind speeds, thereby reducing wind erosion, evaporation and damage farmlands by the wind. It is sometimes referred to as windbreak, although the latter often implies a single strip of trees and other vegetation. A shelterbelt presents a mechanical barrier to the impact of the wind, and separates two zones; the windward and the leeward zones. The windward zone refers to the side from which the wind blows, while the leeward zone relates to the side where the wind passes.

In general, tree or shrub species selected for shelterbelts should have the characteristics of rapid growth, straight stems, wind firmness, good crown formation, deep tap root system and resistance to drought. Some of the tree genera used for windbreaks are *Cassia, Acacia, Casuarina, Leucaena, Eucalyptus, Grevillea, Cupressus, Pinus, Dalbergia, Syzygium, Erythrina, Mangifera, Bambusa* etc.

The main characteristics of shelterbelts are:

1. Shelterbelts have a typical triangular shape by raising tall trees in the centre.
2. A certain degree of penetration by wind is planned as by raising a solid wall of trees, the protection decreases very fast on the leeward side.
3. The ratio of height and width of a shelter belt should be roughly 1:10. Shelterbelts up to 50 m width are considered ideal under Indian condition.
4. Orientation of shelterbelts depends upon the direction and velocity of the prevailing winds. Rows of trees are established at right angles to the prevailing wind.
5. The minimum length of a shelterbelt should be about 25 m.
6. Tree species selected for shelterbelt establishment should have ability for wider adaptability to climatic conditions (drought, frost, extreme temperatures etc.), high growth rate, quick crown formation, developing a strong and deep root system (so that they do not compete for moisture and nutrients with agricultural crops), evergreen foliage, increased land productivity.

Benefits from shelterbelts

Properly placed field shelterbelts provide agronomic and other benefits. The main agronomic benefits include the following:

1. Reduces soil erosion by wind: A shelterbelt modifies the microclimate, mostly in its leeward side. This modified microclimate includes reduced wind speed and, therefore, reduced soil erosion. A significant reduction of wind speed occurs on leeward side for a distance extending to

approximately 20 times the height of the shelterbelt and also 3 to 5 times its height on the windward side. Therefore, a shelterbelt 5 m in height will provide a degree of protection for soils and crops for a total distance of up to 25 times its height i.e. 125 m. Since the zone of protection provided by a single shelterbelt is limited, a series of shelterbelts is required to protect the whole field. The shelterbelts must be planted perpendicular to the direction of the prevailing wind to provide more complete protection.

2. Increases moisture for crop growth: Shelterbelts reduces evaporation, thus providing more moisture for crop growth. It also protects the leeward areas from the desiccating effects of hot wind. Shelterbelts use moisture and nutrients from a greater depth than most annual crops.
3. Reduced wind damage to crops: Crops benefit from the reduced wind speeds in the protected zone. The crop plants are less likely to be twisted by the wind.
4. Potential for increased farm productions: Most of the research conducted around the world reports crop yield increases due to shelterbelts. However, crops vary in their yield response to shelterbelt protection. Drought tolerant crops show the lowest response, forage crops are moderately responsive and weather-sensitive crops such as vegetables show the highest response. Besides, shelterbelts provide potential source of income for farmers (e.g. biomass, timber and non-timber products).

Protein Bank

Protein banks are blocks of forage plants deliberately planted to alleviate fodder shortages in arid, semiarid and mountainous regions, especially during the dry seasons. The forage plants may be leguminous trees and shrubs or herbaceous legumes, and they may be grown in combination with suitable grasses. The fodder trees are pruned regularly to feed livestock. When based on legumes, the fodder banks become important sources of protein and are referred to as protein banks. The important tree and shrub species for this system are *Acacia nilotica, Albizia lebbeck, Leucaena leucocephala, Gliricidia sepium, Sesbania grandiflora, Artocarpus* spp., *Bombax malabaricum, Cordia dichtotoma, etc.*

Trees and Shrubs on Pasture

In this silvipastoral system of agroforestry, MPTs are scattered irregularly or arranged according to some systematic pattern, especially to supplement forage production. Perennial woody fruit crops may also be included which is called hortisilvipastoral system. The number of species with potential for this practice is great. They include *Acacia nilotica, Acacia mangium, Acacia auriculiformis, Gliricidia sepium, Bauhinia* spp., *Leucaena leucocephala, Derris indica, Azadirachta indica, Emblica officinalis, Psidium guajava, Prosopis* spp. and *Tamarindus indica*.

Homegardens

This is the oldest agroforestry practice. Homegardens are characterized by a high species-diversity and usually 3-4 vertical canopy strata. Many species of trees, bushes, vegetables and other herbaceous plants are grown in dense and random arrangements. But some rational control over choice of plants, and their spatial and temporal arrangement should be exercised to reduce competition among the plants and to increase the production. Every homegarden usually consists of an herbaceous layer near the ground, a tree layer at the upper level, and intermediate layers in between. The lower layer is usually divided into two, with the lowermost (less than 1 m height) dominated by different vegetable and medicinal plants, and the second layer (1-3 m height) being composed of food plants such as banana, papaya, yam and so on. The upper tree layer is also partitioned into two, consisting of emergent, fully grown timber and fruit trees occupying the uppermost layer of over 25 m height, and medium-sized trees of 10-20 m height occupying the next lower layer. The intermediate layer of 3-10 m height is dominated by various fruit trees (Tejwani, 1994). Most homegardens also support a variety of animals (cow, goat, sheep, pig) and birds (chicken, duck). Fodder and legumes are widely grown to meet the daily fodder and feed requirements. Thus, homegardens represent land-use systems involving deliberate management of multipurpose trees and shrubs in intimate association with annual and perennial agricultural crops, and livestock within the compounds of individual houses, the whole crop-tree-animal unit being intensively managed by family labour.

Apiculture with Trees

In this system, various honey or nectar producing trees frequently visited by honeybees are planted on the boundary of the agricultural field. The primary purpose of this system is to produce honey. Apisilviculture with *Eucalyptus*, *Gliricidia*, *Grevillea*, *Gmelina*, *Leuceana* and *Albizia* species are more remunerative and a good source of generating additional farm income in rural areas.

Aquaforestry

The aquaforestry system comprises of composite fish culture in farm ponds, and various trees and shrubs (*Leucaena leucocephala*, *Morus alba*, *Gliricidia sepium*, *Moringa olifera*, *etc*.), leaves of which are preferred by fish are planted on the boundary and around fish ponds. Leaves of these trees are used as feed for fish. Inland fish such as *catla*, *rohu*, *mrigal*, common carp, silver carp and grass carp can be grown in the ponds. In the coastal regions farmers are cultivating fish and prawn in saline water and growing coconut and other trees on bunds of ponds. Now fish culture in the mangroves is also advocated, which form a rich source of nutrition to the aquatic life and breeding ground for fish and prawn. Some other modified aquaforestry systems are:

1. A well-balanced system of animal husbandry including goatery, poultry, duck farming, turtles and fishes in the small ponds in homegardens make a balanced system of high moisture, energy and nutrient use efficiency per unit area.
2. In paddy field, fish can easily be reared by planting trees on field bunds or boundary to provide leaves used as fish feed. This system can be practised in high rainfall areas.
3. Coconut plants can also be successfully planted on raised paddy field bunds with an alley space of 5 m width depression which is utilized for pisiculture purpose (Patra, *et. al.*, 2008).

Mushroom in Mixed Tree Species

Cultivation of paddy straw mushroom under the shade of high density plantation of mixed multipurpose tree species is also remunerative. The tree species suitable for the system are *Acacia auriculiformis, Acacia mangium, Dalbergia sissoo, Casuarina equisetifolia, Gmelina arborea, Dalbergia sissoo, etc.*

ROLE OF AGROFORESTRY IN ADAPTING AND MITIGATING CLIMATE CHANGE

Human societies over the ages have depleted natural resources in different ways and degraded their local environments. Indiscriminate cutting down of trees and accelerating the construction works lead to global warming and climate change. Climate scientists believe that human-induced deforestation is responsible for 18-25% of climate change. Climate change threatens the suitability and productivity of crops and livestock and jeopardizes wood and non-wood production. Agroforestry may be promoted to combat the threats of soil erosion and desertification due to climate change (Rao, *et. al.*, 2007; Patra and Mohapatra, 2011).

Agroforestry for Adaptation to Climate Change

Climate change threatens the suitability and productivity of crops and livestock and jeopardizes wood and non-wood production. Agroforestry may be promoted to combat the threats of soil erosion and desertification due to climate change. Adaptation activities can also aim to improve management practices and establish sustainable agroforestry systems.

A wide range of agroforestry systems now exist with a potential to improve productivity, favourably influence microclimate, prevent soil degradation and restore soil fertility and diversify income generating opportunities. If supported by appropriate cultivation, processing and marketing methods, agroforestry products can make a major contribution to the economic development of the millions of poor farmers by meeting their needs for food, feed, fuel and income. Combined yields of tree, crop and livestock products from well planned and well managed agroforestry systems tend to be higher than those from any agricultural systems due to increased and efficient use of scarce resources. Agroforestry thus can both sequester carbon and produce a range of economic, environmental, and socioeconomic benefits.

As adaptation emerges as a science, the role of agroforestry in reducing the vulnerability of agricultural systems to climate change or climate variability needs to be assessed more effectively. Rainfall variability is a major constraint in the semi-arid regions and to the upland farms that do not have access to irrigation. Climate change may translate into reduced total rainfall or increased occurrence of dry spells during rainy seasons in many semi-arid regions. Successful and well-managed integration of trees on farms and in agricultural landscapes often results in diversified and sustainable crop production, in addition to providing a wide range of environmental benefits such as erosion control and watershed services. Therefore, optimizing the use of increasingly scarce rainwater through agroforestry practices such as improved fallow could be one way of effectively improving the capacity of farmers to adapt to drier and more variable conditions. In low-rainfall years, water availability to crops is paramount and seems to be the dividing factor between absolute crop failure and reasonable food production. Buffering agricultural crops against water deficiencies is, therefore, an important function agroforestry would have to play in the adaptation battle. There are other mechanisms such as improved microclimate and reduced evapo-transpiration through which agroforestry practices may improve the adaptive capacity of farmers. Pests, diseases and weeds already stand as major obstacles to crop production in many tropical agroecosystems. By integrating tree and herbaceous species in agricultural landscapes can produce positive interactions that could contribute towards controlling pest and disease outbreaks. The agroforestry practices can also control weeds.

Agroforestry for Mitigating Climate Change

Agroforestry options may provide a means for diversifying production systems and increasing the sustainability of smallholder farming systems. Tree-based cropping systems have some obvious advantages for maintaining production during wetter and drier years.

1. The deep root systems of trees are able to explore a larger soil volume for water and nutrients, which will help during droughts.
2. Increased soil porosity, reduced runoff and increased soil cover lead to increased water infiltration and retention in the soil profile which can reduce moisture stress during low rainfall years.
3. Tree-based systems have higher evapotranspiration rates than row crops or pastures and can thus maintain aerated soil conditions by pumping excess water out of the soil profile more rapidly than other production systems.

Thus, diversifying the production system to include a significant tree component may buffer against income risks associated with climatic variability.

Sustainable Diversification of Agricultural Systems

Diversification of agricultural enterprises is one of the best practices to reduce the risks associated with variable climate. It is an adjustment of the farm enterprise pattern to increase farm income or reduce income variability by reducing risk and exploiting new market opportunities. At the farm level it is the adoption of multiple production activities that are complementary in economic and/or ecological dimensions involving crops, trees and livestock (Dixon, *et. al.*, 2001). Agroforestry systems are a suitable pathway for sustainable diversification of agricultural systems. Agroforestry ensures food security by generating direct benefits to farmers such as food, fodder, feed, fuelwood, live fences and other products. The diversity of crops provides multiple harvests at different times of the year, thereby reducing the risk of crop loss and food shortage. Quality of life of farmers is improved by increasing income due to multiple harvests and sale of products from different components, thereby providing regular income throughout the year.

Improvement in Rain Water Use Efficiency

The presence of trees has positive effect on water budget of the soil and crops growing between or beneath them. There are several mechanisms whereby agroforestry may use available water more effectively than the annual crops (Rao, *et. al.*, 1998). Agroforestry systems with a perennial tree component can make use of the water remaining in the soil after harvest of annual crops and the rainfall received outside the crop season (Ong and Huxley, 1996). A mulch or litter layer increases the infiltration of rain water while simultaneously reducing evaporation from the soil. The changes in microclimate also reduce the evaporative demand and make more water available for transpiration.

Soil and Water Conservation

Trees improve soil fertility by processes of increasing additions to the soil, reduction of losses from soil, and improving soil physical, chemical and biological conditions. Trees have a different impact on soil properties than annual crops in terms of their longer residence time, larger biomass accumulation and more extensive root systems (Rao, *et.al.*, 1998). Trees increase or at least maintain the organic matter levels of the soil. This is mainly through litter fall and continuous degeneration or sloughing-off of roots of standing trees. Pruning materials from the woody perennials used in agroforestry systems add a huge quantity of organic matter to the soil and this is generally high in nitrogen.

Potential to Limit Carbon Emissions and Sequester Carbon

The tree component of the agroforestry systems can be a significant sink for atmospheric carbon. An efficient agroforestry system not only maximizes the benefit it provides but also ensures the link to climate change mitigation. Trees are important carbon warehouses that filter massive quantities of carbon from the atmosphere, trapping it in their biomass (Montagnini and Nair, 2004. Through the natural process of photosynthesis, plants absorb carbon dioxide from the atmosphere and release oxygen. They store this carbon in their leaves, branches, trunks and roots. An average tree can remove about 23 kg of carbon dioxide from the atmosphere annually. In agroforestry systems, the amount of carbon sequestration is further increased. The interactions of the different components of agroforestry systems can help absorb and sequester carbon dioxide and other greenhouse gasses from the atmosphere (Pandey, 2002). Thus, trees in an agroforestry system make it a potential strategy in mitigating climate change.

Microclimate Amelioration

The full genetic potential of many crops can only be exploited under optimum environmental conditions. Any change in these conditions, especially during the reproductive stage, will have a direct impact on the production and economic viability of certain crops (Beer, *et. al.*, 1998). In an agroforestry system, the presence of trees reduces heat and light. Trees bring about favourable changes in the microclimatic conditions by influencing radiation flux, air temperature, wind speed all of which will have a significant impact on modifying the rate and duration of photosynthesis and subsequent plant growth, transpiration and soil water use.

Interventions for Drought Mitigation

Tree canopies lower the temperature and increase relative humidity in an agroforestry system which leads to a lower transpiration rate. Tree litter and pruning materials act as mulch on ground surface that reduces the evaporative loss of soil moisture. The water storage capacity of soil is also increased due to improved soil organic matter. Higher survival and biomass generation under agroforestry is possible due to greater efficiency for photosynthesis, tapping of nutrients and water from deeper layers, efficient utilization of off-season rainfall by the perennial tree component and better environmental conditions.

Protection and Stabilization of Ecosystem

Trees give protection from adverse effects of different kinds of pollutants such as dust, dirt and other physical air pollutants. The dust level in the air can be as much as 75 percent lower on the sheltered side of the tree compared to the windward side. It is estimated that one hectare of a close forest filters about 50 t of dust and dirt every year. Trees also absorb some of the chemical air pollutants.

AGROFORESTRY ADOPTION

There is a growing awareness that agricultural research and development must build upon farmer expertise; identifying, facilitating and building upon local innovation. The concept of Transfer of Technology (ToT) is now increasingly replaced by Participatory Technology Development (PTD). Thus the scientists and extensionists need to develop a more facilitatory role. In order to effectively facilitate PTD it is essential to understand what makes a good innovation. A better understanding of factors influencing the development of optimal technologies can facilitate wider participation and co-operation between farmers, extensionists and scientists, to optimise agroforestry technologies for widespread uptake and diffusion to enhance rural livelihoods.

In the context of an adoption cycle, it is possible to develop a more holistic conception of PTD with reference to dynamic farmer needs, objectives, personal characteristics, capital assets and communication, in addition to the technological characteristics of the innovations themselves. Swinkels and Franzel (1997) developed a three-stage model, in which adoption potential depends on the feasibility, profitability and acceptability of an agroforestry technology. Although feasibility and profitability aspects are clearly defined, the acceptability component depends on a diverse range of factors, including perception of risk, suitability to accepted gender roles, cultural acceptance, and compatibility with other enterprises. To increase the scale of adoption and the impact of innovations, action must be based on an understanding of the dynamics of adoption and the critical factors that determine whether farmers accept, do not accept, or partially accept innovations. Pannell (1999) defined four conditions necessary for farmers' adoption of innovative farming systems.

1. Awareness of the innovation.
2. Perception that it is feasible to trial the innovation.
3. Perception that the innovation is worth trialing.
4. Perception that the innovation promotes the farmer's objectives.

Constraints in Agroforestry Technology Adoption

Institutional Constraints

All the forest lands including hilly, deforested and degraded lands that deserve rehabilitation through agroforestry systems are under the jurisdiction of state forestry departments. In many cases, the forestry officials stick to the classical forestry concept and regard agroforestry systems as incompatible. They believe that farmers' participation is neither suited nor needed. However, people's participation through agroforestry practices could be a potent means of restoring both protective and productive woody vegetation in barren areas.

Government Policy Related Constraints

In India, there is no well defined agroforestry policy either by the state governments or the central government. Even there is no specific policy for felling of trees. Very often the private growers are not allowed to harvest the trees from their own lands at their need which discourage strongly to go for tree cultivation. A clear-cut government policy is also lacking for inter-state transport of forest products including timber, small timber and other minor forest products. Although tree farming requires high initial investment and return is usually delayed there is no policy for financial support to the tree growers or agroforesters through nationalized banks (Patra, 2011).

Sociocultural Constraints

Majority of farmers in developing countries own or cultivate small sized farms. Their immediate priority is food production from each inch of land. They resist displacing food crops with trees. Farmers prefer only high utility perennial species like bamboo and coconuts. Agroforestry systems are also very labour intensive which may cause scarcity at times for other farm activities. Farm families have traditionally developed labour strategies to use family members at various times of the year for different tasks. Thus, they resist changes in the labour practices of the farming system into which they are introduced.

Socioeconomic Constraints

Social acceptability of agroforestry is very closely linked to the economic feasibility of the system. Direct and immediate income that can be derived from a land-use system will be an important criterion in the appraisal of its social acceptability. However, a longer period is required for trees in an agroforestry system to grow to maturity and acquire an economic value. The traditional farmers also do not prefer agroforestry as it requires high initial investment and risk factors are involved for economic returns.

Market Related Constraints

There are no adequate wood based enterprises with low to medium range investments which affect the farmers the most. Marketing is a big issue for forest products as no privilege is allowed in tree marketing like in case of agricultural marketing. Usually minimum support price for the tree products and other forest products is not fixed by any government agency.

Environmental Constraints

Trees serve as hosts to insect pest and diseases that are harmful to agricultural crops. Increased susceptibility to pests and diseases often leads to dependence on potentially harmful pesticides. Trees in agroforestry systems often compete with agricultural crops for light, water and nutrients from the soil.

Technological Constraints

Agroforestry system is very difficult to manage and needs more accuracy with highly skillful management practices. Agroforestry is more complex, less understood and more difficult to apply as compared to monocropping.

To overcome these constraints the agroforestry extension agents should be engaged at grassroots levels. As agroforestry is an integral part of rural development, the role of the extension forester is to explore how natural, human and institutional resources in the community can be developed to bring about rural development through different agroforestry systems. The role of the extension agroforester is to assist the people to come up with their own solutions to the problems that have been identified. This means that the role of the extension forester should be that of a motivator through participation. People should be given a chance to participate actively in the different aspects of planning and implementation of agroforestry systems (Chavangi and Zimmermann, 1987).

CONCLUSION

The impacts of climate change on agriculture is of the greatest concern to most developing countries, because of higher dependence on agriculture, subsistence level of operations, low adaptive capacity and limited institutional support. Thus, some diversification in present agricultural practices is required to ensure protection of environment, food and livelihood securities, poverty alleviation and mitigation of the adverse impacts of pollution and health hazards. Agroforestry systems act as sinks for atmospheric carbon while helping to attain food security, increase farm income, improve soil health and discourage deforestation. In spite of some limitations and constraints, agroforestry has now been recognized as an effective tool to meet all these needs. Thus, it can be used in the war against hunger, inadequate shelter and environmental degradation. With the modern day crisis of shortage of land for forestry and agriculture, agroforestry is well positioned to provide a perfect balance and a viable solution.

REFERENCES

Beer, J., Muschler, R.G., Somarriba, E. and Kass, D. (1998): Shade Management in Coffee and Cacao Plantations – A Review. *Agroforestry Systems*, 38: 139-164.

Bene, J.G., Beall, H.W. and Cote, A. (1977): Trees, Food and People: Land Management in the Tropics, *IDRC*, Ottawa.

Chavangi, A.H. and Zimmermann, R. (1987): A Guide to Farm Forestry in Kenya, *Ministry of Environment and Natural Resources, Government of Kenya*, Nairobi.

Dixon, J.A. Gibbon, D.P. and Gulliver, A. (2001): Farming Systems and Poverty: Improving Farmers' Livelihoods in a Changing World, *Food and Agriculture Organization*, Rome.

FAO. (2011): Forests for Improved Nutrition and Food Security. *Food and Agriculture Organization*, Rome. www.fao.org/docrep/014/i2011e/i2011e00.pdf

Gautam, N.C. and Narayan, L.R.A. (1988): Wastelands in India, *Pink Publishing House*, Mathura.

Mohapatra, A.K. and Patra, A.K. (2011): Importance of Agroforestry in Organic Farming. (*In*) *Recent Developments in Organic Farming* (eds. J M L Gulati & T Barik). *Department. of Agronomy, OUAT*, Bhubaneswar, pp. 366-374.

Montagnini, F. and Nair, P.K.R. (2004): Carbon Sequestration: An Underexploited Environmental Benefit of Agroforestry Systems, *Agroforestry Systems* 61: 281-295.

Nair, P.K.R. (2008): An Introduction to Agroforestry, *Springer (India) Pvt. Ltd.*, New Delhi.

Ong, C.K. and Huxley, P. (eds.) (1996): Tree-crop Interactions: A Physiological Approach, CAB International, Wallingford.

Pandey, D.N. (2002): Global Climate Change and Carbon Management in Multifunctional Forests, *Current Science*, 83: 593-602.

Pannell, D.J. (1999): Social and Economic Challenges in the Development of Complex Farming Systems, *Agroforestry Systems* 45: 393-409.

Patra, A.K. (2011): Agroforestry for Food and Wood, *Science Horizon* 1(7): 24-27.

Patra, A.K. (2013): Agroforestry: Principles and Practices, *New India Publishing Agency*, New Delhi, p. 248.

Patra, A.K. (2013): Agroforestry–A Novel Approach to Climate Change Adaptation and Mitigation in Agriculture. *Science Horizon*, 3(9): 25-28.

Patra, A.K. (2013): Alley Cropping, *Science Horizon*, 3(11): 6-10.

Patra, A.K. and Mohapatra, A.K. (2011): Agroforestry for Climate Change Adaptation and Mitigation, *Agron Activities at a Glance*, 1(1): 14-16.

Patra, A.K. and Mohapatra, A.K., Gantayat, B.P. and Das, S. (2011): Evaluation of *Acacia nilotica* as Bund Plantation in Coastal Odisha, *Journal of Research, OUAT* Special Issue 1(1): 81-85.

Patra, A.K., Mohapatra, A.K., Gantayat, B.P. and Das, S. (2008): Performance of Coconut (*Cocos nucifera*) Based Agrihorticultural System in Coastal Orissa, *Journal of Research, OUAT* 26(2): 53-58.

Rao, K.P.C., Verchot, L.V. and Laarman, J. (2007): Adaptation to Climate Change Through Sustainable Management and Development of Agroforestry Systems, *SAT eJournal*, 4(1): 1-30.

Rao, M.R., Nair, P.K.R. and Ong, C.K. (1998): Biophysical Interactions in Tropical Agroforestry Systems, *Agroforestry Systems*, 38: 3-50.

Swinkels, R. and Franzel, S. (1997): Adoption Potential of Hedgerow Intercropping in Maize-based Cropping Systems in the Highlands of Western Kenya 2. Economic and Farmers' Evaluation. *Experimental Agriculture*, 33: 211-223.

Tejwani, K.G. (1994): Agroforestry in India, *Oxford and IBH Publishing Co. Pvt. Ltd.*, New Delhi.

Tejwani, K. G. (2008): Agroforestry to Meet the Challenges of the Indian Agriculture, *Proceedings of the National Symposium on Agroforestry Knowledge for Sustainability, Climate Moderation and Challenges Ahead*, Indian Society of Agroforestry, Jhansi, pp. 7-8.

Young, A. (2005): Agroforestry for Soil Management, *CAB International*, Wallingford.

Pages: 21-30

NATURAL ECOSYSTEM AND CLIMATE CHANGE
Edited by: Dr. Pawan Kumar 'Bharti'; Dr. Khwairakpam Gajananda
ISBN: 978-93-5056-745-6
Edition: 2015
Published by: Discovery Publishing House Pvt. Ltd., New Delhi (India)

CHAPTER - 2

Global Warming and Microorganisms

Garima Arya and Purshotam Kaushik

ABSTRACT

Global warming is the important problem for all types of livings beings. The earth's atmosphere contained 380 parts/million of carbon in 2007. This is the equivalent to 760 Gt (Giga ton) of carbon, largely in the form of carbondioxide and methane. Both gases are responsible for the global warming. Currently, the most energy production generates carbon dioxide which is a potent green house gas (GHG) that contributes to global warming and local pollution. Global warming presently concerns for every one, water and waste water professional need to be especially aware of the environmental impact of this issue. A land mark study has moved existence of global warming from a subject to a commonly accepted scientific principle.

This review article is synthesis from how some microorganism viz., fungi, actinomycetes and bacteria are capable to reduce the methane and organic compounds. Methanotropic and nitrifying bacteria are also able to oxidize

Department of Botany and Microbiology, Gurukul Kangri University, Haridwar (Uttarakhand) - 249 404, (India).

methane as well as ammonium. This CO and CH_4, must be removed from the atmosphere for good health of each which is live on the earth's atmosphere. Global Warming is a dramatically urgent and serious problem. We don't need to wait for governments to find a solution for this problem: each individual can bring an important help adopting a more responsible lifestyle: starting from little, everyday things. It's the only reasonable way to save our planet, before it is too late.

Key words: Green house gas (GHG), global warming, microorganism, pollution.

INTRODUCTION

Our world is so beautiful, its part of reason we love to be outdoors. The skies, clear lakes and river, soil and fresh air; all are valuable nature sources that make up a healthy and safe environment. Everyone living on the earth needs to do thesis part to help protect these sources, so our world will still be healthy and beautiful many years from now. Pollution involves so many different factors from so many sources that there is no single or simply remedy. Pollution is an evil has born out of development. Mankind will perish if the protection of the environment does not become an integral part of all technological development have to be economically viable and acceptable. Global warming – the most noticeable environmental problem is an unusual rise in earth's temperature mainly due to the accumulation of greenhouse gases. Today global warming has substantial but undefined impacts on our ecosystem which are expected to become more pronounced in the coming years (Jarvis et al., 2009).

Why and How it Happened?

The water vapours, carbon dioxide and methane in the atmosphere from a blanket of gases that does't allow the solar radiation to escape back in to space. This phenomenon Green House Gases (GHG) is essential to maintain the earth's temperature at a habitable level. Unfortunately the human activity has been making the blanket of GHG or enhance the GHE Evaluated concentration of CO_2 absorbed increased amount of radiation and cause a warming of the earth's atmosphere called "Green House Effect"(La Marche et al., 1984). Approximately 86% of world energy production comes from fossil fuels today (Energy Information Administration, 2005), but fossil fuels, especially petroleum, are being exhausted, leading to an energy crisis in the near future (Abhishek 2007 and Rifkin, 2002). Furthermore, the combustion of fossil fuels adds CO_2 to the atmosphere and causes global climate change (IPCC, 2007). To mitigate the adverse effects of an energy crisis and global climate change, society needs to develop carbon-neutral, sustainable energy sources as alternatives to fossil fuels. Throughout the world carbon emission from fossil fuel burning have been usually increased during last 50 years as shown in Figure 2.1.

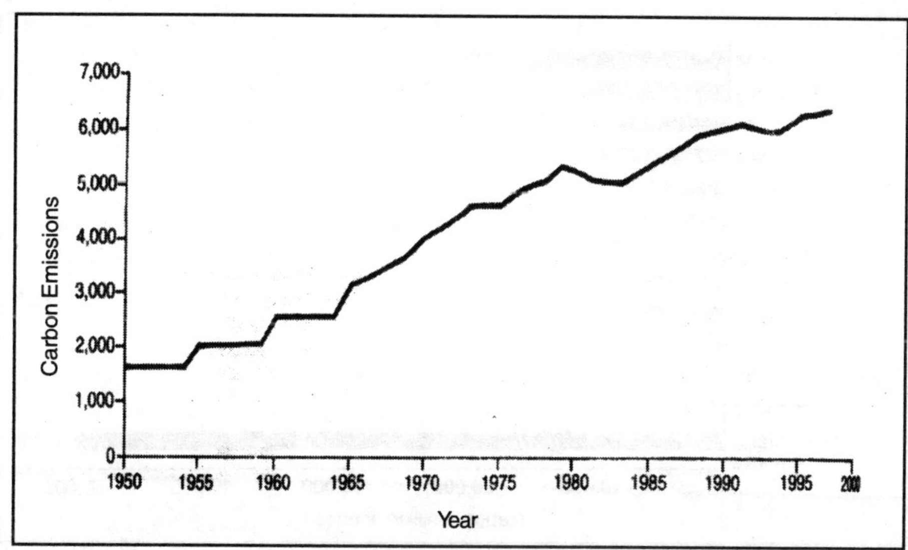

Fig. 2.1: **World Carbon Emission (Million Tonnes) from Fossils Fuel Burning during Last Few Decades**

Global means surface air temperature has increased between 0.3 to 0.6°C since the late 19th century i.e. during last 100 years. This is shown by this following graph.

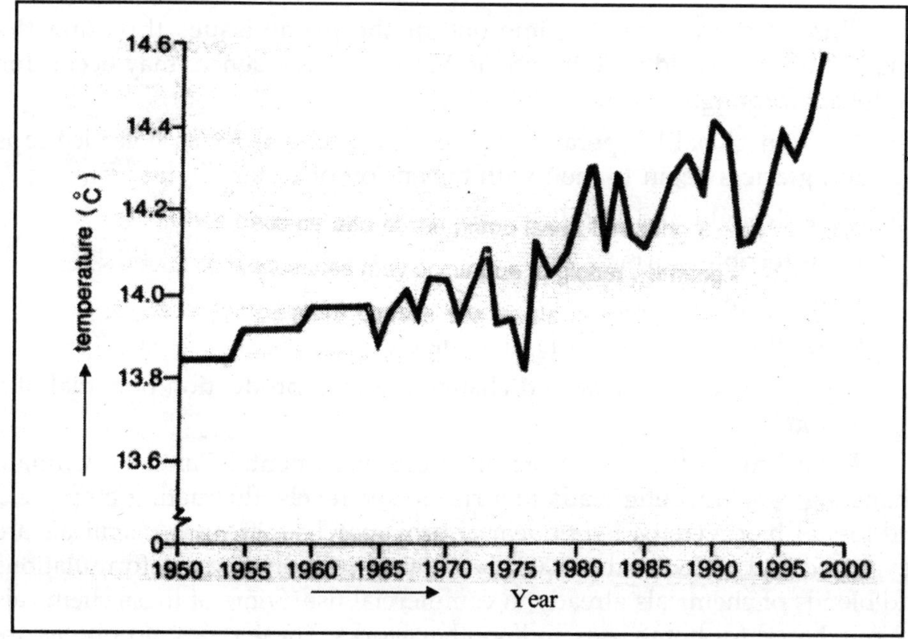

Fig. 2.2: **Global Average Temperature during Last Decades or so**

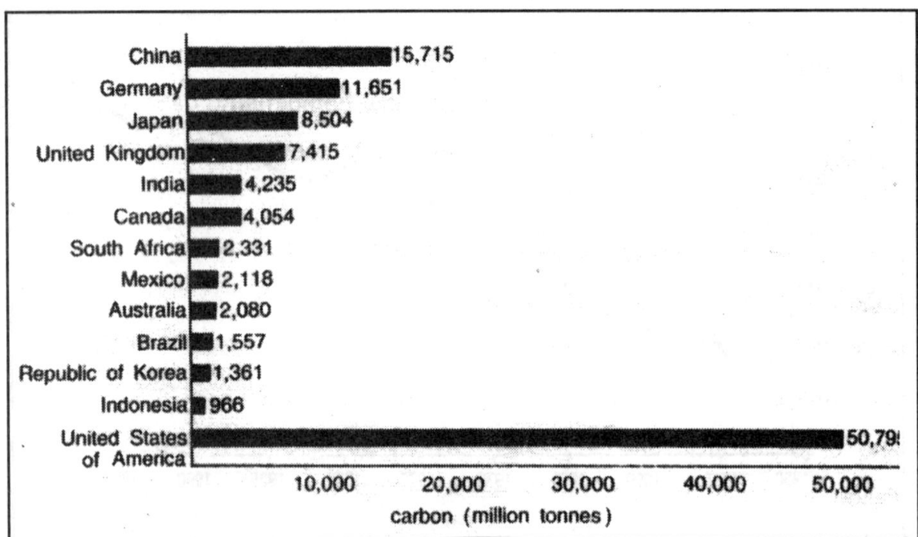

Fig. 2.3: **Graph Shows Carbon Emissions in Different Cities**

As per Intergovernmental Panel on Climate Change (IPCC) estimate global surface temperature would be about 2°C above pre-industrial levels by the year 2030, and about 4°C above pre-industrial levels by the year 2090.

Its Consequences

Climate change has become one of the prime issues threating the sustainability of world's environment. Various consequences may occur due to global warming:

- A rise in global temperature causes sea levels to rise as polar ice caps and glaciers begin to melt with expansion of water.
- More drought and floods.
- More terrible storms.
- Many more hot days.
- More diseases like malaria, dengue etc.
- Impact on ecosystem would change the crop production potential of a region.

According to the 2nd report of Intergovernmental Panel on Climate Change, global warming leads to a rise in sea levels, fluctuating crop yield and loss of biodiversity. Every year approximately 1,000 new chemicals are developed and added to the 7,000 chemicals, 9 million mixture, formulations and blends of chemicals already in commercial use. Some of these chemicals are purchased for home uses and another works. These types of pollutes are able to create various health hazards problems for living beings. In the past, wide fluctuation in the atmospheric carbondioxide concentration occurred independently from the human kind's activities. In the cretaceous period, life thrived in an atmosphere believed to be six time richer in carbondioxide than today (Appenzeller, 1993). Aerosols pollution and increases in cloud cover may to some extent mitigate the effects of increased carbondioxide concentration (Kerr, 1992). It is like impossible to predict with certainly, how disruptive the new houses effect, but every thing is possible. Now governments, scientists, business and industries, agricultural research work station, environmental organization and individuals can help to control pollution.

MICROORGANISM REDUCE THE GLOBAL WARMING

As the world gets warmer everyday and we are trying to decrease the use of any substances that produce green house gases (fossils fuels), the CO_2 levels keep increasing. However, the statistically increase CO_2 levels are based in the production of GHGs. We have forgotten the most abundant form of life in the earth is microorganisms. So now questions are arise how has bacteria been affected by global warming? And what is the role of bacteria in the global warming?

The likelihood of adverse climate change in response to human caused increased in atmospheric CO_2 present an intractable socioeconomic dilemma. Faces the prospect of continuing CO_2 emission, scientist are trying to develop alternative technologies of reducing atmospheric CO and CO_2, especially strategies that involve sequestering rather than decomposing of biomass generated as a result of technologies. To overcome the effects of global warming there is an urgent need to think of various innovative ways for fixing CO_2 through physical, chemical and biological processes. Among the three, the biological fixation using microorganisms has been accepted as a potential measure to mitigate global warming.

It is believed to be an environment friendly and energy efficient process as the biomass formed by fixation of CO2 can be used for the production of bioenergy, microbial biodiesel, biohydrogen. These can serve as an alternative to conventional energy sources such as fossil fuel and hence reduce the pressure to some extent (Bruce, 2008). Till now, in many biological fixation processes, the photosynthetic activity of microalgae have been exploited for mitigating global warming (Wang et al., 2008). But besides microalgae there are some microbes i.e. bacteria and archaea that can too contribute in reducing global warming (Jessup et al., 1998).Theoretically microorganism could remove enough of these GHG from the atmosphere that are threat of global warming would be removed. Some microorganisms like fungi (*Aspergillus, Fusarium, Phoma, Tricoderma*), bacteria (*Cytophega, Cellulomonas, Streptococcus, Vibrio*) and actinomyces (*Nocardia, Streptomyces*) convert carbon dioxide in to various organic compounds (Ward, P.D., 2006). Microbial activities are crucial in term of not only the quantity but also the quality of their contributions.

Under aerobic condition, macro and micro organisms share the ability to biodegrade organic compounds and some biopolymers such as starch, pectin, protein and so on, but microorganisms are unique in their capacity to carry out anaerobic (fermentative) degradation of organic matters. The ability to degrade humic materials, hydrocarbons and many human made synthetic is also virtually unique to microorganism. Methanogens which is the group of Archea (Buckley *et al.*, 2006). Strictly anaerobs are active at redox potential between 350 to 450 mV. They are utilize carbon dioxide as an electron acceptor. They reduce CO_2 using H_2 produced in their fermentation process. If CO_2 is considerd available in carbonate form, following equation may be represented as (Gottschalk 1979):

$$HCO_3\square + H^+ + 4H_2 \xrightarrow[\textbf{Coenzymes}]{\textbf{Methanogens}} CH_4 + 3H_2O + \Delta K\ J/M$$

Methanogens e.g. *Methanosarcina barkeri* are capable to metabolizing acetate, methanol and methylamine to methane and carbon dioxide. *Methanomonas* which is obligate aerobic, utilizing methane in the presence of oxygen as energy source. *Clostridium thermoacetium* and *Acetobacterium woodii* both are facultative chemoautotrophic anaerobic, capable to reducing CO_2 with H_2 to acetate (Sim, Jia Huey., 2008).

$$CO_2 + 4H_2 \longrightarrow CH_3COOH + 2H_2O + \Delta K\ J/M$$

Reducing the rate of global climate change induced by growing levels of greenhouse gases in the atmosphere is recognised as the world's greatest environmental challenge. In parallel with the efforts concentrated on reducing the levels of CO_2 from anthropogenic sources, scientists are increasingly exploring the important role technology can play in effectively managing the long-term risks of climate change. In particular, researchers are focusing on several possible ways in which biotechnology might help to both reduce the emissions of CO_2 in the air, and sequester more carbon from the air into the ground and oceans.

In a recently completed research, American scientists have discovered a more efficient variant of the key enzyme involved in CO_2 sequestration by plants during photosynthesis, the ribulose 1, 5- bisphosphate carboxylase/ oxygenase (RuBisCO). The main aim of the study was to direct the evolution of RuBisCO variants with improved kinetic and biophysical properties that could enable plants to use and convert CO_2 more efficiently. Previous scientific attempts of engineering more efficient RuBisCo enzymes were primarily focused on mutating specific amino acids within RuBisCo and then seeing if the change affected CO_2 conversion. In this study, the researchers used a different approach which consisted in inserting randomly mutating RuBisCO genes into bacteria (as observed *Escherichia coli*) and screening for the most efficient resulting RuBisCO enzymes. In nature, *E. coli* bacteria do not carry the RuBisCO enzyme and they do not effectuate photosynthesis nor do they contribute to the carbon sequestration from the atmosphere. The researchers thus isolated genes encoding RuBisCO and a helper enzyme from photosynthetic bacteria and added them to *E. coli*. Such genetically modified *E. coli* were able to fix and convert CO_2 into consumable energy when the other nutrients were withhold and the bacteria relied on RuBisCO and carbon dioxide to survive under these stringent conditions. (Energy Information Administration US, 2006)

At the recent research, scientists have discovered a mutant enzyme that could enable plants to use and convert carbon dioxide more quickly, effectively removing more greenhouse gases from the atmosphere (Conard, 1995). When the various types of organic compound reach in to soil by the way of animal and plant residues. Carbohydrates, simple sugar, starch, cellulose, hemicellulose, pectin, gums, mucilage, proteins, fats, oils, waxes, renins, alcohols, aldehydes, ketons, tannin, hydrocarbons, alkaloids, pigments and other products are degraded by fungi, actinomycetes and bacteria. Those microorganisms which are involve in the degradation of organic compounds, pesticides and pollutants are shown in table 2.1.

Table 2.1: Shows Microorganism Capable of Utilizing Different Components of Matter as Reported by Several Workers. F – Fungi, A – Actinomycetes, and B- Bacteria

Nature of Substrate in Organic Matter	Genera of Microorganism
Cellulose	
F.	*Aspergillus, Alternaria, Chaetomium, Coprinus, Fomes, Fusarium, Mycothecium, Penicillium, Polyporus, Rhizoctonia, Rhizopus, Trichothecium, Verticillium.*
A.	*Micromonospora, Nocardia, Streptomyces, Streptosporangium.*
B.	*Acromobactor, Angiococcus, Bacillus, Cellulomonas, Clostridium, Cytophaga, Pseupomonas, Vibrio.*
Hemicellulose	
F.	*Aspergillus, Alternaria, Chaetomium, Coprinus, Coriolus, Fomes, Fusarium, Mycothecium, Penicillium, Polyporus.*
A.	*Streptomyces.*
B.	*Acromobactor, Bacillus, Cytophaga, Lactobacillus, Pseupomonas, Vibrio.*
Lignin	
F.	*Clevaria, Clitocybe, Collybia, Flamulla, Hypholoma, Lepiota, Pholiota, Cephalosporium, Humicola.*
A.	*Streptomyces*
B.	*Flavobacterium, Pseudomonas.*

(Table Contd...)

Starch	
F.	*Aspergillus, Alternaria, Chaetomium, Fomes, Fusarium, Polyporus.*
A.	*Micromonospora, Nocardia, Streptomyces*
B.	*Acromobactor, Bacillus, Chromobacterium, Clostridium*
Pectin	
F.	*Fusarium, Verticillium*
B.	*Bacillus, Clostridium, Pseudomonas*
Chitin	
F.	*Aspergillus, Fusarium, Gliocladium, Mucor, Penicillium.*
A.	*Micromonospora, Nocardia, Streptomyces.*
B.	*Acromobactor, Bacillus, Cytophaga, Clostridium, Flavobacterium, Pseudomonas.*
Protein & Nucleic Acid	
F.	*Penicillium, Mortierella.*
A.	*Streptomyces.*
B.	*Bacillus.*
Tanin	
F.	*Aspergillus, Penicillum*
Humic Acid	
F.	*Aspergillus, Polystictus*
Flevic Acid	
F.	*Poria*

According to Rittmann (2006) the developing microbial fuel cells (MFCs) can oxidise organic pollutants and create electricity from pollutants. Rittmann says, MFCs produce no pollution…infact they help to reduce pollution since organic pollution is their fuel sources. As the population on the earth continue to grow at a fast rate. It becomes harder to protect our land, air and water from harmful pollution. The most important way people can fight pollution is to learn as much as possible about how their action affect the environment. Then they can make wise choices that will reduce damage to the planet.

CONCLUSION

It is long part time for a realistic assessment of the likelihood of anything being done on a global warming scale in response to the clear and obvious threat of pollution in respect of global warming. The earth's atmosphere contained 380 parts/million of carbon in 2007. This is equivalent to 760 giga ton of largely in the form of CO_2 and CH_4. These gases must be removed from the atmosphere if the global warming problem is to be significantly reduced or eliminated. Microorganism may have a role in reversing the global warming. They may be used to remove carbon dioxide from the atmosphere.

Investigation of genetically engineered microbes are required which also able to reduce or remove CO_2 and CH_4 from the atmosphere and maintain the levels of atmospheric CO_2 and CH4 that will not cause global warming. In addition, many biofuel production method such as generating biofuel from agricultural, fish and forestry waste produce "biochar" as a by product. This process could also withdraw GHG from the atmosphere. So a lot of precious time has been lost due to negligent attitude towards direct biological impact of global warming. It is therefore, very important to design a proper action against global warming. Microbes as bioresources to cope the problems of global warming to save the our planet earth i.e. Go Green to Cope Global Warming.

REFERENCES

Abhishek, D., Garg, R., and Gadegone, M., 2007. Global Warming and its Impact: A Story of Adaptation, Extinction and Diseases. p. 1.

Appenzeller, T., 1993. Searching for Clues to Ancient Carbon Dioxide. Science 259: 908-909.

Bruce, E.R., 2008. Opportunities for Renewable Bioenergy Using Microorganisms. Biotechnology and Bioengineering 100 (2), 203-212.

Bradshaw, R.M., and Holzapfel, M., 2007. Evolutionary Response to Rapid Climate Change. Science 312: 1477-1478.

Buckley, M., Wall, J., 2006. Microbial Energy Conversion. American Academy of Microbiology, American Society for Microbiology, Washington, DC.

Conard, R., 1995. Soil Microbial Processes Involve in Production and Consumption of Atmospheric Trace Gases. Advance in Microbial Ecology 14: 207-250.

Energy Information Administration US, 2006. Annual Energy Review 2005.

Energy Information Administration US, 2006. Renewable Energy Annual 2004 with Preliminary Data for 2004. Energy Information Administration Office of Coal, Nuclear, Electric and Alternate Fuels US, Department of Energy, Washington, DC.

Gottschalk, G., Braun, M.,and Mayer, F.,1979. *Clostridium aceticum* (Wieringa), a Microorganism Producing Acetic Acid from Molecular Hydrogen and Carbon Dioxide. Archives of Microbiology Volume 128, Number 3, 288-293.

IPCC, 2007. In: Solomon, S., Qin, D., Manning, M., Marquis, M., Averyt, K., Tignor, M.M.B., Miller Jr., H.L., Chen, Z. (Eds.), Climate Change 2007: The Scientific Basis. Contribution of Working Group I to the Fourth Assessment Report of the Intergovernmental Panel on Climate Change. Cambridge University Press, New York, NY, USA.

Jarvis, A., Leedal, D., Taylor, C.J., Young, P., 2009. Stabilizing Global Mean Surface Temperature: A Feedback Control Perspective. Environmental Modelling & Software 24 (5), 665-674.

Jessup, M.S., Geertje, V.K., Wim, G.M., 1998. Something from Almost Nothing: Carbon Dioxide Fixation in Chemoautotrophs. Annual Review of Microbiology 52, 191-230.

Kerr, R.A., 1992. Pollutant Haze Cools the Green House. Science 263: 682-683.

LaMarche, V.C., Jr. and Wallace ,1972. Evaluation of Effects of Past Movements on the San Andreas Fault, Northern California," *Geological Society of America Bulletin* 83, 2665-2676.

Mayer, O., 1989. Aerobic Carbon Mono-oxide Oxidizing Bacteria. In H.G. Schelgal and B. Bowien(eds) Autotrophic Bacteria. Springer, Berlin, 331-350.

National Research Council1991. Global Environment Change: The Human Dimension. National Academy Press. Washington. Paul L E and Frenzel P (23 Feb.1999), Contribution of Methanotrophic and Nitrifying Bacteria to Methane and Ammonia Oxidation in Rhizosphere...Applied and Environment Microbiology. Vol. 65: 1826-1833.

Rifkin, J., 2002. The Hydrogen Economy. Tarcher/Putnam, New York.

Rittmann, B.E., 2006. Microbial Ecology to Manage Processes in Environmental Biotechnology. Trends Biotechnol. 24 (6), 261-266.

Sim, Jia Huey., 2008. Biocatalytic Conversion of CO to Acetic Acid by Clostridium Aceticum—Medium Optimization Using Response Surface Methodology (RSM). *Biochemical Engineering Journal* 40: 2.

Ward, P.D., 2006. Impact from the Deep ? Scientific American Journal. 295: 43-49.

Wang, B., Li, Y., Wu, N., Lan, C.Q., 2008. CO2 Bio-mitigation Using Microalgae. Applied Microbiology and Biotechnlogy 79, 707-718.

Pages: 31-50

NATURAL ECOSYSTEM AND CLIMATE CHANGE

Edited by: Dr. Pawan Kumar 'Bharti'; Dr. Khwairakpam Gajananda

ISBN: 978-93-5056-745-6

Edition: 2015

Published by: Discovery Publishing House Pvt. Ltd., New Delhi (India)

CHAPTER - 3

Environmental Impacts of Hydropower Projects in Upper Satluj Basin

Kesar Chand[1]*, Jagdish Chandra Kuniyal[1] and Dev Dutt Sharma[2]

ABSTRACT

The sum total of all the external conditions affects the environment and all the living beings which exist in it. If the environment is affected by some means then all the animals, plants and human beings are also affected by the stimuli which occur in their behavior and survival. This change occurs by population explosion or distinction, depletion of natural resources and pollution. So anything that affects ecosystem is indeed harmful and needs to be eradicated. Similarly, hydropower is not the biggest source of energy on earth although it has a very less cost because it has many disadvantages. Development of hydropower projects has many positive impacts in the region like economic strengthening, income generation, employment opportunity, infrastructure development, irrigation facility and flood control. While negative impacts are the other side of a coin. Landslides, rock fall, soil erosion, air pollution, water pollution and

1 G.B. Pant Institute of Himalayan Environment and Development, Himachal Unit, Mohal-Kullu - 175 126 (H.P.), India.

2 Department of Geography, Himachal Pradesh University Summerhill, Shimla - 177 005 (H.P.), India.

noise pollution, seismic activity, deforestation, submergence, displacement, health problems, solid waste, public agitation and change in micro-climatic conditions, etc. are of especial significance. Following research work at upper Satluj basin shows the environmental impacts (Water and Soil) which is due to heavy construction of HEPs.

INTRODUCTION

Hydropower is one of the important sources of energy in the Indian Himalayan region (IHR), which is characterized with steep topography; glacier fed perennial rivers with considerable scope for future economic development. The major river systems originating from the Himalayan ranges comprise the Indus, Ganga and Brahmaputra potential for the hydropower development in the region. The harnessing of this available water potential has become important for making progress after introducing hydropower projects in developing or under developing regions. Whenever a series of hydropower projects within a catchment are developed including those under construction or proposed, these projects overlap the ecological boundaries of one another. As a result, their collective impacts often damage the elusive environment. Hydropower projects construction and operation cause may have the downstream impacts. These impacts may include the siltation, water pollution, loss of aquatic habitats etc. (Hakeem and Sankar, 2011).

Making appropriate assessments in terms of above issues, it would be an important task with their implication from the grassroots (local communities) up to the policy level. Today, Hydropower projects are opposed by local people, environmentalist and social activists. This is mainly due to lack of attention paid by project proponents regarding environmental considerations of the projects when these remain under construction phases. As a result, lots of irregularities in environmental perspective occur during construction. Water resources projects are responsible for deteriorating the quality of soil and waters adjoining area of HEPs. Pollution of projects is a multifaceted phenomenon and depends on several factors such as type of scheme (weather run-of-the-river type, storage), climatic condition in the area. In order to assess or monitor the impacts of HEPs on soil and water present study is conducted in upper Satluj basin. Samples are collected upstream to low stream of HEPs and analyzed for physical, chemical properties.

STUDY AREA

The Sutlej River (Shatadru or Sumudri) is the longest of the five rivers that flows through the historic crossroad region of Himachal Pradesh in the northern India. It rises from beyond the Indian boundary in the south facing slope of the Kailash Mountain near Mansarover Lake from the Raksa Taal, as River Longcchen Khabab (Tibet). It is one of the largest among the five rivers of Himachal Pradesh. It enters into Himachal Pradesh at Shipkila (6,608 m) and flows in south-western direction through Kinnaur, Shimla, Kullu, Mandi, Bilaspur and Solan districts. Its length in Himachal Pradesh is about 320 km, having famous tributaries like Spiti, Ropa, Taiti, Kashang, Pangi nullah, Baspa, Yulla khad, Bhaba khad, Rupi khad, and Nauti khad, etc. Many famous settlement areas like Ribba, Kalpa, Sangla Valley, Baspa Valley, Rampur, Tatapani, Kol, Bilaspur, etc. comes under this river basin. Its total catchment area in Himachal Pradesh is 20,000 km^2. Geographical location of Satluj basin is shown in figure 3.1.

There are a number of hydropower projects operating in this basin and many others are also under construction. Majority of hydropower projects are under operation. These are Bhakra Dam (1325 MW), Sanjay Vidyut Pariyojna (120 MW), Baspa-II (300 MW) and Nathpa Jhakri (1500 MW), etc. Besides, hydropower projects under construction are: Ganvi-II (10 MW), Kashang (66 MW), Karcham-Wagtoo (1000 MW), Rampur (412 MW), Koldam (800 MW), etc. (CIA, 2006).

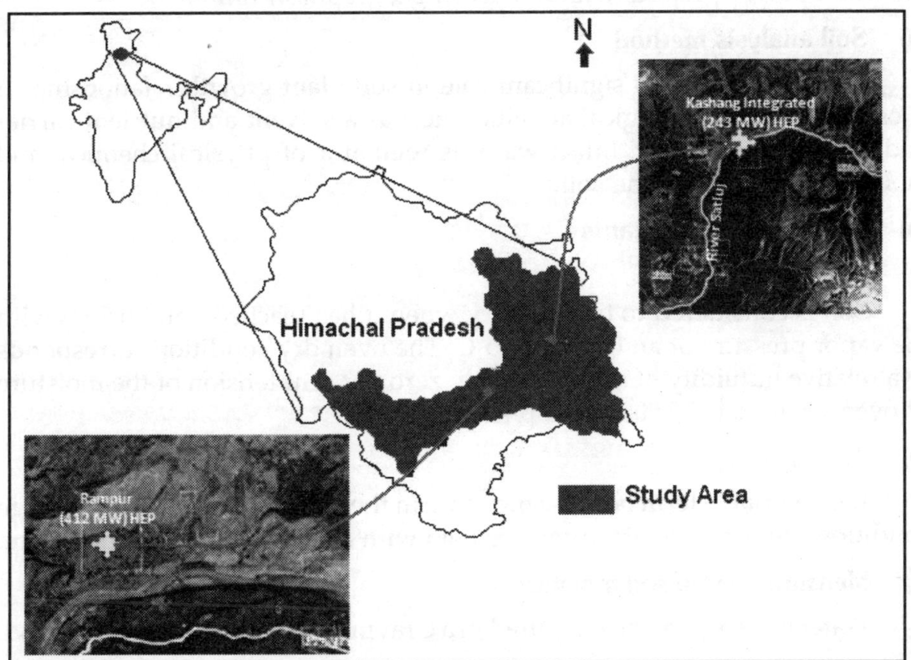

Fig 3.1: **Location of Study Area-the Satluj Basin in Himachal Pradesh**

METHODOLOGY

Shayang (SHP), Tangling (SHP), Karcham Wangtu, Shongthong, Nathpa Jhakri, Rampur and Bhaba HEPs are taken for water and soil sampling in upstream to downstream region at Satluj basin. The lateral study of impacts is supposed to be limited approximately within 1 km lateral distance from both the banks of river, assuming that the downstream impacts mainly confine to the close vicinity of the river valley. The upslope and downslope impact studies, in selected cases, are carried out to assess impacts on water and soil etc. In the study area, selected monitoring sites are identified for assessment of selected parameter like water quality and soil quality. These upslope and downslope impacts will provide the basis for initiating mitigation measures. From each sampling point, triplicate water samples are collected. In this way, a total of 120 water samples and as many soil samples are collected in accordance with the standard sampling guidelines (Radojecvic and Bashlin, 1999). The water samples were collected in 500 mL strong plastic bottles, whereas zip-mounted high-density polythene begs of appropriate size were used to collect about 500 g of soil sample.With a view to analyses soil quality of the project sites and their surroundings, Samples were collected from Up Stream, Dam Site, Pen Stock, Power House and Lowstream sites of the HEPs. Soil pollution is tested in the context to pH, nitrogen (N) phosphorous (P) potassium (K) and moisture content (%) under steep topography surrounding the hydropower projects within a given geographical unit.

(a) Soil analysis method

Water plays a very significant role in soil plant growth relationship. It is essential for physiological activities, acts as a solvent and nutrient carrier and maintains turgidity. Infact water is regulator of physical chemical and biological activities in the soil.

(b) Soil moisture constants

(a) Oven dry

Soil is considered to be oven dry when it has reached equilibrium with the vapor pressure of an oven at 105°C. The oven dry condition corresponds to a relative humidity of approximately zero per cent tension of the moisture at oven dryness is 10,000 atmospheres.

(b) Air dry

It is a variable term because moisture in the air fluctuates. Under average conditions, moisture at air dryness is held with a tension of 1000 atmosphere.

(c) Measurement of soil moisture

Water in a soil may be measured in a Gravimetric and volumetric method.

Gravimetric method

This is the simplest and most widely used method for measuring soil moisture.

Principle

Weighed soil sample is placed in an oven at 105°C and it is dried to constant weight. The weight difference is considered to be water present in soil sample.

Per cent moisture= Loss in weight/Oven dry weight of soil ×100

(d) Soil pH and electrical conductivity

The pH value is a measure of the hydrogen ion activity of the soil water system and expresses the acidity and alkalinity of soil. The pH is a very important property of soil as it determines the availability of nutrients, microbial activity and physical condition of the soil. The methods for determination of pH of the soil solution are mainly measured by Electric pH meter method. pH meter PC 510 (Eutech-part of Thermo Fisher Scientific) is used for the measurement.

(e) Estimation of major soil nutrients

(*a*) ***Nitrogen* (*N*)**

Total Soil N (mainly organic) is generally measured after wet digestion using the well-known Kjeldahl procedure. Total inorganic N is usually determined by distillation of 2 M KCL soil extract.

Kjeldahl Nitrogen

This procedure involves digestion and distillation. The soil is digested in concentrated H_2SO_4 with a catalyst mixture to raise the boiling temperature and to promote the conversion from organic-N to ammonium-N from the digest is obtained by steam distillation, using then titrated with dilute NaOH to raise the pH. The distillate is collected in saturated $H_2 BO_4$; and then titrated with dilute $H_2 SO_4$ to pH 5.0. The method determines ammonium-N, most of the organic-N forms and a variable fraction of nitrate-N in soil. For most soils, the Kjeldhal procedure is a good estimate of total soil N content.

Total N kg/ha=31.36 × actual vol. of $H_2 SO_4$ used in titration.

(*b*) *Phosphorus* (*P*)

(*Olsen and Sommers, 1982*)

Total P measurement involves digestion of a soil sample with a strong acid the dissolution of all insoluble inorganic minerals and organic P forms. Following calculation formula is used in this method for P.

Total P (ppm) = ppm P (from calibration curve) × A/wt×50/V

For total phosphorus in soil:

Where: A=Total volume of the digest (mL)

Wt.= Weight of air-dry soil (g)

V= Volume of digest used for measurement (mL)

(*c*) *Potassium* (*K*)

Highly weathered acid soils (of tropical regions) are more frequently deficient, whereas soils of arid and semi-arid areas tend to be well supplied with K. Soil of arid region are generally adequate in K; a possible exception is sandy soils and irrigated soils grown to high K.

Extractable K (ppm) =ppm K (from calibration curve)×A/Wt.

Where: A=Total volume of the extract (mL)

Wt. = Weight of air-dry soil (g)

(f) Water analysis

An Assessment of water quality is again an important parameter to indicate the level of pollution in HEPs adjacent areas. In this regards, basic water quality parameters like pH, electric conductivity and TDS are tested at different sites of the project. Ionic components and trace metals are estimated by Ion Chromatography in water samples which are collected adjacent areas of HEPs.

(f) *(a)* Ionic and trace metals analysis

Water samples are collected from an adjacent area of HEPs in Satluj basin. Samples were analyzed using an Ion Chromatographic (IC-3000, Dionex Ltd. USA) for major ions and trace metals in water. The details of operating conditions maintained for the analysis for anions, cations and transition metals which are shown in Table 3.1.

Table 3.1: Operating Conditions for the Analysis of Ions by Ion Chromatography

Parameter	Anions	Cations	Transition Matels
Column Flow rate (ml min 1)	Ion Pac AS11 1.50 mL/min	Ion Pac SCS 1 1.0 mL/min	Ion Pac CS5A 1.2 mL/min PCR Flow rate: 0.6 mL/min
Eluent	30mM NaOH	3mM MSA	Oxalic Acid
Detection	Suppressed conductivity	Non-suppressed conductivity	Absorbance Detection using AD 25 at 520 nm
Injection (μl)	10 μL	25 μL	50 μL

RESULTS AND DISCUSSION

Hydropower Potential in River Satluj Basin

Based on primary survey and collection of data from secondary sources, Himachal Pradesh has 21,452 MW total installed capacities for hydropower development. Out of this potential, 1,185 MW capacities were abandoned recently due to environmental considerations by the government. Basin wise potential in Himachal Pradesh is the highest in the Satluj (10,008 MW) followed by the Beas (4,206 MW), the Chenab (2,867 MW), the Ravi (2,478 MW) and the Yamuna (707 MW). A case study conducted in River Satluj Basin, it is revealed that more than 27 large, 4 small and 5 micro projects with the installed capacity of 9,728 MW are likely to be developed under HPSEB. Besides, HIMURJA is planning to develop nearly 69 projects with a capacity of 279 MW in the same basin.

Effectiveness of Environmental Impact Assessment Studies

Study on Environmental Impact Assessment reports of hydropower projects revealed that the methods of collection of baseline data for EIA study had many gaps. It is due to lack of scientific practices being followed from EIA guidelines and legislations. These gaps in individual EIA of the project continued to multiply environmental problems at different developmental stages and planning process. Such gaps also affect adversely the preparation of Catchment Area Treatment plan (CAT) which depends entirely on the level of EIA reports. A systematic protocol for data collection has also an ample scope in these individual EIA. The recommended terms of reference (TOR) by MoEF need to be followed during report preparation. Besides, peoples' participation during public hearing and others is not so satisfactory at the decision-making level. Conducting EIA studies and its report preparation should also be conducted by such organizations as are independent, autonomous, technically sound and free from any interference. Besides, the secondary data being used for EIA report preparation need to be strengthened with the use of primary data to up-date the onsite environmental issues.

In Satluj basin HEPs are developed or commissioned like Nathpa-Jhakri, Bhakra, Baspa-II and Bhaba projects. While Karcham, Wangtoo, Koldam, Rampur, Shongtong Karcham and Kashang hydroelectric projects are under construction. Propose projects are Khab, Luhri, Jangi Thopen, Thopan Powari, Poo Splioo and Yangthang Khab. In Satluj basin out of 37 HEPs, 28 projects were large (>25MW), 7 small (>2 MW to <25 MW) and 2 mini/micro (<2MW) (Fig. 3.2 and table 3.2).

Soil and Water Analysis Adjoining Area of Hydro Power Projects in Satluj Basin

Status of Soil Quality at Adjacent Areas of HEPs in Satluj Basin

Soil study is conducted at adjacent areas of HEPs in Satluj basin. Samples are collected from five points like upstream, dam sites, penstock or tunnel sites, power house sites and lowstream sites of HEPs. Top soil samples (0-20cm) are collected in these sites to know the status of soil quality at adjacent area.

(a) Physical properties of the soil

Physical properties of soil contain soil texture, soil structure, bulk density and soil color. In present study soil texture and soil color are study in the adjacent areas of HEPs in Satluj basin.

Table 3.2: Hydro Power Potenial in Satlaj Basin

Sl.No.	Name	River/Khad
1.	Rongtong	Rongtong Khad
2.	Rukti	Rukti Khad
3.	SVP Bhaba	Bhaba Khad
4.	Ghanvi	Ghanvi Khad
5.	Nogli Stage-I	Nogli
6.	Chaba	Nauti Khad
7.	Bhakra Dam	Satluj
8.	Bhaba Aug. P/H	Shango Khad
9.	Keshang-I	Keshang Khad
10.	Ghanvi-II	Ghanvi Khad
11.	Yangthang Khab	Spiti
12.	Khab -I	Satluj
13.	Khab -II	Satluj
14.	Thopan Powari	Satluj
15.	Baspa Stage-I	Baspa
16.	Sorang	Satluj
17.	Tidong-I	Satluj
18.	Tidong-II	Satluj
19.	Bahairari	Bahajrari Khad
20.	Kashang-II	Keshang Khad
21.	Kashang-III	Keshang Khad
22.	Luri	Satluj
23.	Jhangi Thopan	Satluj
24.	Kuling Lara	Spiti
25.	Lara Project	Spiti
26.	Mani Nadang	Spiti
27.	Lara Sumata	Spiti
28.	Sumta-Kathang	Kothans
29.	Chango Yangthang	Spiti
30.	Ropa	Tidong Khad
31.	Baspa Stage-II	Baspa
32.	Karcham Wangtoo	Satluj
33.	Nathpa Jhakri	Baspa
34.	Kol Dam	Satluj
35.	Rampur	Satluj
36.	Shongtong-Karcham	Satluj
37.	Kut	Satluj

Source: Electric Power Survey, Report released in January 2011

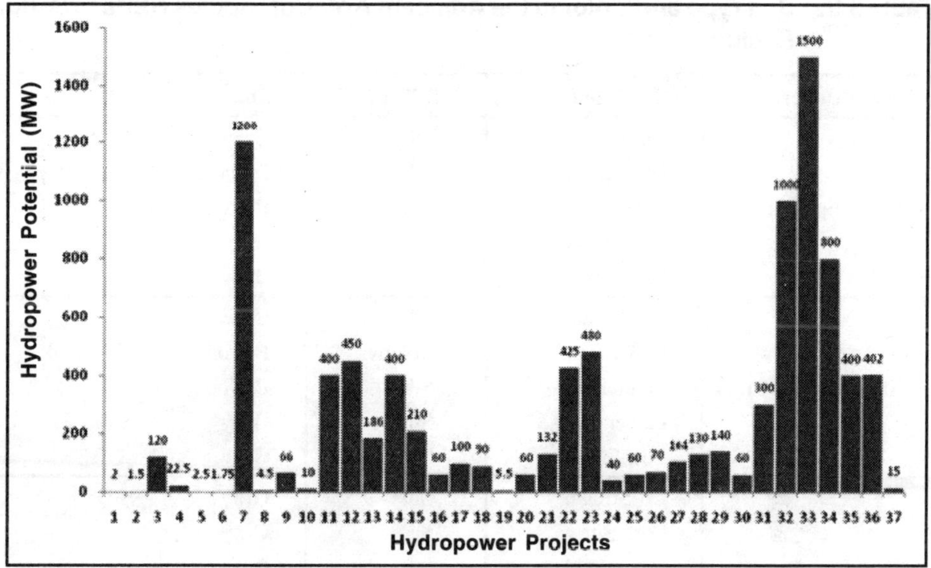

Fig 3.2: **Hydroelectricity Potentiantiality of River Satluj Basin**

Soil Texture

Soil texture is determined by the relative proportions of sand, silt, loamy and clay properties in the soil. In the present study silt and loamy type of soil found, while sand and clay are not found in the adjacent areas of HEPs in Satluj basin (Table 3.3).

Soil Color

The most influential colours in a well-drained soil are white, red, brown and black. White indicates the predominance of silica (quartz), or the presence of salts; red indicates the accumulation of iron oxide; and brown and black indicate the level and type of organic matter. In the present study white (gray) and brown soil observed in the adjacent areas of HEPs in Satluj basin (Table 3.3).

Soil Moisture

Water is a regulator of physical chemical and biological activities in the soil. Average soil moisture contents measured at adjacent areas of HEPs in Satluj basin is 9.89%. Moisture range measured 6.5-14.9% at all the study sites of HEPs. Highest moisture level measured at Shayang SHP (14.9%) and lowest moisture at Shangthong (6.4%).

Table 3.3: Soil Type and Color in the Adjacent Areas of Studies HEPs in Satluj Basin

Project	Location	Soil Type	Color
Shayang (SHP)	Up Stream	Silt	Gray
	Dam Site	Silt	Iron Oxide (red+yellow)
	Tunnel Side	Silt	Brwon
	Power House	Silt	Gray
	Low Stream	Silt	Brwon
Tangling(SHP)	Up Stream	Silt	Brown
	Dam Site	Loamy	Brwon
	Tunnel Side	Silt	Brwon
	Power House	Silt	Gray
	Low Stream	Silt	Gray
Karcham Wangtu	Up Stream	Silt	Gray
	Dam Site	Sil	Gray
	Tunnel Side	Silt	Brown
	Power House	Silt	Brwon
	Low Stream	Silt	Brwon
Shangthong	Up Stream	Loamy	Brown
	Dam Site	Loamy	Gray
	Tunnel Side	Loamy	Gray
	Power House	Loamy	Gray
	Low Stream	Silt	Brwon
Nathpa Jhakri	Up Stream	Silt	Gary
	Dam Site	Silt	Brwon
	Tunnel Side	Silt	Brwon
	Power House	Loamy	Gray
	Low Stream	Loamy	Gray
Rampur	Up Stream	Loamy	Gray
	Dam Site	Loamy	Gray
	Tunnel Side	Silt	Brown
	Power House	Silt	Gray
	Low Stream	Silt	Gray
Bhaba	Up Stream	Silt	Brown
	Dam Site	Silt	Brown
	Tunnel Side	Silt	Brwon
	Power House	Silt	Gray
	Low Stream	Silt	Gray

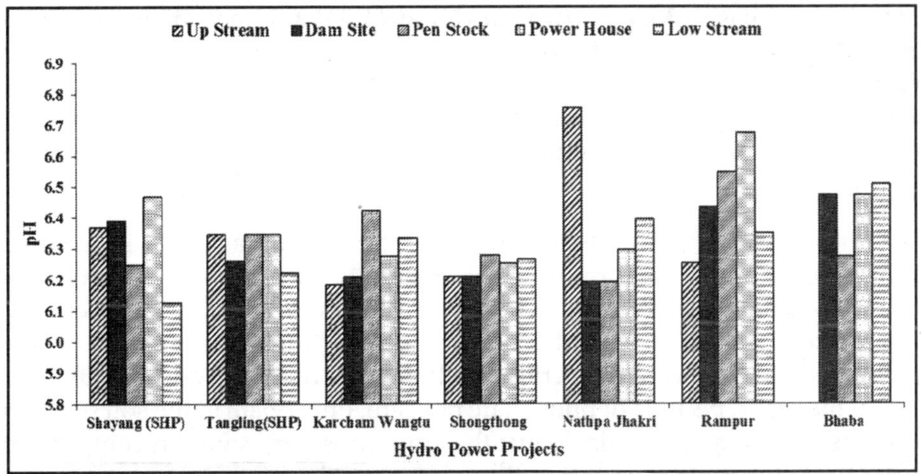

Fig. 3.3: **pH Concentration of Power Projects Upstream to Low Stream in Satluj Basin**

(b) Chemical properties of the soil

pH, EC and TDS

Mean pH is 6.3 measured in Satluj basin. pH range is observed 6.2-6.6 in study projects, maximum is measured at Rampur HEP which is 6.5 and minimum is measured at Shongthong HEP which is 6.2. Maximum upstream pH is measured 6.8 at Nathpa Jhakri and minimum is measured 6.2 at Shongthong HEP. Mean electric conductivity (EC) is measured 122.7 µS at adjacent areas of HEPs. Maximum EC at project EC adjacent areas at Satluj basin masured at power house sites which is 213.7 µS and minimum measured at low stream of the projects which is 27.6 µS. EC ranged between 77.2 to 145.9 µS at HEPs adjacent areas of Satluj basin. Maximum EC is measured at Shongthong HEP which is 77.2 µS and lowest EC measured at Shongthong HEP which is 77.2 µS. Total dissolve solvent (TDS) at penstock or tunnel side found maximum with 108.7 ppm and lowest found at low stream area of the HEPs at Satluj basin. Mean of Total dissolve solvent (TDS) is measured 61 ppm at adjacent areas of HEPs. Maximum TDS is measured at Tangling (SHP) which is 75.7 ppm and minimum found at Shongthong with 38.7 ppm.

Nitrogen (N)

Nitrogen is in organic and inorganic forms in soils. Over 90 percent of soil N is associated with soil organic matter. Nitrogen is in compounds identifiable as part of the original organic material such as proteins, amino acids, or amino sugars, or in very complex unidentified substances in advanced stages of decomposition. These uncharacterized substances resist further microbial degradation and account for the very slow availability of soil N.Nitrogen conversions depend on soil moisture conditions, soil acidity, temperature, and microbial activity.Anthropogenic activitiesare a major cause of slow availability of N in soil. Total nitrogen is measured at HEPs affected area of Satluj basin. Mean Nitrogen (N) at HEPs adjacent areas measured 0.87%. N range measured 0.84-0.93%. Maximum N measured at Karcham Wangtu (0.93%) and minimum at Tangling (SHP) which is 0.84%. Penstock or tunnel side area is observed maximum N at Karcham Wangtu which 0.25%. Pen stock side N is measured minimum which is 0.13% at Tangling (SHP).

Phosphorus (P)

Phosphorus (P) is an essential element classified as a macronutrient. Phosphorus is one of the three nutrients generally added to soils in fertilizers. One of the main roles of P in living organisms is in the transfer of energy. Organic compounds that contain P are used to transfer energy from one reaction to drive another reaction. Soils may contain several hundred to several thousand pounds of phosphate per acre. Phosphate in the soil solution P pool is immediately available but the amount is very small in comparison to the total P in soils. The active P pool is phosphorus that can be released into solution but is generally small in comparison to the fixed P. To determine the need for supplemental P, soil tests are often used to estimate how much phosphate will be available. In present study total P is measured along with the HEPs in upper Satluj basin. Mean P measured 0.82% at adjacent area of upper Satluj basin. P range is measured 0.6% to 1.0%. Maximum P measured at Rampur HEP surrounded area is 0.99% and minimum at Shayang (SHP) which is 0.64%.

Potassium (K)

Mean potassium is measured 8.85% in upper Satluj basin's HEPs. Range of K is measured 7.1% to 11%. Maximum K measured at Bhaba HEP which is 11% and minimum measured at Shongthong 7.1%. In Nathpa Jhakri HEP dam site location K measured maximum which is 13.4%. Minimum measurement of K (3.3%) is found at lower stream of Rampur HEP in adjacent area of the Satluj basin (Figure. 3.4).

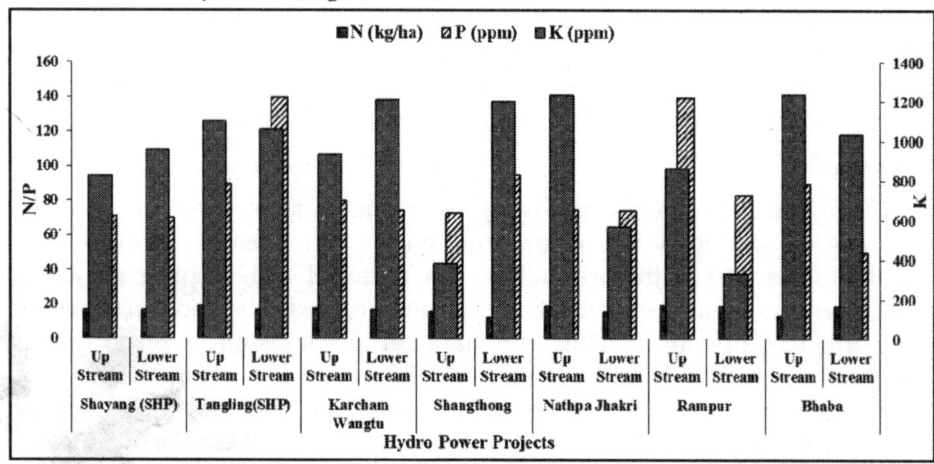

Fig. 3.4: **Soil Nutrients in Power Projects in Adjacent Area of the Satluj Basin**

Soil Quality of Under Construction Projects in Upper Satluj River Basin

In upper Satluj basin three large under construction and two large commissioned HEPs are studies to find out the soil chemical properties NPK. Karcham Wangtu, Shongthong and Rampur HEPs are under construction and Nathpa Jhakri, Bhaba HEPs are commissioned. Chemical properties (NPK) of soil in adjacent areas of projects are analyzed. In under construction projects nitrogen content has observed maximum in Karcham Wangtu HEP which is 0.93% followed by Rampur HEP (0.88%) and minimum at Shongthong HEP (0.84%). Phosphorus content measured maximum at Rampur HEP with (0.99%) followed by 0.84% in Shongthong HEP and minimum at Karcham Wangtu HEP with 0.80%. Potassium content in soil observed maximum at Karcham Wangtu (9.46%) followed by Shongthong (7.11%) and minimum at Rampur HEP with 6.66% (Figure 3.5a). In commissioned projectsBhaba HEP has the maximum concentration of NPK with 0.9%, 0.7% and 11% respectively (Figure 3.5b).

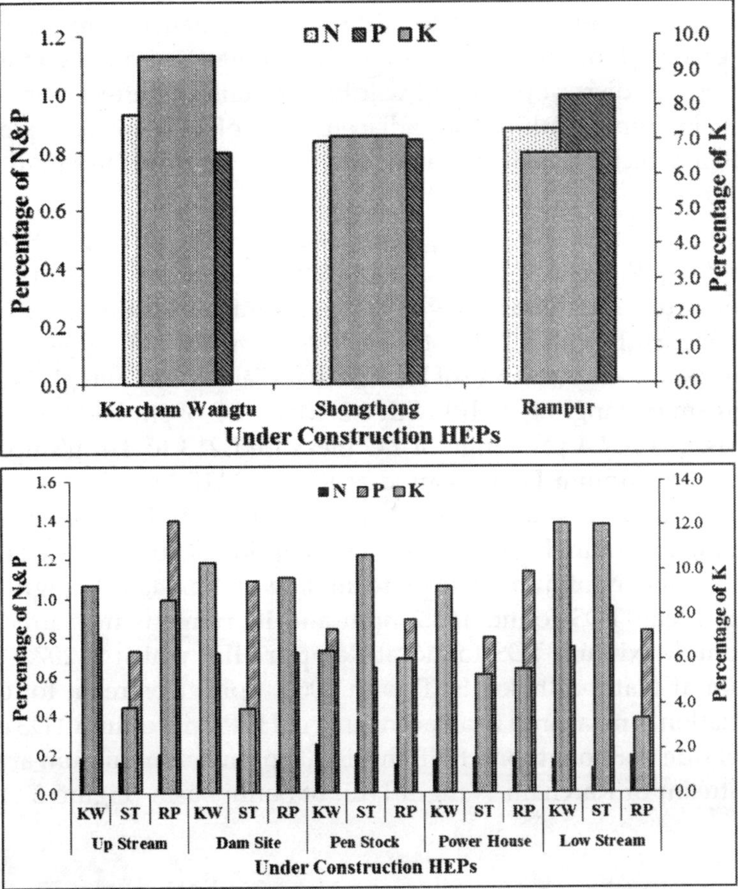

Fig. 3.5 (a & b): **Soil Quality of Commissioned Projects in Upper Satluj River Basin**

Upstream to low stream changes in soil quality due to under construction hydroelectricity project shows the variation in soil contents (NPK). Nitrogen contents observed maximum at Karcham Wangtu HEP penstock side with 0.25% and minimum observed at low stream site of Shongthong HEP with 0.13%. In phosphorus upstream site of Rampur HEP observed maximum with 1.4% and minimum at penstock site of Shongthong HEP. In case of potassium maximum observed at low stream site of Karcham Wangtu HEP and minimum observed same site of Rampur HEP with 3%.

Status of Water Quality at Adjacent Areas of HEPs in Satluj Basin

Hydropower often requires the use of dams, which can greatly affect the flow of rivers, altering ecosystems and affecting the wildlife and people who depend on those waters. Often, water at the bottom of the lake created by a dam is inhospitable to fish because it is much colder and oxygen-poor compared with water at the top. When this colder, oxygen-poor water is released into the river, it can kill fish living downstream that are accustomed to warmer, oxygen-rich water. In addition, some dams withhold water and then release it all at once, causing the river downstream to suddenly flood. This action can disrupt plant and wildlife habitats and affect drinking water supplies. In upper Satluj basin adjacent area of HEPs water qualities are observed in which pH, EC, TDS, Ionic and trace metals are measured upstream to low stream.

Mean pH of water at adjacent area of HEPs in upper Satluj basin measured 6.4. Range of pH is 6.3-6.4 in upstream to low stream. Maximum pH is measured at Rampur which is 6.5 and minimum is measured at Shongthong HEP with 6.2. Upstream to low stream pH value is measured maximum at power house site of Nathpa Jhakri and minimum pH is measured at up stream of Tangling (SHP) with 6.2. Mean EC of studied HEPs in upper Satluj basin is 324.4 µS, range of EC measured 213 to 414 µS upstream to lowstream. Maximum EC measured at Rampur HEP which is 414.9 µS and minimum found at Nathpa Jhakri which is 213.1 µS. EC from upstream to lowstream, maximum EC measured at tunnel side of Shongthong HEP which is 606.7 µS and minimum at lowstream side of Karcham Wangtu which is 138.5 µS. Mean TDS found 162.2 ppm and its range is measured 106.3 to 207.5 ppm. Maximum TDS found at Rampur HEP which is 207.5 ppm and minimum at Nathpa Jhakri HEP with 106.3 ppm. Upstream to lowstream TDS variation is measured in adjacent area of HEPs, maximum TDS measured at tunnel side of Shongthong HEP this is 303 ppm and minimum at 69.3 ppm at low stream of Karcham Wangtu HEP of Satluj basin (Figure 3.6).

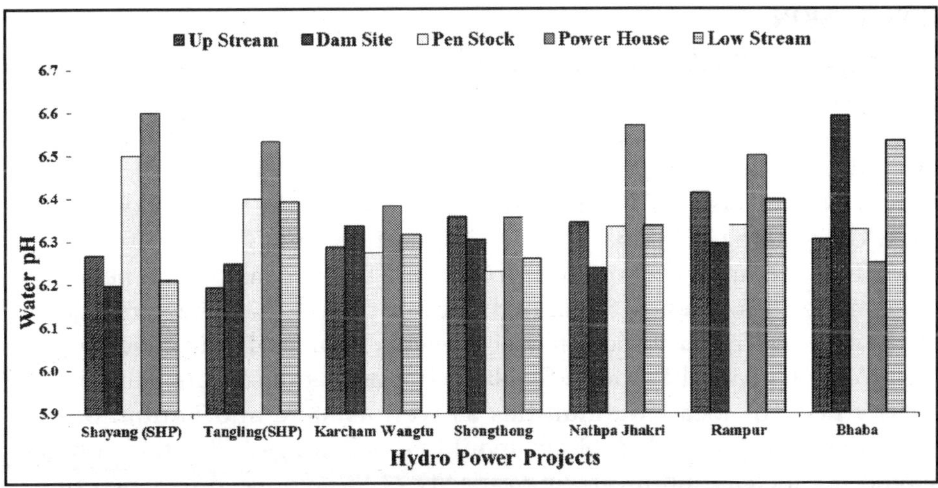

Fig. 3.6: **Project wise Upstream to Low Stream Water pH**

Ionic Components and Trace Metals of Water

Ionic components and trace metals are measured in water samples which are collected adjacent areas of HEPs. In water sample Br^-> Zn> Cl^-> Na^+> K^+ emerged as dominant contributors, whereas PO_4^{3-}> F^-> Co> Li^+ are estimated low levels in water samples (Fig 3.7). In Anions, Cl^- (17.1 mg/L) measured highest and in trace matels Zn (6.3 mg/L) measured highest in adjacent areas of Rampur HEP and in Cations Naz (3.3 mg/L) measured highest in adjacent areas of Bhaba HEP.

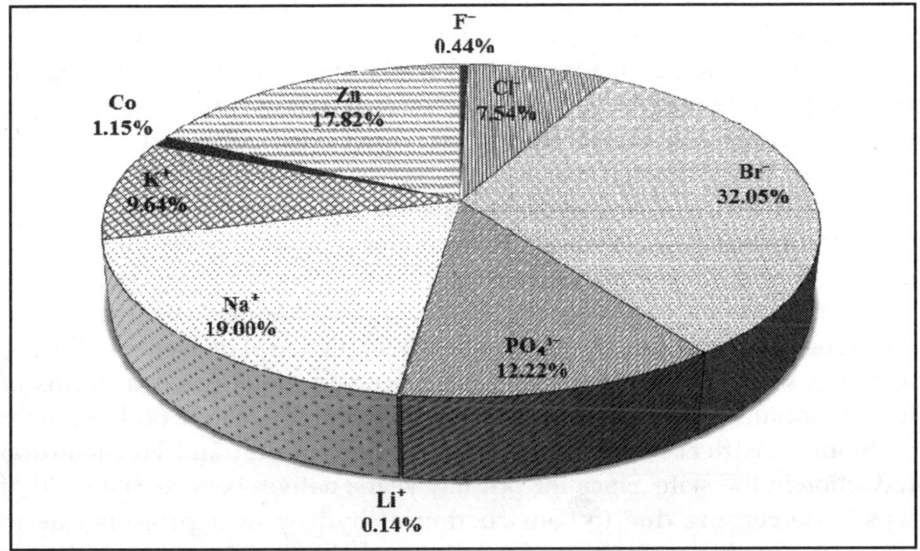

Fig. 3.7: **Ionic and Trace Metals Status in Satluj Basin's HEPs**

CONCLUSION

Himachal Pradesh has vast scope for hydropower development. It is estimated that more than 20,452 MW power could be produced from five river basins. The project authorities of hydropower development in Himachal Pradesh are Himachal Pradesh State Electricity Board (HPSEB), Sutlej Jal Vidyut Nigam Ltd. (SJVNL), National Hydroelectric Power Corporation (NHPC), National Thermal Power Corporation (NTPC), J.P. Groups and HIMURJA. All large hydropower projects are under construction belongs to these authorities/ bodies. Small hydropower projects have been recognized as reliable, eco-friendly and renewable energy sources. It has good scope in region like Himachal Pradesh. Small hydropower projects are fulfilling the energy need of local communities as well as state and nation. So it is recommended that such projects should be encouraged. But their number should not increase until carrying capacity of these projects assessed fully.

Development of hydropower projects has many positive impacts in the region like economic strengthening, income generation, employment opportunity, infrastructure development, irrigation facility and flood control. While negative impacts are the other side of a coin. Landslides, rock fall, soil erosion, air pollution, water pollution and noise pollution, seismic activity, deforestation, submergence, displacement, health problems, solid waste, public agitation and change in micro-climatic conditions, etc. are of especial significance.

In the Satluj basin, positive impacts like construction of roads, dispensaries, schools, temple, bridges and pathway etc. have been noteworthy in and around hydropower projects. Regarding negative impacts, it can be stated that construction of a large number of projects has been changing the hydrological system in the Satluj basin. The actual river path is changing fast due to a diversion of river from its reservoir to dam sites and sometimes beyond this. It is estimated that change in river path will largely be affected between the areas of reservoir to powerhouse of hydropower project. Diversion of river, at present, in all large hydropower projects in the Satluj Basin is a common phenomenon. The diverted rivers are supposed to be altered in terms of micro-climate of the region. Besides, construction of tunnels, blasting activities, plying vehicles, construction of residential colonies, quarrying sites and dumping sites are adversely be affected in terms of physical, social, economic and cultural environment of a region. Both, Kinnaur and Shimla districts which are known for Agricultural and Horticultural production in the state. Since the last few years, natives believe that yield of crops is decreasing due to construction of hydropower projects due to movement of vehicles, blasting, quarrying and change in hydrological cycle are causing in yield to decline.

All these problems are due to lack of good EIA guidelines and legislations. Besides, unscientific methodologies to adopt for baseline data collection and less participation of natives during decision making process have been major issues of concerned. To mitigate these problems, there is an urgent need to refine present policy of development especially in terms of hydropower projects. Besides, study of Cumulative Impact Assessment (CIA) and Strategic Environment Assessment (SEA) are important tasks to achieve an objective of sustainable development in the Indian Himalaya. In present study, soil and water are analyzed to know the status of HEPs and its surrounding in Satluj basin. Physical and chemical parameters of soil are studies to know the status of soil. Silt soil types are observed in adjacent area of the HEPs. Gray color of the soil is dominant in present study and acidic nature of soil is observed in the Satluj basins HEPs. Moisture level is observed maximum at Shyang SHP. Rampur HEP has the maximum pH level and minimum measured at Shongthong HEP. Small hydro-electric project has the maximum EC level and minimum at Shongthong HEP. Maximum TDS measured at Tangling SHP and minimum at Shongthong HEP. Nitrogen measured at maximum Karcham Wangtu HEP and minimum at Tangling SHP. Rampur HEP has the maximum P value and minimum at Shayang (SHP). Potassium observed maximum at Bhaba HEP and minimum at Rampur HEP. Water pH level observed maximum at Bhaba HEP and minimum at Shongthong HEP. EC observed maximum at Rampur HEP and minimum at Nathpa Jhakri HEP. TDS of water observed maximum at Rampur HEP and minimum at Nathpa Jhakri project. Ionic components and trace metals measured highest in under construction HEPs and lowest at commissioned HEPs in adjacent areas of Satluj basin. Ionic components and trace metals are estimated in water samples which are collected adjacent areas of HEPs. In water sample Br^{-}> Zn> Cl^{-}> Na^{+} > K^{+} emerged as dominant contributors, whereas PO_4^{3-}> F^{-}> Co> Li^{+} are estimated low levels in water samples.

REFERENCES

Alshuwaikhat, H.M, (2005) Strategic Environmental Assessment can help Solve Environmental Impact Assessment Failures in Developing Countries, *Environmental Impact Assessment Review*, 25: 307-317.

Bonnell, S. and Storey, K. (2000) Addressing Cumulative Effects Through Strategic Environmental Assessment: A Case Study of Small Hydro Development in Newfoundland, Canada, *Journal of Environmental Assessment Policy and Management*, 2 (4), DOI: 10.1142/S1464333200000485.

Briffett, C., Obbard, J.P. and Mackee, J. (2003) Towards SEA for the Developing Nations of Asia, Environmental Impact Assessment Review 23(2): 171-196.

Buch, V.P. (2000) Need, Environmental Appraisal, Scope and Measurement for Environment Management in Sardar Sarover, Multi-purpose Project. In: Goel, R.S. (eds.) Environment Management in Hydropower and River Valley Projects. Oxford & IBH Publishing Co. Pvt. Ltd., New Delhi, pp. 211-222.

Chandrasekharan, M.E. (1995) Case Study of Reservoir Sedimentation in the Western Ghat Region of Kerala. In: Anonymous (eds.) Environmental Impact Assessment Studies (Case Studies), Pub. No. 248, New Delhi, pp. 192-197.

Chitkara, S.C., Sud, S.C. and Khangura, D.S. (2000) Socio-economic and Environment Review of Bhakra–Beas Projects. In: Goel, R.S. (eds.) Environment Management in Hydropower and River Valley Projects. Oxford & IBH Publishing Co. Pvt. Ltd., New Delhi, pp. 235-246.

Fergusson, J.E. (1990) The Heavy Elements; Chemistry Environment Impact and Health Effects. Pergamon Press plc. Headington Hill Hall, Oxford OX3 OBW, England, pp. 207-234.

Fischer, B. (2003) Strategic Environmental Assessment in Post-modern Times, Environmental Impact Assessment Review 23: 155-70.

Gellhorn, E. (1972) Public Participation in Administrative Proceedings. *Yale Law Journal* 81: 359-387.

Goel, R.S. (2000) Environment Impact Assessment-Trends, Practices and Status in India. In: Goel, R.S. (eds.) Environmental Impacts Assessment of Water Resources Projects. Oxford & IBH Publishing Co. Pvt. Ltd., New Delhi, pp. 241-259.

Goel, R.S. and Aggarwal, K.K. (2000) River Valley Projects and Environment: Concern and Management. In: Goel, R.S. (eds.) Environmental Impact Assessment of Water Resources Projects. Oxford & IBH Publishing Co. Pvt. Ltd., New Delhi, pp. 72-87.

Gupta, V. and Sah, M.P. (2008) Spatial Variability of Mass Movement in the Satluj Valley, Himachal Pradesh during 1990-2006. *Journal of Mountain Science* 5(1): 38-51.

Hakeem, K.A. and Sankar, E.S. (2011) Report on Monitoring of Glacier Lakes/Water Bodies in the Himalayan Regions of Indian River Basins for June 2011, Climate Change and IAD Directorate, Central Water Commission, Govt. of India, New Delhi, pp. 1-15.

Jain, A.P., Kuniyal, J.C. and Shannigrahi, A.S. (1996) Solid Waste Management in Mohal. In Proc. of 22nd WEDC Conference: Discussion Paper: Reaching the Unreached – Challenges for the 21st Century, pp. 328-329.

Kuniyal, J.C. and Sharma, Reeju (2008) Environmental Assessment of Hydropower Projects in the Himalayan Beas Valley of Himachal State, India. In: Singh, Abha Lakshmi and Shahab, Fazal (eds.) Rural Environment Management, B.R. Publishing Corporation, Delhi-52, pp. 227-268.

Kuniyal, J.C. and Jain A.P. (2001) Tourists Involvement in Solid Waste Management in Himalaya Trails: A Case Study in and Around Valley of Flowers. Journal of Environment Systems 28: 91-115.

Kuniyal, J.C., Sharma, Reeju, Kuniyal, C.P., Vishvakarma, S.C.R. and Aggarwal, D. K. (2002) Environmental Assessment of Hydropower Projects in the Beas Valley of Himachal Pradesh: A Local Community Perspective: National Workshop on Mountain Environment and Development: Potential and Progress, Almora (Uttrakhand).

Kuniyal, J.C., Sharma, Reeju, Kuniyal, C.P., Vishvakarma, S.C.R. and Aggarwal, D. K. (2002) Environmental Assessment of Hydropower Projects in the Beas Valley of Himachal Pradesh: A Local Community Perspective: National Workshop on Mountain Environment and Development: Potential and Progress, Almora (Uttrakhand).

Lins, C., Laguna, M. and Soberberg, C. (2004) Small Hydro in Europe, Hydropower and Dams II (3): 30-31.

Liou, M. and Yu Y. (2004) Development and Implementation of Strategic Environmental Assessment in Taiwan, *Environmental Impact Assessment Review* 24: 337-350.

Maria, R.P. (1999) A Training Manual on Strategic Environmental Impact Assessment (SEA)-Current Practices, Future Demands, and Capacity Building Needs. http://www.iaia.org/Non_Members/EIA/SEA/SEAManual.pdf

Mohanty, R.P. and Mathew, T. (1987) Somc Investigations Relating to Environment Impacts of a Water Resource Projects. *Journal of Environment Management* 24: 315-336.

Nair, P.V. and Balasubramanyam, K. (1995) Long-term Environment and Ecological Impacts of Multiple River Valley Projects, KRI Research Report No. 26, Kerala Forest Research Institute, Kerala, India.

Noble, B.F. (2000) Strategic Environmental Assessment: What is it and what makes it Strategic? *Journal of Environment Assessment Policy and Management* 2(2): 203-224.

Noble, B.F. and Storey, K. (2001) Towards Structural Approach to a Strategic Environment Assessment. *Journal of Environmental Assessment Policy Management* 3(4): 483-508.

Panigrahy, Nrusinghanda (2003) Importance of Environment Impact Assessment in Hydropower Projects. In: Mathur, G.N., Goyal, D.P. Chawala, A.S. and Singh, R.B. (eds.) Proc. International Conference on Accelerated Construction of Hydropower Projects. Vol. I, 15-17, Oct. 2003, Gedu Bhutan, pp. X2-X9.

Partida´rio, M.R. and Clark R. (2000) Perspectives on Strategic Environmental Assessment, USA: CRC Press, pp. 3-11.

Pateman, C. (1972) Participation and Democratic Theory, Cambridge University Press, Cambridge.

Prasad, K. (2000) Role of Economic Analysis for Integrated Evaluation of Environmental Impacts. In: Goel R. S. (eds.) Environmental Impacts Assessment of Water Resources Projects, Tata McGraw Hill Publishing Co., New Delhi, pp. 261-267.

Radojevic, M., and Bashlin, V.N. (1999) Practical Environmental Analysis. UK: The Royal Society of Chemistry.

Rana, N., Sati, S.P. and Sundriyal, Y.P. (2007) Socio-economic and Environmental Implications of the Hydroelectric Projects in Uttarakhand Himalaya, India. *Journal of Mountain Science* 4(4): 344-353.

Reddy, U.B. (1991) The Implication of Large Dam: A Case of Narmada Valley Projects. *Geographical Review of India* 53(3).

Samant S.S., Butola, J.S., and Sharma A. (2007) Assessment of Diversity, Distribution, Conservation Status and Preparation of Management Plan for Medicinal Plants in the Catchment Area of Parbati Hydroelectric Project Stage-III in Northwestern Himalaya. *Journal of Mountain Science* 4(1): 34-56.

Sharma, M.P. (2000) Environmental Impacts of Small Hydropower Projects: International Course on Planning of Small Hydro Projects, Roorkee, India, pp. 1-20.

Sharma, S. K, Sharma, V.K. and Gupta, A. (2000) Environment Impact of the Run of the River Hydropower Projects. In: Goel, R.S. (eds.) Environment Management in Hydropower and River Valley Projects. Oxford & IBH Publishing Co. Pvt. Ltd., New Delhi, pp. 267-272.

Sharma, S., Kuniyal, J.C. and Sharma, J.C. (2005) Hydropower Projects in the Beas Valley of Himachal Pradesh: Myths and Facts, XXVII Indian Geography Congress, Bangalore.

Sharma, S., Kuniyal, J.C. and Sharma, J.C. (2007) Assessment of Man-made and Natural Hazards in the Surroundings of Hydropower Projects Under Construction in the Beas Valley of Northwestern Himalaya. *Journal of Mountain Science* 4(3): 221-236.

Sharma, S., Kuniyal, J.C. and Sharma, J.C. (2007) Assessment of Man-made and Natural Hazards in the Surroundings of Hydropower Projects Under Construction in the Beas Valley of Northwestern Himalaya. *Journal of Mountain Science* 4(3): 221-236.

Singh, J.S. (2006) Sustainable Development of the Indian Himalayan Region: Linking Ecological and Economic Concerns, *Current Science*, 90: 784-788.

Singh, V. and Sharma, M.L. (1998) Mountain Ecosystem: A Scenario of Unsustainability. Indus Publishing Co., New Delhi.

Stanley, W. (1996) Machkund Upper Kolab and Nalco Projects in Karaput District Orrisa. Economic and Political Weekly 31(24): 1513-1538.

The´rivel R, Partida´rio M.R. (1996) The Practice of Strategic Environmental Assessment, London: Earth scan Publications, pp. 3-14.

Varshney, R.S. (1995) Hydroelectric Development in the Ganga Valley and its Impact on the Environment. In: Central Board of Irrigation and Power (eds.) Environmental Impact Assessment Studies (Case Studies), Pub. No. 248, New Delhi, pp. 65-76.

Verheem, R. and Tonk, J. (2000) Enhancing Effectiveness: Strategic Environmental Assessment: One Concept, Multiple Forms, Impact Assessment and Project Appraisal 18(3): 177-82.

Webler, T., Kastenholz, H. and Renn, O. (1995) Public Participation in Impact Assessment: A Social Learning Perspective. *Environmental Impact Assessment Review* 15(5): 443-463.

Xiuzhen, C., Jincheng, S. and Jinhu, W. (2002) Strategic Environmental Assessment and its Development in China, *Environmental Impact Assessment Review* 22(2): 101-109.

http://msucares.com/crops/soils/nitrogen.html

Pages: 51-56

NATURAL ECOSYSTEM AND CLIMATE CHANGE
Edited by: **Dr. Pawan Kumar 'Bharti'; Dr. Khwairakpam Gajananda**
ISBN: 978-93-5056-745-6
Edition: **2015**
Published by: **Discovery Publishing House Pvt. Ltd., New Delhi (India)**

CHAPTER - 4

Role of Human Being in Changing Global Environment and its Impact on Human Health

Monika Khanna[1] and Roma Khanna[2]

ABSTRACT

The World Health Organization (WHO) has become increasingly concerned about effect of global environmental change on human health. In addition to climate change, biodiversity and natural disasters, there are a number of human interventions that are direct drivers of environmental change. Impacts can be modified or exacerbated by a local population's current vulnerability, such as population movement into an endemic area for a disease for which they have no immunity. Global changes are likely to impact on the evolution of pathogens and hence of diseases. The paper explores the role of human being in changing environment and its impact on human health.

INTRODUCTION

An environmental problem arises whenever there is a change in the quality or quantity of any environmental factor which directly or indirectly

1 Department of Economics, Govt. Raza PG College, Rampur (UP), India.

2 Department of Economics, K.G.K College, Moradabad (UP), India.

affects the health and well-being of man in an adverse manner. Environmental problems can be studied from two different viewpoints. One is simply to look for adverse effects without regard to their origin in order to detect trends that call for further investigation; the other is to try to understand the cause and effect relationships, which make better prediction and proper management possible.

Some of the environmental problems which are critical at the present time are fairly widely known because of the growing awareness of all levels of society, including governments, general public and the scientific community. However, our present information on the structure and function of the biosphere is not sufficient to allow an accurate evaluation of the total situation, expect to indicate some broad problem areas. There may be serious potential problems of which we are as yet unaware; other known problems may be less serious than we think.

The Commission has made an extensive survey and analysis of those problems which are currently regarded as being of critical importance. The following criteria were used in an attempt to assess the critical nature of the problems to be solved in the near future:

(a) Number of people and nations involved

(b) Geographical distribution of the problem

(c) Temporal distribution of the problem (temporary or long-term effects)

(d) Degree of irreversibility of the effects

(e) Degree of impact on health, standard of living, social structure and economy

(f) Degree of international significance of the problem

Although these criteria overlap and may not be exhaustive, they fonn a useful basis for judgment. The consensus of the Commission's survey was that a fairly restricted number of problems were found to recur time and again. The major critical problem may be summarized as, "the adverse effects of a changed environment on human health and well-being"; The possibility that a changing environment may lead to increased mortality, increased frequency of diseases, lowered nutritional status via decreased agricultural productivity, or lowered psychological value of the environment. Concern has been widely expressed that these possible effects on man may be caused by direct input of toxic substances into the environment or improper land use.

Many global issues are climate-related, including basic needs such as food, water, health, and shelter. Changes in climate may threaten these needs with increased temperatures, sea level rise, changes in precipitation, and more frequent or intense extreme events. Climate change will affect individuals and groups differently. Certain groups of people are particularly sensitive to climate change impacts, such as the elderly, the infirm, children, native and tribal groups, and low-income populations. Climate change may also threaten key natural resources, affecting water and food security. Conflicts, mass migrations, health impacts, or environmental stresses in other parts of the world could raise national security issues for the United States.

Although climate change is an inherently global issue, the impacts will not be felt equally across the planet. Impacts are likely to differ in both magnitude and rate of changing. Some nations will likely experience more adverse effects than others. Other nations may benefit from climate changes. The capacity to adapt to climate change can influence how climate change affects individuals, communities, countries, and the global population.

ROLE OF HUMAN BEING IN CHNAGING ENVIRONMENT

The impact that humans have on the environment and the fundamental role that the environment plays in supporting human well-being, sustainable development will require improved understanding of human-environment interactions and intelligent decisions to guide human actions in ways consistent with maintaining human well-being in the long-run. Human well-being requires, at the very minimum, an acceptable level of safe food, clean air and drinking water, safe shelter (housing) and protection from diseases. Two large problems are facing humanity in this century: (i) nearly half of the world population lives in poverty and (ii) the high level of total energy and materials use are leading to global changes that threaten the life-support system of the planet. Increasing the material well-being of people in developing countries seems to be a global priority, yet bringing the entire world population to levels of consumption prevalent in developed countries, given current technology, is unsustainable.

Climate change and ocean acidulation effects: It dealt with forecasting impacts, assessing ecosystem response and evaluating management strategies in ocean sherry. Another important effect on ocean sherry is due to acidulation of the oceans as a consequence of rising CO2 emission which is poised to change marine ecosystem profoundly by increasing dissolved CO2 and decreasing ocean.

Global warming and human migration: Scientists are predicting human mass migration as a consequence of climate change: millions of people being from rising sea levels and drought, leading to serious consequences for both migrants and receiving societies.

Water and air pollution: Water pollution from human activities, either industrial or domestic, is a major health problem in many countries. Every year, approximately 25 million people die as a result of water pollution.

Energy: The reserves of coal, oil, natural gas and uranium are limited. In addition, their emissions carbon dioxide and radioactive waste cannot be absorbed by Nature. Consequently they are not sustainable sources of energy.

Nor is ethanol from corn, which requires fossil energy input for plowing the fields, distilling the mash, and large quantities of water. The only sustainable energy is renewal energy; solar, wind and hydropower. As demand for renewal energy increases, it becomes important to devise optimal strategies for given demand goals.

Enhancing the Greenhouse Effect: naturally occurring greenhouse gases, keep the Earth warm enough to support life. However, scientific studies have shown that a variety of human activities release greenhouse gases. These include the burning of fossil fuels for producing electrical energy, heating and transportation. By increasing their concentrations and by adding new greenhouse gases like CFCs, humankind is capable of raising the average global temperature.

Land Use Change: As humans replace forests with agricultural lands, or natural vegetation with asphalt or concrete, they substantially alter the way the Earth's surface reflects sunlight and releases heat. All these changes also affect regional evaporation, runoff and rainfall patterns. Land use and the changes in the way it is used effect the global carbon cycle, reduce the world's forests and woodlands, expand the cropped land area, and cause tropical deforestation. As well, there is increased productivity of labor in exploiting land through the application of capital and new technologies. Conversion of land from natural to agricultural use also upsets the balance.

Atmospheric aerosols: Humans are adding large quantities of fine particles (aerosols) to the atmosphere, both from agriculture and industrial activities. Although most of these aerosols are soon removed by gravity and rainfall, they still affect the radiation balance in the atmosphere. Whether this effect adds to or offsets any warming trend depends on the quantity and nature of the particles as well as the nature of the land or ocean surface below. The regional effects, however, can be significant.

Burning of Fossil Fuels for Energy: As humanity burns the organic matter from past geologic periods (or the forests of today) to power the engines and economies of modern society, we are re-injecting our fossil carbon legacy into the atmosphere at incredibly accelerated rate. Carbon dioxide is dumped into the atmosphere at a much faster rate than it can be withdrawn or absorbed by the oceans or living things in the biosphere. The carbon dioxide buildup is a principal controlling factor of the climate change.

IMPACT OF ENVIRONMENTAL CHANGE ON HUMAN HEALTH

The risks of climate-sensitive diseases and health impacts can be high in poor countries that have little capacity to prevent and treat illness. There are many examples of health impacts related to climate change.

- Sustained increases in temperatures are linked to more frequent and severe heat stress.

- The reduction in air quality that often accompanies a heat wave can lead to breathing problems and worsen respiratory diseases.
- Impacts of climate change on agriculture and other food systems can increase rates of malnutrition.
- Climate changes can influence infectious diseases. The spread of meningococcal (epidemic) meningitis is often linked to climate changes, especially drought. Areas of sub-Saharan and West Africa are sensitive to the spread of meningitis, and will be particularly at-risk if droughts become more frequent and severe.
- The spread of mosquito-borne diseases such as malaria may increase in areas projected to receive more precipitation and flooding. Increases in rainfall and temperature can cause spreading of dengue fever.

Certain groups of people in low-income countries are especially at risk for adverse health effects from climate change. These at-risk groups include the urban poor, older adults, young children, traditional societies, subsistence farmers, and coastal populations. Many regions, such as Europe, South Asia, Australia, and North America, have experienced heat-related health impacts. Rural populations, older adults, outdoor workers, and those without access to air conditioning are often the most vulnerable to heat-related illness and death. For more information about the climate impacts on vulnerable populations, please visit the Society Impacts & Adaptation page.

CONCLUSION

Weather and climate play a significant role in people's health. Changes in climate affect the average weather conditions that we are accustomed to. Warmer average temperatures will likely lead to hotter days and more frequent and longer heat waves. Human beings are responsible for causing changes in natural environment and can lead to heat-related illnesses and deaths. Increases in the frequency or severity of extreme weather events such as storms could increase the risk of dangerous flooding, high winds, and other direct threats to people and property. Changes in temperature, precipitation patterns, and extreme events could enhance the spread of some diseases.

REFERENCES

1. Karl, T.R., J.M. Melillo, and T.C. Peterson (eds.) USGCRP (2009). Global Climate Change Impacts in the United States. United States Global Change Research Programme. Cambridge University Press, New York, NY, USA.
2. Gamble, J.L. (ed.), K.L. Ebi, F.G. Sussman, T.J. Wilbanks. CCSP (2008). Analyses of the Effects of Global Change on Human Health and Welfare and Human Systems. A Report by the U.S. Climate Change Science Programme and the Subcommittee on Global Change Research. U.S. Environmental Protection Agency, Washington, DC, USA.

3. EPA (2010). Our Nation's Air: Status and Trends Through 2008. U.S. Environmental Protection Agency. EPA-454/R-09-002.
4. NRC (2010). Adapting to the Impacts of Climate Change. National Research Council. The National Academies Press, Washington, DC, USA.
5. EPA (2006). Air Quality Criteria for Ozone and Related Photochemical Oxidants. U.S. Environmental Protection Agency, Washington, DC, USA.
6. EPA (2009). Integrated Science Assessment for Particulate Matter: Final Report. U.S. Environmental Protection Agency, Washington, DC, USA.
7. http://www.epa.gov/climatechange/impacts-adaptation/health.html
8. http://dimacs.rutgers.edu/SustainabilityReport/friedman8-26-10.pdf
9. http://www.unmillenniumproject.org/documents/Environment-chapter1.pdf
10. http://www.who.int/bulletin/archives/78(9)1148.pdf

Pages: 57-70

NATURAL ECOSYSTEM AND CLIMATE CHANGE
Edited by: **Dr. Pawan Kumar 'Bharti'; Dr. Khwairakpam Gajananda**
ISBN: 978-93-5056-745-6
Edition: **2015**
Published by: **Discovery Publishing House Pvt. Ltd., New Delhi (India)**

CHAPTER - 5

Effect of Climate Change on Pesticide Use

Osadebe, Vivian Ogechi and Echezona, Bonaventure C.

INTRODUCTION

Global climate change is arguably the most severe problem that the world faces today. Our climate influences every aspect of life on this planet from our ability to produce food and therefore our future development, to the distribution of biomes and the level of biodiversity that exists in the world. The earth's climate has changed over the last century and there is new and stronger evidence that most of the warming observed the last 50 years is attributable to human activities.

Once released in the environment, pesticides tend to build up in the fat tissues of living organisms causing serious harm to the health and a potential loss of biodiversity. Agriculture of any kind is strongly influenced by the availability of water. Climate change will modify rainfall, evaporation, runoff, and soil moisture storage. Also changes in the incidence and severity of agricultural pests, diseases, soil erosion, as well as changes in extreme events such as drought and floods are all influenced by climate change. Climate change may allow pest migration or population explosions which may

Department of Crop Science, University of Nigeria, Nsukka, Nigeria.

adversely affect productivity, profitability and possibly even viability. Flowering patterns, breeding behaviours and the timing of migrations are all undergoing changes. The distribution of plants, insects, animals and even soil bacteria is shifting rapidly. Thus, pesticide use is seriously being affected by climate change.

DEFINITION OF TERMS

Pesticide

The United State Environmental protection Agency (USEPA) defines pesticides as "any substance or mixture of substances intended for preventing, destroying, repelling, or mitigating any pest". A pesticide may be a chemical substance, biological agent (such as a virus or bacterium), antimicrobial, disinfectant or device used against any pest. Human label as "pest" any plants or animals that endanger our food supply, health or comfort. Also Food and Agricultural Organization (2002) defined the term pesticide as any substance or mixture of substances intended for preventing, destroying or controlling any pest, including vectors of human or animal disease, unwanted species of plants or animal causing harm during or otherwise interfering with the production, processing storage, transport or marketing of food, agricultural commodities, wood and wood products or animal feedstuffs, or substances which any be administered to animals for the control of insects, arachnids or other pests in or on their bodies. The term includes substance intended for use as a plant growth regulator, defoliant, desiccant or agent for thinning fruit or commodity from deterioration during storage and transport.

CLIMATE CHANGE

Climate change is a long term change in the statistical distribution of weather pattern over periods ranging from decades to millions of years. It may be a change in average weather condition or the distribution of events around the average (e.g. more or fewer extreme weather events). Climate change may be limited to a specific region or may occur across the whole earth. The United Nations Framework convention on climate change defines climate change as "a change of climate which is attributed directly or indirectly to human activity that alters the composition of the global atmosphere and which is in addition to natural climate variability observed over comparable time periods. Climate change is the result of an increase in the concentration of greenhouse gases (GHG) like carbon dioxide (CO_2), nitrous oxide (N_2O), and methane (CH_4). Climate change refers to long-term trends (>30 years). The meaning of climate change is fairly straight forward – a clear, sustained change (over several decades or longer) in the component of climate such as temperature, precipitation atmospheric pressure, or winds.

CLASSIFICATION OF PESTICIDES

Pesticides can be classified by target organism, chemical structures and physical states. According to council on scientific affair (1997), pesticide can also be classed as inorganic, synthetic, or biological (biopesticides). The plant-derived pesticides include the pyrethroids, rotenoids and nicotinoids.

The major classes of pesticides are as follows:

Type of Pesticde	Target Pest Group
Acaricide	Mites, ticks, spiders
Antimicrobial	Bacteria, viruses, other microbes
Attractant	Attracts pests for monitoring or killing
Avicide	Birds
Fungicide	Fungi
Herbicide	Weed
Insecticide	Insects
Molluscicide	Snails and slugs
Nematicide	Nematodes
Piscicide	Fish
Predacide	Vertebrate predators
Repellent	Repels pests
Rodenticide	Rodents
Synergist	Improves performance of another pesticide

Pesticide can further be classified based on their mode of action into contact and systemic pesticide. For contact to be effective they need to be absorbed through the external body surface or the exposed plant tissue. Contact pesticides have to reach their target directly to be effective. Systemic pesticides are those pesticides that can be moved (translocated) from the site of application to another site within the plant or animal where they become effective. Systemic pesticides move from where they are applied to other parts of the plant to reach their target.

In the United States, pesticides are used on 900, 000 farms and in 70 million households. Herbicides are the most widely used type of pesticides. Agriculture uses 75% of all pesticide (Aspelin*et al.*, 1991), but 85% of all U.S. household have at least one pesticide in storage, and 63% have one to five stored (Whitmore, *et al.*, 1992). A survey by Creason and Runge (1992), found that on a per-acre basis urban dwellers use herbicides for lawn care at rates equal to those used by farmers for food production.

BENEFITS AND PROBLEMS OF USING PESTICIDES

Benefits

The benefits derived from using pesticides are:

1. Improved Productivity

Tremendous benefits have been derived from the use of pesticide in forestry, public health and the domestic sphere and of course, in agriculture. Pesticides have had a key role in improving productivity to such an extent that India, a former country of famine has quadrupled grain production since 1951 (Dyanatha and Chand, 1999) and now not only feeds itself but exports produce. Austin (1998) reported that wheat yields in the United Kingdom rose from 2.5 t/ha in 1948 to 7.5 t/ha in 1997. Increases in productivity have been due to several factors including use of fertilizer, better varieties and use of machinery. Pesticides have been an integral part of the process by reducing losses from the weeds, diseases and insect pests that can markedly reduce the amount of harvestable produce. Webster *el al.* (1999) stated that "considerable economic loses" would be suffered without pesticide use and quantified the significant increases in yield and economic margin that result from pesticide use.

2. Protect Crop Losses/Yield Reductions

Herbicides are the most widely used type of pesticide and comprise around 50% of all crops protection chemicals used throughout the world, compared with insecticides and fungicides that are around 17% each (Croplife, 2004). Using herbicides to reduce the drudgery of persistent weeding makes sense, especially in cases of chronic labour shortages. Weed competition is the major constraint that limits yields in many crops. Bridges (1992) reported that losses due to weeds of $4 billion would be $20 without use of herbicides. Chikoye*et al.*, (2005) reported that the average grain yield on farmer's field is still very low in Africa. Among other factors, a significant portion of the yield gap is attributable to poor crop management, notably inadequate weed control. In West Africa, he attributes maize yield losses ranging from 50 % to 90 % to weed competition. Manual weeding is the predominant method of control used by smallholder farms in Africa. However, this method is time consuming, laborious, and very expensive, whereas herbicides were shown to improve yield.

3. Vector Disease Control

Last (2001) defined a vector as any agent (person, animals or microorganism) that carries and transmits an infection. Vector-borne diseases are most effectively tackled by killing the vectors. Insecticides are often the only practical way to control the insects that spread deadly disease such as malaria that results in an estimated 5000 deaths each day (Ross, 2005). Bhatia *et al.*, (2004) wrote that malaria is one of the leading causes of morbidity and mortality in the developing world and a major public health problem in India. In use, insecticide-treated nets have proved to be effective in reducing malaria mortality and morbidity in various epidemiological settings.

4. Quality of Food

The use of pesticide can prevent or reduce agricultural losses to pests and so improve yield, as well as improving the quality of the produce in terms of cosmetic appeal-often important to buyers. They can also improve the nutritional value of food and sometimes its safety. In the developed world, it is now observed that a diet containing fresh fruit and vegetables far out weight potential risks from eating very low residues of pesticides in crops, (Brown, 2004). Increasing evidence (Dietary Guidelines, 2005) shows that eating fruits and vegetables regularly reduces the risks of many cancers, higher blood pressure, heart disease, diabetes, stroke and other chronic diseases. Gianessi (1999) largely attributed all year round availability of inexpensive and good quality fresh fruit and vegetable to the use of pesticide.

5. Other Areas – Transport, Sport Complex, Building

The transport sector makes extensive use of pesticides, particularly herbicides. Torstensson (2001) reported that in Sweden weeds need to be removed from around railway tracks to avoid the risk of train wheels skidding, causing longer acceleration distances and, more seriously, extended braking distances, which could result in the train being unable to stop at signals. Herbicides and insecticides are used to maintain the turf on sports pitches, cricket grounds and golf courses. Insecticides protect buildings and other wooden structures from damage by termites and wood boring insects.

PROBLEMS OF PESTICIDES USAGE

Despite their numerous advantages, there are some potential hazards or risks associated with pesticide usage. Some of the undesirable side effects of pesticide use usually stem from a lack of understanding of the impact of the chemical on the environment, compounded by indiscriminate and overuse of the product. Some of these effects may be:

1. *Reduction of beneficial species:* Non-target organisms, including predators and parasites of pests, can also be affected by pesticide application. The reduction of these beneficial organisms can result in changes in the natural biological balances. Losses of honeybees and other pollinating insect can also be a problem(Osborn, 1986).
2. *Drift of sprays and vapour:* Jury *et. al.*,(1987) reported that pesticides can affect other areas during application and can cause severe problems in different crops, livestock, waterways and the general environment. Care in the methods of application and the weather conditions under which it is carried out can reduce drifts. Environmental pollution from careless application and runoff can result in wildlife and fish losses.

3. *Residue in Food:* There is possibility of pesticides in human food, either by direct application onto food, or by biomagnifications along the food line. Not all levels are undesirable but unnecessary and dangerous levels must be avoided through good agricultural practice (Forget, 1991).
4. *Ground water Contamination:* Chemical can reach underground aquifers if there is persistent products use in agricultural areas (El-sebae, 1983).
5. *Resistance:* Overuse of the same pesticide can encourage resistance in target pest as reported by Plapp and Wang (1983).
6. *Poisoning hazards:* Poisoning and other health effects to operators can occur through excessive exposure if safe handling procedures are not followed and protective clothing not worn. Poisoning risks depend on dose, toxicity, duration of exposure and sensitivity (Osborn, 1986).
7. *Other possible health Effects:* As pesticides used now have been through rigorous testing, most health problems stem from misuse, abuse or overuse (Tardiff*et al.*,1988).

We know that many people have concerns about the uncertain effects of pesticides. However, we really need pesticides for the growth of our economy. We need fruits and vegetables to live and sometimes weeds, pests, and other disease make it harder for us to get proper nutrition. Nowadays, there are hazardous chemicals in everything from shampoo to tooth paste (Forget, 1991). We cannot avoid the use of chemical in everyday products. Yet, we can make ourselves aware of the use of pesticides and use them wisely.

EFFECTS OF CLIMATE CHANGE ON PESTICIDE USAGE

Climate change is real and already taking place, according to the IPCC's most recent Assessment Report (IPPC, 2007). According to the report, the impact of climate change and their associated costs will fall disproportionately on developing countries threatening to undermine achievement of the millennium Development Goals, reduce poverty, and safeguard food security. The climate is changing because of the way people live these days, especially in richer, economically developed countries and that includes the EuropeanUnion. The power plants that generate energy to provide us with electricity and to heat our homes, the cars and planes that we travel in, the factories that produce the goods we buy, the farms that grow our food all these play a part in changing the climate by giving off what are known as 'greenhouse gases', (European Commission, 2005).

Food production will be particularly sensitive to climate change, because crop yields depend directly on climatic conditions (temperature and rainfall patterns). In tropical regions, even small amounts of warming will lead to declines in the amount of crops harvested (Parry *et al.*, 1999). In cold areas, crop harvests may increase at first for moderate increases in temperature but then fall. Higher temperatures will lead to large declines in cereal (e.g. rice, wheat) production around the world (Stern, 2006).

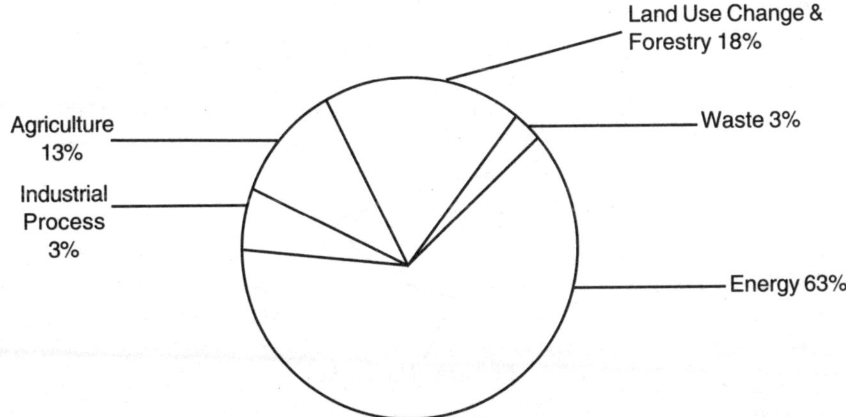

Fig. 5.1: Share of Global Green House Gas Emission by Sector, in Year 2000

Source: Drawn from data from WRI (2008)

Agriculture, including land use change and forestry accounts for nearly one-third of global GHG (Green House Gases) emissions (WRI, 2008). Further analysis of figure 1 indicates that agriculture alone contributed 13 percent of total global GHG (Green House Gases) in year 2000. Emissions from this sector are primarily methane (CH_4) and dinitrogen oxide (N_2O), making the agricultural sector the largest producer of non-CO-$_2$ emissions. Indeed, 60 percent of total global non-CO_2 emissions came from this source in year 2000(WRI, 2008). Certain GHG emissions arising from agricultural activity are accounted for in other sectors, such as those relating to manufacture of equipment, fertilizers, and pesticides, plus on-farm use of fuels and the transportation of agricultural products (Mark *et al.*, 2008). Emission from agriculture comes from four principal sub-sectors: agricultural soils, livestock and manure management, rice cultivation, and the burning of agriculture residues and savanna for land clearing.

The problem of pesticide misuse is well- known and is a widely-held concern for researchers, farmers and environmentalists. Once released into the environment, pesticides tend to build up in the fat tissues of living organism, causing serious harm to health and a potential loss of bio-diversity (Palikhe, 2002). The sole reliance on chemical pesticides for plant protection has created serious problem. In addition, problems of pest outbreaks, resistance and resurgence of pests demand more pesticides. There is a significant decline in population of birds, earthworms, natural predators like ladybird beetles, and spiders as a result of pesticide misuse (Osborn, 1986).

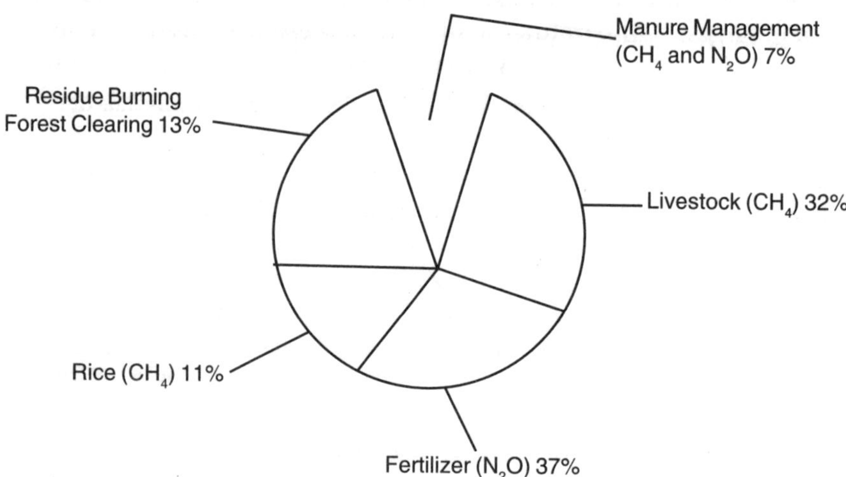

Fig. 5.2: **Represents the Share of Pollutants Derived from each of these Sectors**

Source of emission from the agricultural sector (2000).

Source: Drawn from data presented on USEPA (2006).

IMPLICATION OF CLIMATE CHANGE FOR PEST AND DISEASES

Conditions are more favourable for the proliferation of insect pests in warmer climates (Cannon, 1998). Longer growing seasons will enable insects such as grasshoppers to complete a greater number of reproductive cycle during the spring, summer and autumn (Bale *et al.*, 2002). Warmer winter temperature may allow larvae to overwinter thus causing greater infestation during the following crop season (Bale *et al.*, 2002). Altered wind patterns may change the spread of both wind-borne pests and of the bacteria and fungi that are the agents of crop disease (Chakraborty*et al.*, 2000). Crop-pest interactions may shift as the timing of development stages in both hosts and pests is altered (Harvell *et al.*, 2002). The possible increases in pest infestations may bring about greater use of chemical pesticides to control them.

INSECT PESTS

Climate change is likely to alter the balance between insect pests, their natural enemies and their hosts. One of the most important effect of climate change will be to alter the synchrony between host and insect pest development. The predicted rise in temperature will also generally favour insect development and hence bringing about the use of more pesticides use (Harrington *et al.*, 2001).

FUNGAL DISEASES

The impact of pathogens whose reproduction or dispersal is clearly affected by temperature is relatively predictable. Warmer temperature may in particular favour certain thermophilic rust fungi and increase the activities of some weak pathogens. An increased incidence of drought would probably favour diseases caused by fungi whose activity is dependent on host stress, particularly root pathogens. This of course will increase the use of fungicides to combat these diseases caused by this fungi (Harvell *et al.*, 2002).

INSECT POPULATIONS

Most studies have concluded that insect pests will generally become more abundant as temperature increases (Lewis,1997). Global climate change is expected to increase the frequency and the intensity of insect outbreaks through direct effects of climate change on insect populations, as well as through disruption of community interactions. Global warming will increase pest populations, including weeds, invasive species, insects, and insect-borne diseases, which will likely lead to large increase in the use of pesticides. Researchers at the university of Washington have found that insect species that adapt to warmer climates also will increase their maximum rates of population growth, meaning that global warming will likely lead to increased insect populations. Study's authors say that this " warmer is better" phenomenon is likely to have wide spread effects on agriculture, public health and conservation, (Frazier *et al.*, 2005).

Additionally, climate change is expected to increase the range of some insect populations. For example, the red imported fire ant, an invasive pest originally from South American has currently occupied much of the south east, expected to expand its range into the eastern U.S. over the next century, with the help of global climate change (Morrison *et al.*, 2005). Also many species of parasitic wasps have been used as biological control in agriculture and climate change may compromise their ability to control pests, leading to increased use of pesticide (Stireman*et al.*, 2005).

INSECT-BORNE DISEASES

With the boom in insect populations, scientists also hypothesize that there will be increases in insect- borne disease such as malaria, dengue fever, and viral encephalitis (Sutherst, 2004). Scientists believe that climate change will increase transmission by shifting insects' geographic range, increasing reproductive and biting rates of the insects, and by shortening the pathogen incubation period (Patz*et al.*, 1996). In fact, research shows that malaria zones are already increasing world wide. A report by the World Health Organisation (2004) on malaria suggested that 60% of the world will be in a malaria zone by 2100.

WEEDS

Fast growing weeds are able to adapt to change reproductive patterns as quickly as over a 7-years period, an ability which will lead to their expansion in response to global warming. According to a study by researchers at the

University of California, Irvine, those plants with short life cycles can adapt more quickly to change than those that reproduce slowly (Franks *et al.*, 2007). In their study, they found that the annual plant *Brassica rapa*, or field mustard, flowered significantly earlier than usual during a period of drought. Droughts, which are expected to become more frequent, especially in arid regions, cause abbreviated growing seasons. The ability of *Brassica rapa* to adapt in just a few generations shows how weeds will likely keep up with any attempts to develop crops that can adapt to global warming (Washington post, 2007).

Another study finds that increased levels of atmospheric carbon dioxide cause poison ivy (*Rhusradicans* L.) to grow larger and more poisonous (Mohan *et al.*, 2006). An additional expected result of rising carbon dioxide levels is an increase in invasive plants. One study finds that in plant communities, high levels of carbon dioxide stimulate the growth of invasive plant species more than native species (Ziska and George, 2004).

PEST OUTBREAK

With the global climate change, prediction of disease outbreaks will be more difficult because of the rapidly changing climate and unstable weather. Environment instability and increased incidence of extreme weather, may reduce the effectiveness of pesticides on targeted pests or result in more injury to non-target organisms. Biological control may be affected either negatively or positively. Overall, the challenge to agriculture from pests probably will increase.

HOW TO MITIGATE THE PROBLEMS

According to Huq (2006), mitigation refers to efforts to reduce greenhouse gas emissions. Mitigation may also refer to efforts to capture greenhouse gases through certain kinds of land use such as tree plantation. This will reduce global warming, as the greenhouse layer in the atmosphere will not be so thick and its warming, blanket-like effect will be lessened. Mitigation is the main response that must be made to prevent future impacts of climate change.

Some ways to achieve this are:

1. *Use of legumes:* If legumes could be integrated into the production system with the addition of manure through recycling farm waste, the amount of nitrogen fertilizers from outside the agriculture system could be reduced.
2. *Reduced grower input cost:* In modern agriculture greater energy input in the form of mechanical force, fertilizers and pesticide are required. Thus there is a stronger need to reduce grower input cost with concomitant increase in yield and quality with reduced environment impact.

3. *Diversification of crop varieties:* If the crop varieties are diversified, the chances of an outbreak in terms of pests could be greatly reduced. Thus pesticide use could be reduced or even eliminated.
4. *Improved control:* Improved controls on the use and distribution of pesticide will reduce some of the harmful effect of pesticide such as killing of some of the beneficial insects and some pollinators.
5. *Minimizing the harzards and risks from use of pesticides:* this can be done by proper regulation of its use.
6. *Organic farming methods:* Organic farming methods combine scientific knowledge and modern technology with traditional farming practices based on thousands of years of agriculture. In general, organic methods rely on naturally.

ADAPTATION STRATEGIES

The word "adaptation" has evolved from the term "adapt," which means "making things/conditions/situation better by changing " (Ahmed, 2006). Adaptation to climate change is therefore the process through which people reduce the negative effects of climate on their health and well-being and adjust to the new situation around them. 'In a nutshell adaptation is being better prepared or adapting to climate change, not fighting it, but learning to live with it (Rahman, 2008).

A wide varieties of adaptive actions may be taken to lessen or overcome adverse effects of climate change on agriculture. At the levels of farms, adjustments may include the introduction of later-maturing crop varieties or species, sowing earlier, adjusting timing of field operations, conserving soil moisture through appropriate tillage methods and improving irrigation efficiency. Adaptations such as changing planting dates and choosing longer seasons varieties are likely to offset losses or further increase yields.

CONCLUSION

Climate change may bring new opportunities (e.g. new crop option), but also will pose new risks and challenges for farmers and specifically:

1. Invasive insects, disease and weed pests are likely to benefit most from climate change, leading to increased pesticide and herbicide use.
2. Reductions in biodiversity are likely, because climate change will tend to favour aggressive invasive species at the expense of endangered species that are poor at migrating and adapting to change.

In conclusion, to reduce climate change and impact, agriculture should make a full transition to integrated production (and ultimately organic farming) abandoning high-input agriculture, and move away from our current dependency on synthetic agrochemicals. The transition can deliver climate-neutral agriculture, producing high-quality food and feed.

REFERENCES

Ahmed, A.U. (2006). Bangladesh Climate Change Impacts and vulnerability: A Dhaka: Climate Change Cell, Bangladesh Department of Environment.

Aspelin, A.L. Grube, A.H and Kibler, V. (1991). Pesticide Industry Sales and Usage: 1989 Market Estimates. EPA Economic Analysis Branch, Washington, D.C.

Austin, R.B. (1998) Yield of Wheat in the UK: Recent Advances and Prospects. Annual Meeting of the Crop Science Society of America.

Bhatia, M.R., Fox-Rushby, J and Mills, M. (2004). Cost Effectiveness of Malaria Control Intervention when Malaria Mortality is Low: Insecticide Treated Nets Versus in-house Residual Spraying in India. Social Science and Medicine 59: 525.

Bale, J.S., Masters, G.J., Hodkinson, I.D., Awmack, T.M., Brown, V.K., Butterfield, J., Buse, A., Coulson, J.C., Farrar, J., Good, J.E.G., Harrington, R., Hartley, S., Jones, T.H., Lindroth, R.L., Symrnioudis, I., Watt, A.D. and Whittaker. J. B. (2002). Herbivory in Global Climate Change Research In: Direct Effects of Rising Temperature on Insect Herbivores. Global Change Biology 8: 1-16.

Bridge, D.C. (1992) Crop Losses Due to Weeds in Canada and the United States. Weed Science Society of America.

Brown, L. (2004) UK Pesticides Residue Committee Report 2004 (available online: http://www/pesticidegov.uk/uploadedfiles/web. Assets/PRC/PRC Annual Report 2004).

Cannon, R.J.(1998). The Implications of Predicted Climate Change for Insect Pests in the UK, with Emphasis on Non-indigenous Species. 4: 785-796.

Chikoye, D., Udensi, E.U. and Fontem L. (2005). Evaluation of a New Formulation of Altrazine and Metolachlor Mixture for Weed Control in Maize in Nigeria, Crop Protection 24: 1016.

Council on Scientific Affairs, American Medical Association (1997). Educational and Informational Strategies to Reduce Pesticide Risks. Preventive medicine 26 (2): 20-24.

Creason, J.R. and Runge, C.F. (1992) Use of Lawn Chemicals in the Twin Cities. Public Report Services Number 7, Water Resources Research Centre, Univesity of Minnesota.

Croplife International at: http://www.croplife.org/def.aspx. Accessed March 2011.

Chakraborty, S., Tiedemann, A.V., and Teng, P. S.(2000). Climate Change: Potential Impact on Plant Diseases. Environ. Poll. 108: 317-326.

Dayanatha J. and Ramesh, C. (1999). National Centre for Agricultural Economics and Policy Research (ICAR), New Delhi, India. From Agro-chemicals News in Brief Special Issue.

Dietary Guidelines for Americans 2005. U.S Department of Health and Human Services. U.S. Department of Agriculture.

El-sebae, A.H.(1983). Overview of Environmental Chemistry and Toxicology of Pesticide Use in Egypt. Arab Symposium on Environment, UNSCO, University of Jordan.

European Commission (2005) Climate Change –What is it all About ? An Introduction for Young People. Luxembourg: Office for Official Publications of the EUROPEAN Communities. ISBN 978-92-79-09544-3 pp. 4.

Forget, G. (1991). Pesticide and Third World. J. Toxicol. Environ Health 32: 11-31.

Food and Agricultural Organization of the United Nations (FAO), (2002). International Code of Conduct on the Distribution and Use of Pesticides. Retrieved on 25-10-2007.

Franks, S.J. Sim, S and Weis, A.E. (2007) Rapid Evolution of Flowering Time by an Annual Plant in Response to a Climate Fluctuation Processing's of the National Academy of Sciences. Published Saline Before Print, 10.10 73/pnas. 0608379104. Available online at hppt://www.climatecrisis.net/takeaction.

Frazier, M., Huey, R.B. and Berrigan D (2005). Thermodynamics Constrains the Evolution of Insect Population Growth Rates: "Warmer is Better". American Naturalist 168: 512-520.

Gianessi, L. (1999) Beneficial Impacts of Pesticides Use for Consumers, In Ragsdale N and James. S.(eds), Pesticides. Managing Risks and Optimizing,, American Chemical Society Symposium Series # 734 American Chemical Society, Washington, D.C. United State of America p. 207.

Huq, S. (2006) Learning to Live with Climate Change. London: International Institute for Environment and Development (IIED).

Harrington, R., Fleming, R. and Woiwood, I.P.(2001). Climate Change Impacts on Insects Management and Conservation in Temperate Regions: Can They be Predicted? Agricultural and Forest Entomology 3: 233-240.

Harvell, C.D., Mitchell, C.E., Ward, J., Altizer, S., Dobson, A.P., Ostfeld, R.S. and Samuel, M.D.(2002). Climate Warming and Disease Risks for Terrestrial and Marine Biota. Science 296: 2158-2162.

IPCC (2007) Summary for Policy Makers. Climate Change 2007: Synthesis Report. Fourth Assessment Report of the Intergovernmental Panel for Climate Change [Availableonlineathppt://www.ipcc.ch/pdf/assessment---report/ar4/syr/ar4syr spm.pdf].

Jury, W.A., Winer, AM., Spencer, W.F. and Focht, D.D.(1987). Transport and Transportation of Organic Chemicals in the Soil-air-water Ecosystem. Rev. Enviro. Contain. Toxicol 99: 119-16.3

Last, J ed. (2001). A Dictionary of Epidemiology. New York: Oxford University press. pp. 185. ISBN: 978-0195141696.

Lewis, T. (1997). Thrips as Crop Pests. CAB International, Cambridge: University Press. p. 740.

Mark, W.R, Mandy, E., Gary, Y., Lan, B. Saleenul H., Rowena, V. (2008). Climate Change and Agriculture: Threats and Opportunities Federal Ministry for Economics Cooperation and Development Eschborn Germany. p. 6.

Mohan, J.E., Ziska, L.H.., Sicher, Jr., George, K., Thomas, R.B. and Schlesinger, W.H. (2006). Poison Ivy Grows Larger and more Poisonous at Elevated Atmospheric CO_2. Proceedings of the National Academy of Sciences 103 (24): 9086-9089.

Morrison, L.W., Korzuklin M.D. and Porter S.D. (2005) Predicted Range Expansion of the Invasive Fire Ant, *Solenopsisinvicta.*

Osborn, D. (1986) Effects of Pesticides on Non-target Organisms. In Richardson, M.L. (Ed.) Toxic Hazard Assessment of Chemicals, The Royal Society of Chemistry, London. pp. 247-258.

Patz, J.A., Epstein, P.R., Burke, T.A. and Balbus J.M. (1996). Global Climate Change and Emerging Infectious Diseases AMA 275 (3).

Plapp, F.W.Jr., and Wang, T. C.(1983). Genetic Origins of Insecticide Resistance. In: Georghiou, G.P. and Saito, T. (Eds.) Pest Resistance to Pesticides. Plenum Press, New York. pp. 47-70.

Parry, M.L., Fischer, M., Livermore C., Rosenzweigh, C. and Iglesias, A. (1999). Climate Change and World Food Security: A New Assessment. Global Environmental Change 9: S51-S67.

Palikhe, B.R. (2002). Pesticide and Environment. Agriculture and Environment Journal. pp 38.

Rahman, N. (2008) Environmental Heros. Star Weakened Magazine February 15th, 2008, 8-13.

Ross, G. (2005) Risks and Benefits of DDT, The Lancet 366(9499): 1771.

Stireman, J.O., Dyer, L.A. and Janzen, D.H. (2005). Climatic Unpredictability and Parasitism of Caterpillars: Implications of Global Warming. Proceedings of the National Academy of Sciences of the United States of America 102: 17384-17387.

Stern, N. (2006). Report on the Stern Review: The Economics of Climate Change.HM Treasury: London.

The United Nations Framework Convention on Climate Change. (1994). http/unfccc.int/essentialbackgrond/convention/background/items/1349.php.

Tardiff, R.G and Rodricks, J. V(Eds.). (1988). Toxic Substances and Human Risks: Principles of Data Interpretation. Plenum Press New York. p. 40.

U.S. Environmental Protection Agency (2007). What is a Pesticide?.epa.gov. Retrieved on September 15, 2007.

U.S. Environmental Protection Agency (USEPA) (2006) Global Mitigation of Non CO_2 Greenhouse Gases. Office of Atmospheric Programs, Washington D.C. USA.

Washington Post Tuesday, January 9 2007 Page A09 : Weeds Adapt Quickly to Climatic Change".

World Health Organization (WHO) (2004). Factsheet 94 Malaria. Available online at: http://www.rbmo.who.int/docs/AMD/factsheet.

Webster, J.P.G, Bowles, R.G. and Williams N.T (1999). Estimating the Economic Benefits of Alternative Pesticide Usage Scenarios". Wheat Production in the United Kingdom. Crop Protection 18: 83.

Whitemore, R.W. Kelly, J.E. and Reading P.L. (1992). National Home and Garden Pesticide Use Survey Final Report. Research Triangle Institute, Research Triangle Park N.C.

World Resources Institute (WRI) (2008) Climate Analysis Indicators Toolkit (CAIT) [January 2008, available online at: http?//cait.wri.org/]

Sutherst, R. V.(2004). Global Change and Human Vulnerability to Vector-Borne Disease. Clin. Microbiol. Rev(1): 136-173.

Ziska, L.H and George, K. (2004). Rising Carbon Dioxide and Invasive, Noxious Plants: Potential Threats and Consequences. World Resource Review 16: 427-447.

Pages: 71-86

NATURAL ECOSYSTEM AND CLIMATE CHANGE
Edited by: **Dr. Pawan Kumar 'Bharti'; Dr. Khwairakpam Gajananda**
ISBN: 978-93-5056-745-6
Edition: **2015**
Published by: **Discovery Publishing House Pvt. Ltd., New Delhi (India)**

CHAPTER - 6

The Contribution of Ruminant Animals to Climate Change and its Mitigation Strategies

Oyeagu Chika E.[1], Akpa Martins O[2], and Ani Augustine O.[1]

ABSTRACT

In this chapter, an attempt was made to discuss methane production by ruminants which are a potent greenhouse gas. Enteric methane emissions produced by ruminant animals is a major source of Greenhouse gas in agriculture and is formed in the rumen through a process called enteric fermentation. The negative effects of climate change tend to be high in our environment as a result of increase in the production of these gases which reduces the rate of livestock production, as it affects livestock performance. The relationship between greenhouse gases, greenhouse effect, global warming and Climate change was highlighted. Global warming is projected to have significant impacts on conditions affecting livestock, including temperature, carbon dioxide, glacial run-off, precipitation and the interaction of these elements. At the same time, livestock production has been shown to produce significant effects on climate change, primarily through the production and

1 Department of Animal Science, University of Nigeria, Nsukka, Nigeria.

2 Department of Animal/Fisheries Science and Management, Enugu State University of Science and Technology, Enugu, Nigeria.

release of greenhouse gases such as carbon dioxide, methane, and nitrous oxide. Methane production by ruminants has become a major concern since it contributes to unsafe environment (climate change). Hence, this paper attempts to review various ways of mitigating methane production by ruminants. With adequate reduction of enteric methane emission, a decrease in greenhouse gases in the atmosphere is assured, it will improve the efficiency of converting plant material into milk and meat in the humid tropics and this will result in maximum returns to livestock farmers and availability of milk and meat to the consumers at affordable prices.

Key words: Climate change, enteric methane, ruminants, greenhouse gases.

INTRODUCTION

In Nigeria, livestock production is declining due to longer dry period and threatening forage scarcity. Climate change is a global concern because the changes associated with it have the potential to alter Livestock production and subsequently the lives of people (Vaclav, 2003). These global changes not only threaten to deprive humans of their lands but also end the lives of animals that cannot adapt to the chaotic weather.

Climate change especially indicated by prolonged drought is one of the most serious climatic hazards affecting the agricultural sector of the continent. As most of the agricultural activities in Nigeria hinge on rain, any adverse changes in the climate would likely have a devastating effect on the sector.

Global warming is projected to have significant impacts on conditions affecting livestock, including temperature, carbon dioxide, glacial run-off, precipitation and the interaction of these elements. At the same time, livestock production has been shown to produce significant effects on climate change, primarily through the production and release of greenhouse gases such as carbon dioxide, methane, and nitrous oxide, but also by altering the Earth's land cover which can change its ability to absorb or reflect heat and light, thus contributing to radiative force (Hansen, 2005).

Methane is a potent greenhouse gas that contributes to global warming (Johnson and Johnson, 1995). Over the past three centuries, the amount of atmospheric methane has grown by 2.5-fold (lassey, 2008). Most methane that is emitted from livestock originates in the fore stomach, also called the rumen of ruminants (Beauchemin and McGinn, 2005) and this source of methane is called enteric Methane. Hence, only about 10% of the total methane from ruminant is from manure. While the digestion process enable ruminant to convert forages into usable energy, a portion of the feed energy (3 to 12%) is used to produce enteric methane and it is released into the atmosphere as the animal breath (Johnson and Johnson, 1995). However, about 25% of the enteric methane produced by the 16.25 million cattle is generated by the dairy industry. Most of the remaining 75% is produced by beef cattle, (Beauchemin and McGinn, 2005).

According to Smith *et al.*, (2007) agriculture produces 10-12 percent of total global anthropogenic greenhouse gas emissions, contributing 50 percent of all anthropogenic methane. Ruminant livestock animals are a major source of total anthropogenic emissions producing an estimated 80 million tons of methane annually accounting for 33 percent anthropogenic emissions of methane (Beauchemin *et al.*, 2008). Minimizing the production of methane can improve efficiency of livestock production and it is an environmentally sound practice. This paper therefore looked at some developed ways of reducing methane production from ruminants which are major contributors to global warming (CONAM 2001).

METHANE

Methane is a greenhouse gas, it effects the ozone layer in the atmosphere and it contributes to global warming or global climatic change (Fraser *et al.*, 1986). The largest agricultural sources of methane (CH_4) are managed ruminant animals and rice production (Levine, 1994). Methane is emitted from 3 sources within livestock production systems:

- From digestive processes in animals (enteric fermentation);
- From anaerobic decomposition processes in animal manure; and
- From anaerobic decomposition processes of waste products from animal processing.

Methane emissions are an important contribution to global greenhouse gas emissions. The IPCC (2007), reported that methane is more than twenty times as effective as CO_2 at trapping heat in the atmosphere.

Methane production by ruminants has been estimated in the past by several authors. The earliest figures on world-wide production rate were published by Hutchinson (1949), who estimated the CH_4 emission by large herbivores to be 45Tg/year for the 1940's. Ehhalt (1974) calculated a global CH_4 production of 100 Tg CH4 for 1970 from domestic ruminants. This would constitute 20-35% of the total input of methane to the atmosphere, which is now estimated by various authors to be in the range 300-500 Tg/year (Khalil and Rasmvsen, 1983; Crutzen and Gidel, 1983; Seiler, 1984).

Global CH_4 emissions are difficult to predict because specific biochemical components of diets are often overlooked in empirical models. Important differences in feed components of the diets used in extensive and intensive capacity are often overlooked and these systems are viewed as similar. This can result in over – and underestimates of enteric derived CH_4 emissions regionally; especially, where diet components may differ based on the availability of nutrients. Kebreab *et al.* (2008) suggested that international panel on climate change (IPCC) values overestimate CH_4 emissions by 12.5% and underestimate CH_4 emissions by 9.8% for daily and feedlot cattle, respectively. Due to the regional differences in animal species, diets and production systems globally, it is very difficult to determine accurate CH_4 emissions.

THE RELATIONSHIP BETWEEN GREENHOUSE GASSES (GHG), GREENHOUSE EFFECTS (GHE), GLOBAL WARMING (GW) AND CLIMATE CHANGE

The Earth is wrapped in the blanket of air called the 'atmosphere', which is made up of several layers of gases (Vaclav, 2003). The sun is much hotter than the Earth and it gives off rays of heat (radiation) that travel through the atmosphere and reach the Earth. The rays of the sun warm the Earth, and heat from the Earth then travels back into atmosphere. The gasses in the atmosphere stop some of the heat from escaping into space (Mckay *et al.,* 1991). These gases are called GHG, e.g. water vapour, carbon dioxide, methane, nitrous oxide and ozone. These gasses are important in order to keep the Earth warm (to sustain life on earth) and the natural process between the sun, the atmosphere and the Earth is called 'Greenhouse Effect', because it works the same way as a greenhouse, (Levine, 1994; Hansen, 2005).

The atmosphere has a number of gasses, often in tiny amounts, which trap the heat given out by the Earth (Hansen, 2005). To ensure that the Earth's atmosphere remains constant, the balance of these gasses in the atmosphere must not be upset, but these gases keep increasing in the atmosphere and because of the constant increase of the greenhouse gases in the atmosphere, more heat is trapped which makes the Earth warmer (Solomon *et al.,* 2007). This is known as Global warming. However, as more heat is trapped on Earth. The planet will become warmer, which means the weather all over Earth will change (Ifeanyi – Obi *et al.,* 2012). This change in the weather is termed climate change which refers to all changes in climate as a result of human activities or natural variations (Akinro *et al.,* 2008; Ifeanyi – Obi *et al.,* 2012). Warrick and Barrow (1991) observed that climate change is a long term shift in the climatic pattern of a specific location, region or planet measured by changes in features associated with average weather components, such as temperature, wind patterns and precipitation. Over the past 100 years, the earth's average surface temperature has risen by around 0.74°C (Direct Gov., 2010). Most scientists agree that global temperature will rise further (by how much depends on future emissions of greenhouse gases) and if the temperature rise is high, changes are likely to be so extreme that it will be difficult to cope with them (Ifeanyi – Obi *et al.,* 2012).

RUMINANT PHYSIOLOGY

Ruminating animals have various physiological features which enable them to survive in nature. One feature of ruminants is their continuously growing teeth. During grazing, the silica content in forage causes abrasion of teeth. Abrasion of the teeth is compensated by continuous tooth growth throughout the ruminant's life, as opposed to humans or other non-ruminants whose teeth stop growing after a particular age (Steinfeld *et al.,* 2006). Most ruminants do not have upper incisors; instead they have a thick dental pad to thoroughly bite food (Ditchkoff, 2000). Camels and llamas are exceptions; their dentition shows traces of vestigial central incisors in the upper jaw.

RUMEN MICROBIOLOGY

Vertebrates lack the ability to hydrolyze beta [1-4] glycosidic bond of plant cellulose due to the lack of an enzyme cellulase. Thus ruminants must completely depend upon the microbial flora, present in rumen or hindgut, so as to digest cellulose. Digestion of food in rumen is primarily carried out by the rumen micro flora which contain dense populations of several species of bacteria, protozoa, sometimes yeasts and fungi and it is estimated that 1mm of rumen contains 10-50 billion bacteria, 1 million protozoa and several yeasts, fungi (Yavitt, 1992). As the environment inside a rumen is anaerobic, most of these microbial species are obligate or facultative anaerobes which can decompose complex plant material such as cellulose, hemicellulose, starch, proteins. Hydrolysis of cellulose results in sugars which are further fermented to acetate, lactate, propionate, butyrate, carbon dioxide and methane (Boadi *et al.*, 2004). During grazing, ruminants produce large amount of saliva. Estimates are within 100 to 150 litres of saliva per day for an adult cow (Hackmann and spain, 2010). The role of saliva is to provide ample fluid for rumen fermentation and as a buffering agent (USDA, 2004). Rumen fermentation produces large amounts of organic acids and thus maintaining the appropriate pH of rumen fluids is a critical factor in rumen fermentation.

METHANOGENIC ARCHAEA

The methanogenic archaea constitute a large and diverse group of Archaea (Boone *et al.*, 1993). Methanogenic species were cultured from the rumen for enumeration and isolation of methanogens. They have unique features that separate them from bacteria and the eukaryotes (Balch *et al.*, 1979; Woese *et al.*, 1990). The methanogens are the only recognized ruminal microbes belonging to the Archaea and are an integral part of the rumen microbial ecosystem (Hungate, 1966; Miller, 1995; Wolin, 1979). By scavenging hydrogen gas, methanogens play a key ecological role in keeping the partial pressure of hydrogen low so that fermentation can proceed efficiently (Wolin, 1982).The methanogens are the only recognized ruminal microbes belonging to the Archaea and are an integral part of the rumen microbial ecosystem (Hungate, 1966; Wolin, 1979; Miller, 1995). By scavenging hydrogen gas, methanogens play a key ecological role in keeping the partial pressure of hydrogen low so that fermentation can proceed efficiently (Wolin, 1982).

Although about 70 methanogenic species belonging to 21 genera have been identified from anaerobic environments, and a range of different methanogens co-exist in the rumen (Sharp *et al.*, 1998; Tajima *et al.*, 2001; Whitford *et al.*, 2001), to date only seven ruminal species have been isolated and purified. The population densities of methanogens in the rumen appear to be influenced by diet and in particular by the fibre content of the diet (Kirchgessner *et al.*, 1995). The methanogens classified as archaea have a distinctly different cell wall structure from true rumen bacteria (Woese *et al.*1990).

RUMINANT ANIMAL AND METHANE PRODUCTION

Ruminant animals are those that have a rumen. A rumen is a multichambered stomach found almost exclusively among some artiodactyls mammals, such as cattle, sheep and goat, enabling them to eat cellulose – enhanced tough plants and grains that monogastric (i.e., "Single – chambered stomached") animals, such as pigs, poultry etc cannot digest (Steinfeld *et al.*, 2006). Ruminants are unique in their ability to convert plants on non-arable land to protein. This characteristic allow ruminants to utilize land and feed that would otherwise be in – used for human food production. At the same time, ruminant livestock is an important contributor to CH_4 in the atmosphere (IPCC; 2000; USDA, 2004). Methane is produced from the microbial digestive processes of ruminant livestock species such as cattle, sheep and goats. Non – ruminant livestock such as pigs, and poultry produce less CH_4 than ruminants (USDA, 2004).

In ruminant livestock, enteric fermentation is strongly affected by quantity and quality of their diet (Johnson and Johnson, 2005). Production of CH_4 in ruminants is directly correlated to a loss of metabolizable energy and has been studied in depth during performance studies that aimed at improvements of feed efficiency (Mosier *et al.*, 1998b; Jungbluth *et al.*, 2001). The primary source of CH_4 from ruminant livestock is from the process of enteric fermentation during rumination (Jungbluth *et al.*, 2001; Casey *et al.*, 2006; Sun *et al.*, 2008). Methane production from enteric fermentation is considered the primary source of global anthropogenic CH_4 emissions accounting for approximately 73% of the 80 Tg of CH_4 produced globally per year (Johnson and Johnson, 2005). Initial microbial breakdown (essential in ruminant digestion) occurs in the rumen, or large fore – stomach, where microbial fermentation converts fibrous feed into products digested and utilized by the animal (Boadi *et al.*, 2004; USDA, 2004). Rumination promotes digestion of cellulose and hemicelluloses through hydrolysis of polysaccharides by microbes and protozoa, which is followed by microbial fermentation generating H_2 and CO_2. Methane is produced as a by – product of enteric fermentation and carbohydrate digestion and is expelled through the mouth via eructation (Monteny *et al.*, 2001).

Cattle typically lose 2-12% of their injested energy as eructated CH_4 (Johnson and Johnson, 1995). Many factors affect CH_4 emissions from livestock including feed intake, animal size, diet, growth rate, milk production, and energy consumption (Johnson and Johnson, 1995; Jungbluth *et al.*, 2001). Diet and level of production directly affect CH_4 emission rate (Holter and Young, 1992; Jugbluth *et al.*, 2001; Sun *et al.*, 2008). For example, CH_4 outputs are estimated to range from 3.1 to 8.3% of gross energy intake for dry, non-lactating cows and from 1.7 to 14.9% of gross energy intake for lactating cows (Holter and Young, 1992).

VULNERABILITY OF LIVESTOCK SECTOR TO CLIMATE CHANGE

Livestock sector contributes to climate change as discoursed earlier in this paper and it is also affected by the climate (Singh *et al.*, 2012). Climate change affects livestock both directly and indirectly. Houghton *et al.* (2001) concluded that directs effects from air temperature, humidity, wind speed and other climatic factors influence animal performance: growth, milk production, wool production, egg production and reproduction. The impact of climate change on animal production has been categorized by Rotter and Van de Geijn (1999) as:

(a) availability of feed grain

(b) Pasture and forage crop production and quality

(c) Health, growth and reproduction and

(d) Disease and their spread.

Animal health may be affected by climate change in four ways: Health-related diseases and stress, Extreme weather events, Adaptation of animal production systems to new environments, and Emergence or re-emergence of infectious diseases, especially vector borne disease which are critically dependent on environmental and climatic conditions. The livestock production is an integral part of mixed farming systems practiced in Africa, especially Nigeria.

Mandal *et al.* (2002a) stressed that, crossbred cows are negatively correlated with temperature – humidity index and that, climatic condition impact on milk production has been also observed for local cows which are more adapted to the tropical climate. According to Tailor and Nagda (2005), heat stress has detrimental effects on the reproduction of cattle, sheep, goat, poultry etc. Upadhya *et al.*, (2007) stated that thermal stress on livestock has been reported to decrease estrus expression and conception rate. The outbreak of the disease was observed to be correlated with the mass movement of animals which in turn is dependent on the climatic factors (Sharma *et al.*, 1991). Singh *et al.* (1996) reported that higher incidence of clinical mastitis in dairy animals during hot and humid weather was due to increased heat stress and greater fly population associated with hot humid conditions. In addition, the hot-humid weather conditions were found to aggravate the infestation of cattle ticks like: *Boophiluls microplus*, *Haemaphysalis bispinosa* and Hyalomma anatolicum (Basu and Bandhyopadhyay, 2004; Kumar *et al.*, 2004).

When temperature rise above the thermo neutral or confort zone, heat stress results. Under this condition, the animal goes off feed and spends much time on non-productive hebaviours as panting, urination, salivation and sweating (Onyimonyi, 2012). Alaku (2010), observed that when an animal is subjected to high ambient temperatures, it attempts some compensatory measures in this order; increased skin blood flow through vasodialation of the blood vessels near the surface; initiation of sweating; increased though shallow respiration (panting), changes in behaviour pattern; increased use of water (e.g. water intake increases, wallowing etc.); increased body temperature; changes in the use of body water and changes in hydration when and if these measures fail to renew equilibrium of heat balance or shift it to a new plateau, there ensure progressive stages of failure of the heat regulation mechanism. There follows diarrhea, general weakness, staggering, convulsion and finally death due to hyperthermia. Hence, continuous exposure to high ambient temperatures leads to changes in the functioning of the endocrine glands (Onyimonyi, 2012). It has been documented that, the ideal environment for a laying hen is 18.3-23.9°C, using poultry as a case study (Onyimonyi, 2012). When temperatures exceed this level, there is a drastic reduction in feed intake, low body weight for age, drop in egg production, small size eggs, reduced shell quality and threatened survivability of the birds (Sobayo *et al.*, 2010).

MITIGATION STRATEGIES OF METHAN PRODUCTION BY RUMINANTS

Numerous ways of lowering CH4 emissions are under investigation. Some of these technologies are experimental and require development, but beef and dairy sectors could implement a few immediately. There are increasing body of research that demonstrate the possible reduction of methane by changing the diet or the management.

(a) Feeding higher grain diets

Feeding high grain diets to cattle unequivocally lowers the formation of CH4 in the rumen. With grain diets, the percentage of the energy consumed that is converted to CH4 in the rumen is typically reduced to about 3%, from the 6.5% or more that is common for animals fed primarily forages (Beauchemin and McGinn, 2005). For the feedlot sector, decreasing the duration of the backgrounding phase, in which high forage diets are fed, would decrease the industry's contribution to greenhouse gas emissions (McCaughey *et al*, 1999). However, for this drop in CH4 production to occur, the finishing diet needs to contain starch-based grain rather than high-fiber byproduct feeds (e.g., screenings, millrun). Starch containing grains lower CH4 formation in the rumen by forming more propionate and less acetate (Benchaar *et al*, 2001).

Feeding high grain diets also causes the rumen environment to become more acidic, which inhibits the growth of rumen methanogens. While increased use of grains in ruminant diets reduces enteric CH4 emissions (Lassey, 2008).

(b) Grain type

The extent to which high grain diets lower CH4 emissions depends on the source of grain. For example, greater reductions are achieved with corn than with barley. Beauchemin and McGinn, (2005) found out that beef cattle, fed diets containing mainly corn grain, produce about 30% less CH4 than diets containing mainly barley grain.

(c) Fats and oilseeds

Supplementing diets with fats and oils (excluding sources that are protected from digestion in the rumen) lowers enteric CH4 emissions. Reductions greater than 40% have been achieved, but reductions of 10 to 25% are more commonly reported (Beauchemin *et al*, 2008). Incorporating fat in the diet as an energy source lowers the carbohydrate content, which is the substrate for CH_4 formation.

Fats also lower the number of protozoa in the rumen, many of which are physically associated with the methanogens. Some fats may depress CH4 emissions because they are toxic to the rumen methanogens. Fats rich in unsaturated fatty acids, such as found in prairie oilseed crops, also reduce CH4 formation in the rumen because they compete with methanogens for H_2 (Chaves *et al*, 2006). With each 1% fat that is added to the diet, CH4 production is reduced by about 5.6% (Beauchemin *et al*, 2008).

Most oilseeds require mechanical processing prior to feeding to ensure the fat interacts with the rumen microbial populations. Another potential fat source is corn distiller's dried grains, which contains 10 to 15% fat. Incorporating 20% corn distiller's grains into the ration is expected to lower CH4 production by about 10 to 15%. Cost is the major limitation of using fat feeding to lower CH4 emissions. In addition, added fat can negatively affect animal performance by decreasing fibre digestion and feed intake (McCaughey *et al*, 1999), but making sure that total dietary fat is kept below 6% of the diet helps avoid this negative effect.

(d) Use of legumes

Methane emissions are lower from animals fed legume forages (i.e. alfalfa, clover) compared with those fed grasses, McCaughey *et al*, (1999),Benchaar *et al*, (2001),but this relationship is also influenced by the maturity of the forage at the time of consumption(Chaves *et al*, 2006). The lower CH4 observed with legumes is attributed to lower fiber content and faster rate of passage of feed through the rumen. While this strategy has promise, farmers are often reluctant to replace grass with legumes because of pasture management issues and bloat risk.

(e) Use of corn silage and small grain silages

Use of corn silage and small grain silages, rather than grass silage, and hay, can also lower CH4 production. The high starch content of grain-based silages favours the production of propionate rather than acetate in the rumen (O'Mara *et al*, 1998). These forages also promote high dry matter intake and have a faster rate of passage through the rumen. Furthermore, replacing grass silage or hay with grain silage often improves animal performance, thereby lowering CH4 emissions per unit of animal product (O'Mara *et al*, 1998).

(f) Ionophores

Ionophores such as monensin are antimicrobials that are used in commercial beef and dairy cattle diets to modulate/regulate feed intake, control bloat, and improve feed efficiency. Monensin causes a change in the bacterial species in the rumen resulting in an increased proportion of propionate. At times, monensin may also cause a decrease in the numbers of rumen protozoa in the rumen, which provide a habitat for the rumen methanogens. Decreases in CH4 production of up to 10% (Beauchemin *et al*, 2008) are possible with monensin, depending upon the dose but the reduction in CH4 is not always sustained over time. This limits the usefulness of monensin as a long-term solution to CH4 abatement (Guan *et al*, 2006).

(g) Immunization

Wright *et al*, (2004), has proposed that it may be possible to immunise Ruminants against their own methanogens with associated decreases in methane output. Shu *et al*. (1999) have shown that such an approach can successfully reduce the numbers of *Streptococci* and *Lactobacilli* in the rumen.

(h) Probiotics

The most widely used microbial feed additives (live cells and growth medium) are based on *Saccharomyces cerevisiae* (SC) and *Aspergillus oryzae* (AO). Their effect on rumen fermentation and animal productivity are wide ranging and this has been reviewed by several authors (Martin and Nisbet, (1992). There is very limited information on their effect on methane production and all of this is in vitro. AO has been seen to reduce methane by 50%, (Newbold, 1992), which were directly related to a reduction in the protozoa population (45%).

On the other hand, addition of SC to an in vitro system reduced the methane production by 10% initially, though this was not sustained (Mutsvangwa *et al*, 1992). In other experiments with AO and SC, an increase in methane production has been reported, Martin and Nisbet, (1992), Martin *et al*, (1989), while Mathieu *et al*. (1996), reported that SC addition did not affect methane in vivo. This suggests that more research is required. Lassey, (2008), found that, methane production by ruminant's addition of soluble carbohydrates gave a shift in fermentation pattern in the rumen which give rise to a more hostile environment for the methanogenic bacteria in which passage rates are increased, ruminal pH is lowered and certain populations of protozoa, ruminal ciliates and methanogenic bacteria may be eliminated or inhibited. The work of Lana *et al*. (1998), supports this theory confirming that rumen pH regulates methane production.

(i) Reducing CH_4 by Increasing Feed Conversion Efficiency

One of the approaches in lowering enteric CH4 emissions is to improve the efficiency of converting feed to meat and milk. By reducing the amount of feed it takes to produce animal products, less enteric CH4 is generated, because CH4 emissions are related to feed intake (Benchaar *et al*, 2001). This increased efficiency of production can be achieved through animal breeding and improved nutrition.

(j) Reducing CH_4 by Increasing Animal Productivity

One of the approaches is to increase the productivity of individual animals so that fewer animals are required to produce the same amount of product. In this case, the total amount of CH_4 produced per kilogram of milk or meat declines, but CH_4 emissions per animal increase. Overall, however, a reduction in CH4 occurs because animal numbers decrease (O'Mara *et al*, 1998) and for the beef industry, improved feeding, and animal genetics, can reduce the time cattle are on feed. This has a major impact on lifetime CH_4 emissions. In addition, improving reproductive performance of cattle can reduce total CH_4 emissions from the herd by reducing the number of replacement heifers required. This approach is particularly attractive as there are economic incentives to improve reproductive efficiency even without consideration for potential reductions in CH_4 emissions.

In general, the approach of reducing CH_4 emissions by increasing animal productivity works best when a supply management system limits the total amount of product produced, as in the case of milk production within the Canadian dairy sector. It is estimated that since 1990, CH_4 emissions from the Canadian dairy industry have decreased by 24%, simply due to improved efficiency of milk production and a concomitant decrease in cow numbers (Environment Canada, 2002). However, beef cattle numbers have increased over that time and so have the total greenhouse gas emissions. Canadian dairy and beef producers could potentially lower enteric CH_4 emissions by up to 25% by implementing some of the currently available solutions. Further reductions may be possible in the future as new technologies are developed.

BENEFITS OF REDUCING ENTERIC METHANE EMISSIONS.

Reducing enteric CH_4 emissions decreases greenhouse gases in the atmosphere and improves the efficiency of converting plant material into milk and meat (Guan *et al*, 2006). At the same time, this reduction may improve the competitiveness of livestock sector. Reducing CH_4 emissions can increase animal performance by conserving energy that could be redirected to milk production or weight gain. This is in line with the findings of McAllister and Newbold, (2008), that a 20% reduction in CH_4 could allow growing cattle to gain an additional 75 g/d of weight or dairy cows to produce 1 L/day more milk.

CONCLUSION

Essentially, we must be aware of the fact that any livestock production system that meets the goals of social responsibility in terms of animal welfare or other societal concerns may also have some negative impacts on the environment that must be recognized in order to be addressed. The manipulation of the ruminal fermentation has tremendous potential for improving animal physiology, nutrition and subsequently, production. It is important to reduce the enteric methane emissions from ruminants, because methanogenesis corresponds to dietary energy loss as well as contributes to global warming. Therefore, in considering ethical animal production practices, special consideration needs to be given to the impacts of the system on the environment.

REFERENCES

Akinro, A.O; Opeyemi, D.A. and Ologunagba, I.B. (2008). Climate Change and Environmental Degradation in the Niger Delta Region of Nigeria: Its Vulnerability, Impacts and Possible Mitigations. Research Journal of Applied Sciences. 3(3); pp. 167-173.

Alaku, S.O. (2010). Introduction to Animal Science. Jee Communications. Enugu.

Balch WE, Fox GE, Magnum LJ, Woese CR, and Wolfe RS (1979). Methanogens: Re-evaluation of a Unique Biological Group. Microbiol. Rev. 43: 260-296.

Beauchemin, K.A. and McGinn, S.M. (2005). Methane Emissions from Feedlot Cattle Fed Barley or Corn Diets. J. Anim. Sci. 83: 653-661.

Beauchemin, K.A., Kreuzer, M., O'Mara, F. and McAllister, T.A.(2008). Nutritional Management for Enteric Methane Abatement: A Review. Austr. J. Exp. Agric. 48: 21-27.

Benchaar, C., Pomar, C. and Chiquette, J. (2001). Evaluation of Dietary Strategies to Reduce Methane Production in Ruminants: A Modelling Approach. Can. J. Anim. Sci. 81: 563-574.

Boadi, D; Benchaar, C; Chiquette, J; and Masse, D (2004). Mitigation Strategies to Reduce Enteric Methane Emissions from Dairy Cows: Update Review. Can. J. anim. Sci. 84, 319-335.

Boone DR, Whitman WB, and Rouviere P (1993). Diversity and Taxonomy of Methanogens. In JG Ferry (eds.). Methanogenesis: Ecol. Physiol. Biochem. Genet. Chapman and Hall, New York. pp. 35-80.

Casey, K; Bicudo, J; Schmidt, D; Singh, A; Gay, S; Gates, R; Jacobson, L; and Hoff, S (2006). Air Quality and Emissions from Livestock and Poultry Production/Waste Management Systems, p. 40. Animal Agriculture and the Environment: National Center for Manure and Waste Management White Papers.

Chaves, A.V., Thompson, L.C., Iwaasa, A.D., Scott, S.L., Olson, M.E., Benchaar, C., Veira, D.M. and McAllister, T.A. (2006). Effect of Pasture Type (Alfalfa vs Grass) on Methane and Carbon Dioxide Production by Yearling Beef Heifers. Can. J. Anim. Sci. 86: 409-418.

CONAM (Consejo Nacional del Ambiente) (2001). Communication Nacinal del Peru a la Convention de las Nacions Unida sobre Cambio Climatico. Primera Communication. Consejo Nacional del Ambiente, Lima, Peru, p. 118.

Crutzen, P.J. (1983). Atmospheric Interactions – Homogeneous Gas Reactions of C, N and S Containing Compounds. In: The Major Biogeochemical Cycles and Their Interactions (scope 21), eds. B. Bolin and R. B. Cook. John Wiley, Chickester, pp. 69-112.

Directgov (2010). Causes of climate change. http://www.direct.gov.uk/en/environmentandgreeneerliving/thewiderenvironment.

Ditchkoff, S.S. (2000). "A Decade Since "Diversification of Ruminants": Has Our Knowledge Improved?". *Oecologia* 125: 82-84. doi:10.1007/PL00008894. https://fp.auburn.edu/sfws/ditchkoff/PDF%20publications/2000%20-%20Oecologia.pdf

Ehhalt, D.H. (1974). The Atmospheric Cycle of Methane. Tellvs 26, 58-69.

Environment Canada (EC). (2002). Canada's Greenhouse Gas Inventory 1990-2001. http://www.ec.gc.ca/pdb/ghg. Wright, A.D.G., Kennedy, P., O'Neill, C.J., Toovey, A.F., Popovski, S., Rea,

Fraser, P.I., Rasmussen, R.A; Creffield, J.W; French, J.R. and Khalil M.A.K. (1986). Termites and Global Methane – Another Assessment. J. Atmos. Chem. In Press.

Guan, H., Wittenberg, K.M., Ominski, K.H. and Krause D.O. (2006). Efficacy of Ionophores in Cattle Diets for Mitigation of Enteric Methane. J. Anim Sci. 84: 1896-906.

Hackmann. T.J., and Spain, J.N. (2010). "Ruminant Ecology and Evolution: Perspectives Useful to Livestock Research and Production". *Journal of Dairy Science*, 93: 1320-1334.

Hansen, J. (2005). A Slippery Slope: How much Global Warming Constitutes "Dangerous Anthropogenic Interference. Climate Change 68(333): 269-279. Doi: 10.1007/s 10584-005-4135-0.http://www.springerlink.com/content/x283127781675v51/?p=799ebc88193f4ecfa8ca76f6e28f45d7.

Holter, J.B. and Young, A.J. (1992). Methane Prediction in Dry and Lactating Holstein Cows. J. Dairy Sci. 75, 2165-2175.

Hungate RE (1966). The Rumen and its Microbes. Academic Press, New York. Jarvis GN, Strompl C, Burgess DM, Skillman LC, Moore ERB, Joblin KN (2000). Isolation and Identification of Ruminal Methanogens from Grazing Cattle. Curr. Microbiol. 40: 327-332.

Hutchinson, G.E. (1949). A Note on Two Aspects of the Geochemistry of Carbon. Am. J. Sci. 247, 27-32.

Ifeanyi-Obi, C.C.; Etuk, U.R. and Jike-Wai O. (2012). Climate Change, Effect and Adaptation Strategies; Implication for Agricultural Extension System in Nigeria. Greener Journal of Agricultural Sciences. ISSN: 2276 – 7770. Vol 2(2), pp. 053-060, March, 2012.

IPCC (2007). Climate Change 2007: Synthesis Report. Contributions of Working Groups 1, Ii and Liito the Fourth Assessment Report of the Intergovernmental Panel on Climate Change. Geneva: IPCC.

IPCC. (2000). Good Practice Guidance and Uncertainty Management in National Greenhouse Gas Inventories. Intergovernmental Panel on Climate Change (IPCC), IPCC/OECD/IEA/IGES, Hayama, Japan.

Johnson, K.A. and Johnson, D.E. (1995). Methane Emissions from Cattle. J. Anim. Sci. 73: 2483-2492.

Jungbluth, T; Hartung, E. and Brose, G. (2001). Greenhouse Gas Emissions from Animal Houses and Manure Stores. Nutr. Cycl. Agroecosystem. 60, 133-145.

Khalil, M.A.K. and Rasmuscen, R. (1983). Sources, Sinks, and Seasonal Cycles of Atmospheric Methane. J. Geophysics Res. 88, 5131-5144.

Kirchgessner M, Windisch W, Muller HL (1995). Nutritional Factors Affecting Methane Production by Ruminants, In Engelhardt WV, Leonhard-Marek S, Breves G, Giesecke D (eds.). Ruminant Physiology: Digestion, Metabolism, Growth and Reproduction. Ferdinand Enke Verlag, Stuttgart. pp. 333-343.

Lana R.P., Russell J.B. and Van Amburgh M.E. (1998). The Role of pH in Regulating Methane and Ammonia Production, J. Anim. Sci. 76 (1998) 2190-2196.

Lassey, K.R. (2008). Livestock Methane Emission and its Perspective in the Global Methane Cycle. Austr. J. Exp. Agric. 48: 114-118.

Martin S.A. and Nisbet D.J. (1992) Effects of Direct Fed Microbials on Rumen Microbial Fermentation, J. Dairy Sci. 75 (1992) 1736-1744.

Martin S.A., Nisbet D.J. and Dean R.G. (1989). Influence of a Commercial Yeast Supplement on the *in vitro* Ruminal Fermentation, Nutr. Rep. Int. 40 (1989) 395-403. 250 Methane Production by Ruminants.

Mathieu F., Jouany J.P., Senaud J., Bohatier J., Berthin G., Mercier M. (1996). The Effect of Saccharomyces Cerevisiae and Aspergillus Orizae on Fermentations in the Rumen of Faunated and Defaunated Sheep; Protozoal and Probiotic Interactions, Reprod. Nutr. Dev. 36 (1996) 271-287.

McAllister, T.A. and Newbold, C.J. (2008). Redirecting Rumen Fermentation to Reduce Methanogenesis. Austr. J. Exp. Agric. 48: 7-13.

McCaughey, W.P., Wittenberg, K. and Corrigan. D. (1999). Impact of Pasture Type on Methane Production by Lactating Beef Cows. Can. J. Anim. Sci. 79: 221-226.

McKay, C; Pollack, J. and Courtin, R. (1991). "The Greenhouse and Antigreenhouse Effects on Titan". Science 253 (5024): 1118-1121. Doi:10.1126/science.11538492. PMID 11538492. Edit.

Miller TL (1995). Ecology of Methane Production and Hydrogen Sinks in the Rumen, In: Engelhardt WV, Leonhard-Marek S, Braves G and Giesecke D (eds.). Ruminant Physiology: Digestion, Metabolism, Growth and Reproduction. Ferdinant Enke Verlag, Stuttgart. pp. 317-331.

Monteny, G.J., Groenestein, C.M; and Hilhorst, M.A. (2001). Interactions and Coupling Between Emissions of Methane and Nitrous Oxide from Animal Husbandry. Nutr. Cycl. Agroecosyst. 60, 123-132.

Mosier, A.R., Duxbury, L.M; Freney, J.R., Heinemeyer, O; Minami, K. and Johnson, D. (1998b). Mitigating Agricultural Emissions of Methane. Climate Change 40, 39-80.

Mutsvangwa T., Edward I.E., Topps J.H., Paterson G.F.M. (1992). The Effect of Dietary Inclusion of Yeast Culture (Yea-Sacc) on Patterns of Rumen Fermentation, Food Intake and Growth of Intensively Fed Bulls, Anim. Prod. 55 (1992) 35-40.

Newbold C.J. (1992) Probiotics – A New Generation of Rumen Modifiers? Med. Fac. Landbouww University of Ghent 57/4b (1992) 1925-1933. Mathers J.C., Miller E.L., Some Effects of Chloral Hydrate on Rumen Fermentation & Digestion in Sheep, J. Agric. Sci. (Camb.) 99 (1982) 215-224.

O'Mara, F.P., Fitzgerald, J.J., Murphy, J.J. and Rath, M. (1998). The Effect on Milk Production of Replacing Grass Silage with Maize Silage in the Diet of Dairy Cows. Livest. Prod. Sci. 55: 79-87.

Onyimonyi, A.E. (2012). Climate Change and Livestock Production in Nigeria: Effect and Adaptation Options. Critical Issues in Agricultural Adaptation to Climate Change in Nigeria. A Production of the Faculty of Agriculture, University of Nigeria, Nsukka. ISBN: 978-8128-84-x. p. 73-84.

Seiler, W. (1984). Contribution of Biological Processes to the Global Budget of CH_4 in the Atmosphere. In: Current Perspectives in Microbial Ecology, eds. M.J. Klug and C. A Reddy. American Society for Micro – biology, Washington, DC, USA, pp. 468-477.

Sharp R, Ziemer CJ, Stern MD, Stahl DA (1998). Taxon-specific Associations Between Protozoal and Methanogen Populations in the Rumen and a model rumen system. FEMS Microbiol. Ecol. 26: 71-78.

Shu Q., Gill H.S., Hennessy D.W., Leng R.A., Bird S.H., Rowe J.B. (1999). Immunisation Against Lactic Acidosis in Cattle, Res. Vet. Sci. 67 (1999) 65-71.

Singh, S.K; Meena, H.R.; Kolekar, D.V. and Singh, Y.P. (2012). Climate Change Impacts on Livestock and Adaptation Strategies to Sustain Livestock Production. J. Vet. Adv 2(7): 407-412.

Smith P, Martino D, Cai Z, Gwary D, Janzen H, Kumar P, McCarl B, Ogle S, O'Mara F, Rice C, Scholes B and Sirotenko O, (2007). Agriculture. In: Climate Change 2007: Mitigation. Contribution of Working Group 111 to the Forth Assessment Report of the Intergovernmental Panel on Climate Change. Eds B. Metz, O.R. Davidson, P.R. Bosch, R. Dave & L.A. Meyer. Cambridge University Press, Cambridge: United Kingdom and New York, NY, USA.

Sobayo, R.A; Oguntona, E.B; Osinowo, O.A; Eruvbetine, D; Bamgbose, A.M; Oso O.A; Fafiolu, A.O; Bawala, T.O. and Adeyemi, O.A. (2010). Effect of Ascorbic Acid Supplementation on the Performance and Egg Quality of Laying Birds in a Humid Environment. Proc. Of the 13th Ann. Conf. of the Ani. Sc. Association of Nigeria (ASAN). pp. 196-199.

Solomon, S; Qin, D; Manning, M; Chen, Z; Marquis, M' Averyt, K.B; Tignor, M; and Miller, H.L. (2007). Climate Change 2007: The Physical Science Basis; Contribution of Working Group 1 to the Fourth Assessment Report of the Intergovernmental Panel on Climate Change, Cambridge University Press, ISBN 978-0-521-88009-1 (pb: 978-0-521-705967).

Steinfeld, H; Gerber, P; Wassenaar, T; Castel, V; Rosales, M, and De Haan, C (2006). Livestock Long Shadow. Food and Agriculture Organization of the United Nations. http>//www.fao.org/docrep/010/a0701e00.HTM.

Sun, H; Trabue, S.L; Scoggin, K; Jackson, W.A; Pan, Y; Zhao, Y; Malkina, I.L; Koziel, J.A. and Mitioehner, F.M. (2008). Alcohol, Volatile Fatty Acid, Phenol, and Methane Emissions from Dairy Cows and Fresh Manure. Journal of Environ. Qual. 37, 615-622.

Tajima K, Nagamine T, Matsui H, Nakamura M, Aminov RI (2001). Phylogenic Analysis of Archael 16S rRNA Libraries from the Rumen Suggests the Existence of a Novel Group of Archaea not Associated with known Methanogens. FEMS Microbiol. Lett. 200: 67-72.

USDA (2004). U.S. Agriculture and Forestry Greenhouse Gas Inventory: 1990-2001. Global Change Programme Office, Office of the Chief Economist, USA.

Vaclav Smil (2003). The Earth's Biosphere: Evolution, Dynamics, and Change. MIT Press. P. 107. ISBN 978-0-262-69298-4.

Warrick, R.A. and E.M. Barrow (1991). Climate Change Scenarios for the UK. Transactions of the Institute of Geographer, 16: 397-399.

Whitford MF, Teather RM, Forster RJ (2001). Phylogenetic Analysis of Methanogens from the Bovine Rumen. BMC Microbiol. ttp://www.biomedcentral.com/1471-2180/1471/1475.

Woese CR. Kandler O, Wheelis JL (1990). Towards a Natural System of Organisms: Proposal for the Domains Archaea Bacteria and Eucarya. Proc. Natl. Acad. Sci. USA. 87: 4576-4579. doi: 10.1073/pnas.87.12.4576.

Wolin MJ (1979). The Rumen Fermentation: A Model for Microbial Interactions in Anaerobic Ecosystems, In: Alexander M (Ed.). Adv. Microb. Ecol. Vol. 3. Planum Press, New York and London. pp. 49-77.

Wolin MJ (1982). Hydrogen Transfer in Microbial Communities, In: Bull AT, Slater JH (Eds.). Microb. Interact. Commun. Vol. 1. Academic Press, London. pp. 323-356.

Wright, A.D.G., Kennedy, P., O'Neill, C.J., Toovey, A.F., Popovski, S., Rea, S.M., Pimm, C.L., and Klein, L. (2004). Reducing Methane Emission in Sheep by Immunization Against Rumen Methanogens. Vaccine 22: 3976-3985.

Yavitt, J.B. (1992). Methane, Biogeochemical Cycle. pp. 197-207 in Encyclopedia of Earth System Science, Vol. 3. Acad.Press, London, England.

Pages: 87-167

NATURAL ECOSYSTEM AND CLIMATE CHANGE

Edited by: **Dr. Pawan Kumar 'Bharti'; Dr. Khwairakpam Gajananda**

ISBN: 978-93-5056-745-6

Edition: **2015**

Published by: **Discovery Publishing House Pvt. Ltd., New Delhi (India)**

CHAPTER - 7

Management Strategies for Rodents within Different Ecosystems

Abd El-Aleem Saad Soliman Desoky

INTRODUCTION

Rodent pests in urban and rural areas have been present in different situations in the world. In general, most of them inflect economic losses and public health problems (Dolbeer, 1999).

In many countries due to lack of studies to establish either control programmes or reduction of rodent population and to estimate risk or losses have not been possible. Only control activities on rodents were reduced environment and items were performed. Thus, specific treatments were made, and many animals were eliminated by poisoning, but quickly new animals move to occupy the vacant area and exploit the resources of untreated areas. These campaigns are an expensive way of "harvesting" some rodents, and usually they are not useful for eliminating or controlling population that endanger or damage people's economy or public health. On the other hand, most of the materials and strategies of control have been designed to be used in developed countries (Singleton and Brown, 1999).

Department of Plant Protection, Faculty of Agriculture -Assiut University, Assiut, Egypt.

Current address: **Plant Protection Department (Zoology), Faculty of Agriculture, Sohag University, Sohag, Egypt.**

Rodentia is one of the most important mammalian orders which have a great effect on the environment. Directly, through their destructive feeding habits and indirectly as a stable food items for many predators in the food chains. In Egypt changes in the agroecosystem, during the last 40 years, have had a great effect on the distribution and abundance of field rodent population (El-Sherbiny, 1987 and Abd EL-Galil, 1997).

Thus, great efforts should be done to develop rodent control programmes. Control methods must not only fulfill the requirement of protecting crops, but also in a safe efficient and economic manner (Abdel-Gawad, 2001).The main options available for non-chemical control and non-lethal chemical control methods may be cost effective, but they rarely achieve rapid knock-down of pest population that is possible with properly used chemical rodenticides. However, they can be integrated with chemical control except perhaps vertebrate predators which may be vulnerable to secondary poisoning from some persistent (Keshta 2003). The main objectives of this studies aim to develop an effective strategy for implementation of rodent management programmes in cultivated and newly reclaimed agro ecosystems in Egypt. Information regarding rodent species composition as well as habitat and food preference is very important and rarely found in local literature. Therefore, the field and laboratory studies of this investigation were an attempt to add some knowledge to fill the gap in current information of this subject. So, the present work was initiated to study the following main points:

1. Species composition of rodents in cultivated and reclaimed lands.
2. Determination of the population density of rodents by using different methods.
3. Colours preference of rodent bait.
4. Food preference of rodent baits.
5. Rodent Control.

REVIEW OF LITERATURE

Analytical review of literature was made to through a beam of light on rodents in Egypt, as well as, abroad. The reported references include the species composition of rodents and the fluctuations of the population density of rodents collected by different methods. Also, food and colour preferred in rodent baits and control measures of rodents.

The main sources of publications were Agriculture Research Review, Hebriden Naturalist, Ecology Modelling, Acta Oecologica, International Biodeterioration, Ecosystem and Environment, Indian Journal of Agriculture Sciences, Pharmacology Biochemistry and Behavior, Newzealand Journal Ecology, Mammalian Biology, Crop protection, East Grinstead, Pytoparasitica, Science for Conservation, Assiut Journal of Agricultural Sciences, Journal of Stored Products Research, Scientific Conferences of Agricultural Sciences,

Animal Behavior, Journal of Arid Environment, Applied Entomology and Phytopathology, Wildlife Research. Also, approved thesis and dissertations in file at different colleges and institutional libraries.

SPECIES COMPOSITION OF RODENTS

Most publications dealing with rodents in cultivated and reclaimed lands were found among general surveys in different agro ecosystems. However, the present review covers the most important literature published in Egypt and abroad. Six rodent species were concerned as shown in table 7.1. One species belonged to family cricetidae, named lesser garbia *Gerbillus gerbillus* Olivier and five species of family muridae were recorded. Species of family muridae include field rat *Arvicanthis niloticus* Desmarest, grey bellied rat *Rattus rattus alexandrinus* Linnaeus, white bellied rat *Rattus rattus frugivorus* Linnaeus, Norway rat *Rattus norvegicus* Berkenhout and house mouse *Mus musculus* Linnaeus.

DETERMINATION OF THE POPULATION DENSITY OF RODENTS BY USING DIFFERENT METHODS

The present review covers the most important articles concerned with the population density of the common rodents inhabiting cultivated area, reclaimed lands and River Nile bank. Rodent species concerned include *Gerbillus gerbillus* (Olivier), *Arvicanthis niloticus* (Desm.), *Rattus rattus alexandrinus* (Linn.), *Rattus rattus frugivorus* (Linn.), *Rattus norvegicus* Berk., and *Mus musculus* Linn. Authors have reported that the population density of rodent species concerned herein was determined by several methods. Traps were usually applied to determine the population density and surface activity of rodents, traps were usually applied. Sometimes, traps are not enough and in such cases alternative methods should be applied e.g. feces, active burrows and food consumption ... etc., (keshta, 2003).

Trapping Method

Most publications concerned with the population density of the common rodents collected by trapping method was done by several authors such as: Abdel-Gawad (1974), (1979) and (1987); Hussien (1991); Ibrahim (1995); El-Deeb *et al.,* (1996); Embarak (1997); Ebaid *et al.,* (1999); Felicion *et al.,* (2002); AbdEl-Galil (2005); Cavia *et al.,* (2005) and Baghdadi (2006).

In Assiut Governorate of Egypt, Abdel-Gawad (1974) reported that the peak number was recorded during March, May, September and October for *A. niloticus* Desm. *R. r. frugivorus* (Linn), *R. r. alexandrinus* (Linn). and *R. norvegicus* Berk., while low density was recorded in January and July in the cultivated and suburban areas. Also, Abdel-Gawad (1979) in Assiut area of Egypt, recorded that *A. niloticus* (Desm.) which was the predominant species in the clay-soil cultivated areas the highest density was during Summer (June) and Autumn (September to November) which coincided with harvesting of Winter and Summer crops.

Table 7.1: List of Rodent Species in Cultivated and Reclaimed Lands in Arid Ecosystems as Reported by Several Authors

Family Species	Common Name	Author(s), Year and Country
Fam. Cricetidae: *Gerbillus gerbillus* (Olivier)	**Lesser garbia**	Abdel-Gawad *et al.,* (1982), Egypt; Abdel-Gawad (1987), Egypt; Greaves (1989), Rome; Egypt; Abd El-Galil (1997), Egypt; Mourad (1997), Egypt; El-Deeb *et al.,* (1999), Egypt and Al-Gendy (2004), Egypt.
Fam. Muridae: 1. *Arvicanthis niloticus* (Desmarest)	**Field rat, grass rat, Nile rat and Nile grass rat**	Abdel-Gawad (1974), Egypt; Abdel-Gawad *et al.* (1982), Egypt; Ali (1985), Egypt; El-Bahrawy (1986), Egypt; Abdel-Gawad (1987), Egypt; Abazaid (1990), Egypt; El-Fekey (1990), Egypt; Abd El-Karim (1991), Egypt; Embarak (1997), Egypt; El-Nashar (1998), Egypt ; Ahmed (2001), Egypt; Al-Gendy (2004), Egypt; AbdEl-Galil (2005), Egypt; Baghdadi (2006), Egypt and Ahmed (2006), Egypt.
2. *Rattus rattus alexandrinus* (Linnaeus)	**grey bellied rat white bellied rat**	Abdel-Gawad (1974), Egypt; Abdel-Gawad *et al.*, (1982), Egypt; Ali (1985), Egypt; El-Bahrawy (1986), Egypt; Abazaid (1990), Egypt; Embarak (1997), Egypt; Al-Gendy (2004), Egypt; Baghdadi (2006), Egypt; Ahmed (2006), Egypt.
3. *Rattus rattus frugivorus* (Linnaeus)		Abdel-Gawad (1974), Egypt; Abdel-Gawad *et al.*, (1982), Egypt; Ali (1985), Egypt; El-Bahrawy (1986), Egypt; Abdel-Gawad (1987), Egypt; Abazaid (1990), Egypt; El-Fekey (1990), Egypt; Embarak (1997), Egypt; Mourad (1997), Egypt; El-Deeb *et al.*, (1999), Egypt; Al-Gendy (2004), Egypt and Baghdadi (2006), Egypt.

(Table Contd…)

Family Species	Common Name	Author(s), Year and Country
4. *Rattus norvegicus* Berkenhout	**Norway rat, Brown rat and Sewer rat**	Abdel-Gawad (1974), Egypt; King (1984), New Zeland; Ali (1985), Egypt; El-Bahrawy (1986), Egypt; Abazaid (1990), Egypt; Girard *et al.*, (1990), Oklahoma; Abd El-Karim (1991), Egypt; Dowing and Murphy (1994), New Zeland; Ibrahim (1995), Egypt; Yossef (1996), Egypt; AbdEl-Galil (1997), Egypt; Mourad (1997), Egypt; El-Deeb *et al.*, (1999), Egypt; Welhong *et al.*, (1999), New Zland; Ahmed (2001), Egypt; Castillo *et al.*, (2003), Argentina; Al-Gendy (2004), Egypt and AbdEl-Galil (2005), Egypt.
5. *Mus musculus* Linnaeus	**House mouse**	King (1984), New Zeland; Ali (1985), Egypt; El-Bahrawy (1986), Egypt; Parshad *et al.*, (1987), India; Abazaid (1990), Egtpt; El-Fekey (1990), Egypt; Girard *et al.*, (1990), Oklahoma; Abd El-Karim (1991), Egypt; Dowing and Murphy (1994), New Zeland; Ibrahim (1995), Egypt; Miller and Miller (1995), Island; Yossef (1996), Egypt; Mourad (1997), Egypt; El-Nashar (1998), Egypt; El-Deeb *et al.*, (1999), Egypt; Welhong *et al.*, (1999), New Zland; Ahmed (2001), Egypt; Blackwell (2001), New Zland; Castillo *et al.*, (2003), Argentina; Al-Gendy (2004), Egypt; Baghdadi (2006), Egypt; Ahmed (2006), Egypt.

Asran *et al.*, (1985) in Fayoum Governorate of Egypt, found that the population density of *A.niloticus* (Desm.) differed from location to location, from district to another and from month to month, forming a cycle with two peaks per year. One was in May and the other in November. The population occurred in cattle farms followed by field and citrus orchards. Abdel-Gawad (1987) in wady El-Assiuty area, Assiut Governorate of Egypt, studied rodent population. He found three species, *Arvicanthis niloticus* (Desm.), *Rattus r. frugivorus* (Linn.) and *Gerbillus sp* (Olivier), representing about 59.72%, 29.42%, and 10.87%, respectively. The population density could be arranged according to different seasons in a descending order as follows: spring, autumn, summer and winter.

Abazaid (1990) in Qena Governorate of Egypt, recorded the seasonal fluctuations of *R.r.frugivorus* (Linn.) and *R.r.alexandrinus* (Linn.) in the poultry farm. The highest population was trapped in Autumn (50%), followed by Summer (31.39%), Spring (11.44%), then Winter (7.14%). Hussien (1991) in Beni-Suef of Governorate Egypt, found that *Mus musculus* Linn, was 54% during June 1988-1989 and minimum was 8.3% during February in the same year. During January no pregnant 0% was recorded. El-Deeb *et al.*, (1992) in Fayoum, Minia and Sharkia governorates of Egypt, studied the population dynamics of *A.niloticus* (Desm.) during 1988. They recorded that population densities of *A.niloticus* (Desm.) showed two peaks after the harvesting periods of Winter (wheat and barley) and Summer (maize and rice) crops. The highest density of pregnancy rate was recorded during September and the lowest during November. Asran (1994) In Abu Qurkas district, Minia governorate of Egypt, found the relative percentage of *Arvicanthis niloticus* (Desm.) in Spring, Autumn, Winter and Summer were 35.3%, 30.6%, 29.6% and 28.5%, respectively. Ibrahim (1995) in Ismailia, Minoufia and Beheira governorates of Egypt recorded that the highest population of rodents during the months directly followed the Winter crops harvesting while the lowest caught numbers were during winter season in certain different habitats. *R. norvegicus* Berk., was found with moderate numbers during months of summer and autumn and completely absent throughout the rest of year months. On the other hand *M.musculus* Linn., started to be found from April and its number gradually increased to reach the maximum during November. El-Deeb *et al.*, (1996) in three Governorates Ismailia, Menofia and Behira of Egypt, studied that population dynamic of rodent species. The results showed that the highest rodent population density was recorded during the summer months directly followed the winter crop harvesting. However the lowest caught numbers were during winter season. *Rattus rattus* (Linn.) species was abundantly recorded in the field crop during spring. Embarak (1997) in Assiut of Egypt, studied the fluctuations of the population density of rodents in cultivated area in two successive years. Results indicated that the highest density was recorded in summer and the least density in winter of three species of rats include *R.r.frugivorus* (Linn.), *A. niloticus* (Desm.) and *R..r. alexandrinus* (Linn.). Ebaid *et al*., (1999) in Ismailia and Alexandria Governorates of Egypt, studied female sexual status of *Gerbillus gerbillus* (Olivier) and *Meriones shawi* (Thomas) rodent were studied under the field conditions of two reclaimed areas at Egypt, i.e. serabium village (Ismailia Governorate) and 6th October farm (Nubaria area, Alexandria Governorate). The results obtained showed that *G. gerbillus* (Olivier), the average percentages of female reached the maximum during September and October at serabium area and during November at 6th October. While, males outnumbered females during the rest month. On the other hand, pregnant females were completely disappeared during winter month at serabium areas and summer month at 6th October farm. Females reached the maximum during April, August at Serabium area and during March, November at 6th October farm (5 embryos/females in all cases). The highest ratio of pregnant females was recorded during July, while the lowest was on August.

Felicion *et al*., (2002) in Brazil, studied the population dynamics of *Mus musculus* Linn., were studied through capture-mark-recapture in grass land between fragments of Atlantic forest from March 1998 to February 1999. The results showed that *M.musculus* Linn., reached highest population size by the end of dray seasons. Cavia *et al*., (2005) In Argentina, studied the distribution of the rodent *Akodon azarae*, the abundance of rodent *Akodon azarae* decreased in field before and after harvest. Baghdadi (2006) in Assiut Governorate of Egypt, reported that the highest seasonal index was recorded in spring, while the lowest one in winter of rodent species viz., *Arvicanthis niloticus* (Desm.), *R.r. frugivorus* (Linn.), *R.r. alexandrinus* (Linn.) and *Mus musculus* Linn. In general, males were outnumbered females. Mature surpassed immature stages allover the two years. The highest density of immature stage in spring in the field crops and woodlands.

Feces Method

Limited information concerned the using of feces method for studying and determining the population density of rodents. However, several authors reported feces method for determining the infestation by rodents such as (Ahmed, 2001 and Keshta, 2003).

In the approach Meehan (1984) in UK, found that *Rattus norvegicus* Berk., dropping tend to be spindle shaped (20mm) and generally were grouped together. *Rattus rattus* (Linn.) dropping were on average somewhat smaller more sausage shaped (15mm) and more scattered . *Mus musculus* Linn., dropping were much smaller (spinal shaped 6mm). *Rattus norvegicus* Berk., produce about 40 droppings a day, and *Mus musculus* Linn., about 8.

Maclennan *et al*., (2000) in Shiant Island, studied the distribution and abundance of *Rattus rattus* (Linn.) by feces sampling.

Active Burrows Method

Most publications concerned with the population density of the common rodents collected by active burrows method was done by several authors such as: Yunker and Guirgis (1969); Abdel-Gawad and Maher Ali (1982a); Ali (1985); Ali (1991) and Shehab *et al.,* (2000). Al-Gendy (2004).

Yunker and Guirgis (1969) in Cairo of Egypt, studied *gerbillus spp* burrows in the desert and semi desert near Cairo. Burrows in semi desert were sometimes dug among root of plant. Occupied burrows were plugged with sand during the warm period of the year March through December and opened during the cooler wet season January and February.

Abdel-Gawad and Maher Ali (1982a) in Assiut of Egypt, found that the active burrows technique could used to estimate the population density of rodents during control operation. Ali (1985) in Sohag Governorate of Egypt, studied the fluctuations of rodent active burrows in five cultivated areas. Data results the activity of the rodents increased in spring, summer and autumn, and decreased in winter. The highest peak was recorded in July.

Ali (1991) in Sohag Governorate Egypt, stated that estimated reduction in population density of rodent by active burrows in treated and untreated (control) areas.

Shehab *et al.,* (2000) in Syria, estimated the decrease or increase of population density of *Microtus socialis* with active burrows. Al-Gendy (2004) in Egypt, studied the population density of large jirds of rodents by active burrows. He found that the population density of large jirds in wheat crops were 79% during November, as follows 67.-, 52, 33, 32 and 16% encountered during March, December, April, February and January while for peanut crops was 100% during May followed July 44% and June 32%.

Food Consumption Method

Abdel-Gawad and Maher Ali (1982) in Assiut Governorate of Egypt, found that the food consumption technique can be used to estimate the population density of rodents during control operation.

Baghdadi (2006) in Assiut Governorate of Egypt, studied the population density of rodent species in the building with food consumption. He found that the highest population was observed during the spring season followed by autumn (3123 and 2788.7g) and (2320 and 2173.6g) respectively, through the years of study. The lowest density was observed during winter (1561.3 and 1985g) and summer (1577.6 and 2100g) seasons during the two years of study.

COLOUR PREFERENCE OF RODENT BAITS

Coloured baits tested for attracting rodents occupied the attention of several authors such as:

Meehan (1984) in UK, found that rats and mice are almost certainly colour blind, but yellow and green are more attractive as they are seen as a very light grey. Ali (1985) in Qena Governorate of Egypt, found that as for colour preference, no significant difference was observed in the consumption of rodents to eight coloured baits, but the rodent preferred the grey, yellow and red baits than the other baits (blue, green, brown, violet and orange)

Sherwin and Glen (2003) found that mice can discriminate amongst colours and laboratory mice preferred white cages over black, green and particularly, red ones.

FOOD PREFERENCE OF RODENT BAITS

Most publications concerned with food preference of the common rodents was done by several authors such as: Abdel-Gawad and Maher Ali (1982b); El-Deeb *et al.*,(1985); Saied (1985); Abazaid (1990); Abd el-Rahman *et al.*, (1991) Shafi *et al.*, (1992); Jackson (2001); Ahmaed (2006) and Baghdadi (2006).

Abdel-Gawad and Maher Ali (1982b) in Assiut Governorate of Egypt, found that crushed maize and sorghum were the most preferable baits for all species of rodents in Upper Egypt and can be recommended as carriers for rodenticides. El-Deeb *et al.*, (1985) in Beni-Seuf of Egypt, obtained that the most preferable foods for Nile rat *A. niloticus* (Desm.) were wheat followed by maize and sorghum. The least accepted baits were dried bagasse and cotton seed cake. Saied (1985) in Egypt, found that *Acomyes cahirinus* prefers the crushed maize which mixed with sesame oil than the cotton seed oil.

Abazaid (1990) in Qena Governorate of Egypt, studied three items in triple or double cup tests for their acceptability to three species of rodents. In double cups test, the bagasse was found to be more preferred than wheat or crushed maize for the three species. Also, in the triple cups test, bagasse was more preferred for *R.r. frugivorus* (Linn.) and *R.r. alexandrinus* (Linn.) than crushed maize and wheat. For *A. niloticus* (Desm.), the consumption was nearly equal from bagsse and crushed maize, but higher than that from wheat. Abdel-Rahman *et al.*, (1991) in Ryan of Qatar state, mentioned that acceptance of non toxic bait by the rat population, was related to their calories and nutritional values. Peanuts and wheat were the most favorable. While maize, barley and rice were the lowest accepted by the rats. Peanuts and wheat were the best carriers for rodenticides followed by maize, barley and then rice. Shafi *et al.*, (1992) in Pakistan, stated that in order to increase poison bait acceptance, six taste additives yeast, egg shell, egg yolk, sheep blood, chicken blood and minced meat were incorporated 2% (w/w) individually in a bait base of wheat flour and broken rice. Under no-choice tests (single feed), *R. norvegicus* Berk., showed potential for preference of additive baits. In paired-choice tests (two feed), baits with yeast and egg shell were significantly preferred against plain bait (reference). Yeast additive was first and egg shell second in order of preference. A similar order of preference was observed in three feed choice tests. Yeast additive, which was highly preferred in choice tests, increased acceptability (palatability) by 68.2% and 60.1% of the bait containing brodifacoum and bromadiolone, respectively.

Jackson (2001) in USA, reported rodenticides bait can control be effected. Grain bait mixtures (often with flavors, sugar, and vegetable oil added) are the basis of most control programmes. Some baits are palletized; others, left in granular form. Shelf-life is good as long as the bait is protected from environmental extremes. For sewer and moist environments, wax blocks have been marketed. Fresh fruits, vegetables or meats were highly attractive to rodents. Ahmed (2006) in Assiut Governorate of Egypt, reported that under laboratory condition crushed maize, crushed sorghum and crushed wheat was the most preferred food to the Nile rat, *A.niloticus* (Desm.) and house mouse, *Mus musculus* Linn., followed by long sorghum, barley, crushed broad bean and cobs+ 4% molas. Baghdadi (2006) in Assiut Governorate of Egypt, reported that under laboratory condition wheat, peanut, maize and sunflower was the most preferred food to the Nile rat, *A.niloticus* (Desm.) followed by short sorghum, sugarcane refuse and 4% molas+ sugarcane refuse.

RODENT CONTROL

Rodent damage a variety of agricultural crops throughout most regions of the world. In developing countries where the economy depends on agriculture, rodent infestation can pose a serious threat of not only reduced income but also widespread dangerous diseases. Damage range from negligible destruction of growing plants to total crops loss. Thus, great efforts should be done to develop rodent control programmes. Control methods must not fulfill the requirement of protecting crops, but also in a safe efficient and economic manner. However, in this review three method of rodents curative applied control method were considered these methods are mechanical control, biological control and chemical control.

Mechanical Control

Most publications concerned with the Mechanical control of the common rodents was done by several authors such as: Maher Ali (1972); Maher Ali and Abdel-Gawad (1982); Abazaid (1997) El-Eraky *et al.*, (2000); Abdel-Gawad (2001a); Al-Gendy (2004); Ahmed (2006) and Baghdadi (2006).

Maher Ali (1972) in Assiut Governorate of Egypt, reported that in case of large food stores, it is highly advisable to destroy all vegetations (weeds) in order to deter any rodents foraging in the surrounding area from approaching close to the building.

Maher Ali and Abdel-Gawad (1982) in Assiut Governorate of Egypt, studied that the application of anticoagulants and zinc phosphide for the control of the Nile grass rat *A.niloticus* (Desm.) was compared with burning of weeds harboring rodents. It was found that anticoagulants are superior to the other two methods, the burning of weeds comes next.

El-Eraky *et al.*, (2000) in Assiut Governorate of Egypt, found that mechanical control by laser-land operation has given great success. By this method a complete reduction in rodent active burrows was achieved after 10 days as compared with 50.6% in Qunitox rodenticides respectively. Abdel-Gawad (2001a) in Assuit Governorate of Egypt, studied that two common rodenticides, super caide 0.004% and zinc phosphide 5% and four mechanical viz., laser- land leveling, deep irrigation, destroying burrows and traps were evaluated for their efficacy for rodent control in maize fields. The results showed mechanical control methods achieved great success in rodent control as compared with the chemical control was ranged between 94.2% in the laser treatment method and 74.5% in the trap method with an average of 89.65% and 94.6% in handing destroy method. Al-Gendy (2004) in Sharkia of Egypt, pointed that the active burrows of rodents decreased by crashing in three consecutive days through all period of study except April. Ahmed (2006) in Assiut Governorate of Egypt, studied that mechanical control of rodents in broad bean, wheat, maize and sorghum fields by handling destroying of burrows and erased the wasted materials. It was more effective in controlling rodents than chemical methods. Baghdadi (2006) in Assiut Governorate of Egypt, found that the ploughing and brushing woods operation led to complete reduction in rodent numbers during the first five months of ploughing and brushing woods operation comparing with untreated area. Whereas; the number of rodent was increased gradually from May to November.

Biological Control

The rodent population in nature can be groaned by the Naturally Occurring Biological Control Agents (NOBA) such as pathogens, parasites and predators.

Most publications concerned with Biological control of the common rodents was done by several authors such as Hussain and Ahmad (1990); Fitzgerald (1991); Dielenberg *et al.*, (1999); Keshta (2003); Al-Gendy (2004).

Hussain and Ahmad (1990) in Egypt, found that animals like cats, snakes and dogs were known to kill and eat rats under most field or godown conditions. Cats can catch a full grown rat, but adult rats were too large and aggressive and often injures the cat when a capture attempt was made Cats therefore, generally confine their attention to mice and small immature rats. Dogs and snakes can kill rats but not in such effective quantities, as to result in rodent control. For dogs, cats and snakes, like all predators, only catch the rodents that were easily available. Fitzgerald (1991) in Island, reported that in some Island ecosystems, domestic cats maintain rodent populations at low levels. Although, they also often prey upon endangered species. It was believed that, in some ecosystems at least, the beneficial effects of reducing the rodent population could outweigh the damage done to the endemic prey species. Dielenberg *et al.*, (1999) studied the efficacy of predatory odors avoidance for rodents. Results showed that rats exposed to the cat collar displayed a robust avoidance response, spending about 70% of a 20-min session in the hide box compared to 25% in control rats .This avoidance response was completely reversed in rats given a low dose (0.375mg/kg) of midazolam. During the test phase, rats exposed to the cat odor on the previous day showed elevated levels of hiding when returned to the test apparatus without the cat odor present.

Keshta (2003) in Shark El-Ewainat of Egypt, reported that wild animals were in wild cats *Felis sylvestrs*, sand fox *Vulpes ruepelli* and Arab wolf *Vulpes cana*. They encountered all over the year. The wild cat is diurnal. In general the efficiency average of the present predators against the distributed rodents in the tested area were arranged descendingly as follows. *Jaculus sp* 35.3%, *Gerbillus sp* 30.7%, *Meriones sp* 30.2%, Mus *sp* 25.2%. Al-Gendy (2004) in Sharkia governorate of Egypt, surveyed the rodent predators. He found that carnivorous species were cat *Felis silvestris*, weasel *Mustela nivalis* and mongoose Herpestes ichneumon, red fox *Vulpes vulpes*, snakes, dog *Canis lupus*.

Chemical Control

Most publications concerned with the chemical control of the common rodents was done by several authors such as: Kitahara (1981); Abdel-Gawad and Farghal (1982); Helal and Zedan (1982); Zaghloul and Zakaria (1986); Parshad *et al.*, (1987); Mikhail (1988); Ali (1991); Asran *et al.*, (1992); Gill (1992); Parshad and Malhi (1995); Vaziri and Farid (1995); Chander-sheikher *et al.*, (1996); Abazaid (1997); Khan *et al.*, (1998); Dielenberg *et al.*, (1999); Moran (1999); El-Eraky *et al.*, (2000); Hygnstrom *et al.*, (2000); Farghal *et al.*,(2000); Shehab *et al.*, (2000); Yaghoobi-Ershadi *et al.*, (2000); Abdel-Gawad (2001b); O'Connor and Booth (2001); Twigg *et al.*, (2002); Eisemann *et al.*, (2003); Keshta (2003); Moran (2003); Shriprakash *et al.*, (2003); Kaur and Parshad (2005); Johnston *et al.*, (2005); Ahmed (2006) and Baghdadi (2006).

Kitahara (1981) in Japan, studied the poisonous effects of a rodenticide, Zinc phosphide 1% with three different dosages (200, 400and 800g/0.4 ha) against the japans field vole, *Microtus montebelli* in three areas. The control effectiveness of the rodenticide was estimated by the reduction in the vole density, and was shown to be proportional to the increasing dosage of the poison (47.6% in 200g application area, 76.0% in 400g and 86.7% in 800g area). However, the percentage (ratio) of the bait consumption to the total dosage at each area decreased: 53.7, 36.2, and 30.5%, respectively. Abdel-Gawad and Farghal (1982) in the central hospital in Assiut of Egypt, found that *A. niloticus* was more susceptible to Warfarin (0.04%) than *R. norvegicus* in all maturity stages (early, medium and mature). Helal and Zedan (1982) in Assiut Governorate of Egypt, used Difenacoum at 0.005% against *R. norvegicus* and *R.r. alexandrinus*. They found that the LT_{50} and LT_{95} and values were 5.5 days and 21 days. Zaghloul and Zakaria (1986) in Kuwait reported that Warfarin offered for 4 days at a concentration of 0.025% had a low toxicity against *Mus musculus*. Also, complete mortalities were obtained in both sexes by using feeding tests with Brodifacoum 0.005% for one day. Parshad *et al.*, (1987) in India, studied the Poisoning of rodents with 2·4% Zinc phosphide and 0·005% Brodifacoum and Bromadiolone baits resulted in an 80·8-97% reduction in census bait taken and 100% in track marking activity in the case of Zinc phosphide. However, on two separate farms, 88·8 and 92·8% control success could be achieved with two treatments of Brodifacoum at 15 day intervals and Zinc phosphide at 54 day intervals respectively. Mikhail (1988) in certain Egyptian regions found that Warfarin was more toxic than Racumin to the combined roof rat, *R. rattus*. The males showed a slight higher susceptibility to tested anti coagulant rodenticides than females.

Ali (1991) in Sohag Governorate of Egypt, studied efficacy of anticoagulant rodenticides using multiple feeding for 6 days under field condition. He found in multiple dose that Racumin and Matikus the highest percentage of rodents control success 98.5% and 95% consequently. Asran *et al.*, (1992) evaluated the efficacy of 6 anticoagulant rodenticides against Nile rat, *A. niloticus*. Results indicated that 0.005% Flocoummafen, 0.005% Brodifacoum anticoagulants were the most effective followed by 0.005% Diphacinone, 0.006% Chlorophacinone, .019% Sulphaquinoxaline, 0.005% Bromadiolone and 0.05% Warfarin. The reduction caused by the above mentioned six rodenticides was 91.2 %, 85.4%, 82.8%, 76.8% and 64.2%, respectively. Gill (1992) in UK, determined the toxicity of the anticoagulant Flocoumafen to three universal commensal rodent pest species, *R. norvegicus*, *R. rattus* and *Mus domesticus* and four tropical rodent species not native to UK, *Meriones shawi*, *Acomys cahirinus*, *A. niloticus* and *Mesocricetus auratus*. In the 1-day no-choice tests, Flocoumafen gave 97.5% mortality of Warfarin-resistant laboratory rats, 100% mortality of Difenacoum-resistant rats, 92% mortality of *R. rattus*, 75% mortality of warfarin-resistant *M. domesticus* Linn., and 100% mortality of *A. niloticus*. In the choice tests, Flocoumafen was generally palatable and gave 100% mortality of Warfarin-resistant and susceptible *R. norvegicus*, and Warfarin-susceptible *R. rattus* but only 65% mortality was obtained with Warfarin-resistant *M. domesticus* and 60% mortality of *A. niloticus*, Flocoumafen at 0·005% (w/w) as a single-feed rodenticide was not toxic to *Merions shawi* (Thomas) and Merions *auratus*. Parshad and Malhi (1995) in India, studied the efficacy Racumin to three species of South Asian rodents, *Bandicota bengalensis, Tatera indica* and *Rattus rattus* in laboratory and field experiments. Species-specific differences occurred between the efficacy of 0.75% Racumin tracking powder (RTP) used for contact poisoning, and 0.0187, 0.0375 and 0.075% Racumin baits (RB), prepared by mixing the concentrate with cracked wheat, powdered sugar and peanut oil (96:2:2), used for poison baiting. *B. bengalensis* was most susceptible to the toxic effects of Racumin as both RTP and RB caused 80-100% mortality after short exposures (15 min and 3 h) to a floor/runway treated with 1 g/rat of RTP in forced contact and simulated runway techniques and 1-2 days of choice feeding of 0.0187 and 0.0375% RB in feeding tests. These treatments were less effective against *T. indica* and least effective against *R. rattus*. In pen experiments, in which the runway was treated with 2g of RTP, 100 and 60% mortality from groups of 5 rats each of *B. bengalensis* and *T. indica* occurred, respectively. Vaziri and Farid (1995) in Iran, studied the efficacy of the rodenticides, Bromadiolone 0.005%, Chlorophacinone 0.006% plus Sulphaguinoxaline 0,019% against *Rattus norvegicus* and *Nesokia indica* under field conditions. The results showed that Bromadiolone gave 88.4% mortality of *Nesokia indica* in Karaji and 90.13% mortality in Djiroft. However, Chlorophacinone plus sulfaquinoxaline gave 86 and 85.15% mortality, respectively, in these areas. Chander-sheikher *et al.*, (1996) tested the rodenticide baits containing Zinc phosphide 2.5%, Bromadiolone 0.005%, Flucoumafen 0.00% and Cholecalciferol 0.075. Results indicated that the above mentioned rodenticides were most effective when applied through burrow baiting, leading to a 61.11, 83.64, 84.61 and 36.36% reduction in the number of active burrows, respectively. In Pakistan, the baiting technique was evaluated and developed for the control of rats in rice field Khan *et al.*, (1998) both acute and anticoagulant baits were used against *Bandicota bengalensis* and *Nesokia indica*. The results showed efficacy of 2% zinc phosphide formulation 97.5%, 96.7%, 95.2% for grain, wax cake and plain cake respectively. Efficacy of 0.005% Brodifacoum estimated mortality was 98.8% and 98.95% respectively.

Moran (1999) in Israel, studied that wheat grain bait, treated with sodium fluoroacetate, is used to control field rodents

Hygnstrom *et al.*, (2000) in USA, examined the efficacy of in-furrow applications of 2% Zinc phosphide at planting for control of rodent damage in no-till corn. In three independent field studies. The population in the most severely damage fields ranged from 104 to138 active colonies/ha. Zinc phosphide reduced yield loss in the three studied areas by 7-34%. Farghal *et al.*, (2000) in Qena Governorate studied the toxicity of three anticoagulant i.e. Farobaid, Caid and Supercaid against *A. niloticus* under field conditions, Farobaid gave complete control to *A. niloticus* inhabited tomato field after 20 days of treatment. The LT50 and LT95 values were 3.1 and 21 days. Supercaid reduced 77.3% of *A. niloticus* population in sugarcane field after 21days of treatment, with LT50 and LT95 values of 8.2 and 43 days. Caid gave 59% reduction in *A. niloticus* inhabited sugarcane after 20 days of treatment. The LT50 and LT95 values were 16 and 100 days. The acute rodenticides, Quintox reduced 70% of *A. niloticus* population in corn field after 20 days of treatment. The LT50 and LT95 values of 10 and 82 days. Storm completely eradicated *R. norvegicus* after 6 days of offering poisoned baits. The LT50 and LT95 values were 4.4-6.0 days in 1995 and 4.0-5.8 days in 1996. Shehab *et al.*, (2000) in Syria, studied the efficacy the poisoned bites prepared by mixing 95.5g bite base (water added until 40% moisture) + 2g vegetable oil + 2.5% Zinc phosphide. Inside the opening of each active burrow. The results showed that the reduction in the active burrows, after 24 hour of treatment, were: 83.97% and 81.86% for grains of wheat and corn, However, the other bite bases were 74.95%, 65.13%, 58.78%, respectively. Yaghoobi-Ershadi *et al.*, (2000) in Iran, used Zinc phosphide to control gerbilline rodents by opened burrows. The average reduction of rodent holes was at 87.4% for one year after the first baiting in the intervention area. Abdel-Gawad (2001b) in Assiut Governorate of Egypt, studied the rodent control in the student buildings of Assiut University during ten successive years from 1991 to 2000. Zinc phosphide 3% was used through July as quick acting poison outside the buildings one time during the first year to reduce the high density of rodents and avoid to the bait shyness. The anticoagulant rodenticide, Retak (Difenacoum 0.005%) followed the treatment of Zinc phosphide twice a year one during February and the other through July month, outside and inside the building. The results revealed that there were three species of rodent outside and inside the student buildings of Assiut University. The most prevalent rodents were *Rattus rattus alexandrinus* (Linn.) 42.6%, *Arvicanthis niloticus* (Desm.) 36.2%, *Rattus norvegicus* Berk., 21.2% .The reduction in rodent population after the treatment with Zinc phosphide was 76.8% from the initial population. The decrease in rodent density during the years of study which treated with anticoagulant rodentcide was about 69.8% during 1994, 80.7% in 1995 and 1998. Using Zinc phosphide treatment for one time followed by anticoagulant rodenticide twice a year and removing the garbage daily showed great effect on rodent population reduction in the university cities, and it may be useful in closed places such as hospitals and animal production farms . O'Connor and Booth (2001) in New Zealand, studied the sensitivity to brodifacoum for the four rodent species include *Ratus norvegicus, R. rattus, R. exulans* and *Mus musculus* Linn., was determined. Results indicated that the LD50 in rodents ranged from 0.17mg/kg to 0.52mg/kg. Twigg *et al.*, (2002) in Australia. found the efficacy of 2.5% Zinc phosphide wheat bait in dry storage for about 3,5 tears against house mice in the canola in the central wheat belt region of western Australia. Eisemann *et al.*, (2003) in USA, studied the utilizing of Zinc phosphide as a population control against the Norway rat, roof rat, house mouse. The efficacy of Zinc phosphide under laboratory and field condition have been conducted against the three species of mice, *Peromyscus mainiculatus, Acomys cahirinus, Mus musculus* Linn. All studies reported efficacy rates for mouse control using ZP higher than 70%. Moran (2003) in Israel, tested Cholecalciferol whole wheat bait in no-choice laboratory experiments as rodenticides for the field rodent species *Microtus guentheri* and *Meriones tristrami*. The LD_{50} was 40.86 and 32.17 days. Shriprakash *et al.*, (2003) studied The efficacy bait formulated with two acute rodenticides, Uoroacetamide and Zinc phosphide and two second generation anticoagulants, Bromodialone and Difethialone at diferent concentrations against laboratory-bred wild type rats, *Rattus rattus* (Linn.). The mortality data clearly indicated that Uoroacetamide was more effective than Zinc phosphide at all three concentrations and produced complete mortality at 2% and 3%. In contrast, the Zinc phosphide bait did not show appreciable mortality and caused lower bait acceptance and palatability. The mortality patterns were significantly different and there were decrease in mortality caused at some concentrations .Bromodialone admixed cereal-based bait did not cause any deference mortality pattern among rats. However, the mortality pattern was inurned by concentration and duration of exposure. Bromodialone at the higher concentration (0.0075%) showed less effectiveness than at 0.005% which caused 100% mortality after 96 h exposure. There was no marked deference in bait acceptance and palatability ratio at concentrations of 0.0025% and 0.005%. The Difethialone admixed cereal-based bait caused 100% mortality even at 0.0013% concentration. Johnston *et al.*, (2005) in California, found that efficacy zinc phosphide bait with pre-baiting 100 and 60% mortality was achieved control rodent pests, respectively. Kaur and Parshad (2005) in South Asia, studied the efficacy of 0.0375% Racumin to control the lesser bandicoot rat, *Bandicota bengalensis*. Tthe results showed high success in rice and wheat cropping. Ahmed (2006) in Assiut Governorate of Egypt, found that the application of phosphide zinc singly was the superior in controlling rodents, while supercaid only had lowest effect. Whereas, using both rodenticide together achieved a moderate effect. Baghdadi (2006) in Assiut Governorate of Egypt, observed that the females of *A. niloticus* were more tolerant to all rodenticides than males at different poisoned baits under laboratory conditions. The acceptance of rats to the poisoned bait considerably differed according to the type of bait. The Bromadilone carried on crushed maize has the most acceptance to rats, While Brodifacoum carried with sunflower was the lowest. On the other hand, time required to death differed according to the type of rodenticide and bait carrier. Brodifacoum carried with wheat was the most effective, while the lowest effective was recorded when Chlorophacinone with sorghum. Also, the effectiveness of rodenticides for mortality time was related to the concentration of the rodenticide. The Bromadilone 0.005% was more effective than Brodifacoum 0.004%.

MATERIALS AND METHODS

Species Composition of Rodents in Cultivated and Reclaimed Lands

The present work was carried out in three different agro ecosystems in Assiut Governorate (Figure 7.1) these areas were described as follows:

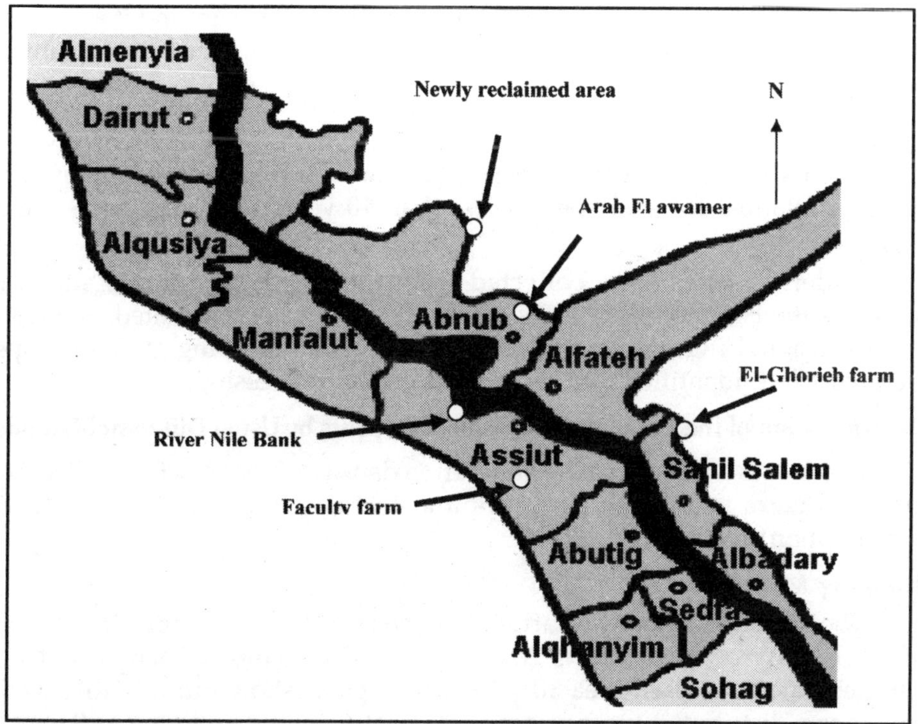

Fig. 7.1: A Map Showing the Position of Assiut Governorate and the Studied Areas

Cultivated Area

The cultivated area used was the experimental station of the Faculty of Agriculture, Assiut University. It is a rather mosaic agro ecosystem (old land) that has been planted with vegetables, field crops and orchards.

River Nile Bank

It is located in the Western beach of the River Nile in Assiut town.

Reclaimed Areas

Three areas with different reclamation periods were selected to carry out this study:

The Experimental Station of the Faculty of Agriculture, El-

Ghorieb, Assiut University

It is located at the Eastern desert (25km. North East of Assiut city) and fringe of the alluvial agriculture land in the Eastern side of the River Nile. It has been planted from along period about (50 years) with isolated patches of vegetables, wheat, Egyptian clover, alfalfa and certain orchards.

The Experimental Station of the Agriculture Research Center

(ARC) in Arab El- Awamer, Assiut Governorate

It is represented as a reclaimed area from about 20 years and it is located at the Eastern desert (20km. South East of Assiut city). It has been planted with vegetables, field crops and fruit trees.

Newly Reclaimed Area

It is located at the Eastern desert (25 km. South East of Assiut city). It has been planted for short period less than 10 years with vegetables, field crops, orchards.

Rodent species were collected from the above mentioned sites by applying the common wire traps (photo 1). Each trap was baited by bread and distributed twice every 15 days at 6 pm. Next morning at 7 am, traps were checked, identified and recorded for data processing.

Determination of the Population Density of Rodents by Using Different Methods

In order to a determine the population density of rodents, four collecting methods were used such as: (trapping, feces, active burrows and food consumption) method.

Trapping Method

The present method was carried out two areas in the experimental station of the Faculty of Agriculture; Assiut University included Faculty and El-Ghorieb Farms. In each area 30 wire-box traps as shown in (photo1) were baited and distributed twice every 15 days at 6pm and collected at 7am.

The captured rodents were classified and recorded. The Percentage of every species was estimated as a percent from total rodents captured during the year dominant percentage (D%). Also, trap index the seasonal density and sex ratio were estimated.

$$\text{Dominant percentage} = \frac{\text{Number of rodent species}}{\text{Total rodents captured}} \times 100$$

$$\text{Trap index} = \frac{\text{No. rodent captured}}{\text{Total traps distributed}}$$

Feces Method

The feces method was carried out at two sites in Assiut Governorate. The first site was the building of poultry farm in the experimental station of the faculty of Agriculture, Assiut University (photo 2). However, the second site at the building of the experimental station of ARC in Arab El-Awamer.

In each site, feces in three square meters were collected and counted as an index for the changes in rodent population at each inspected date (once monthly).The percent of feces was estimated as a percent for overall year total as follows:

$$\text{Population \%} = \frac{\text{Number of feces in area unit during month}}{\text{Total number of feces during year}} \times 100$$

Active Burrows Method

This method was carried out in newly reclaimed area in about one Feddan (photo 3). This area was cultivated with wheat, barley, peanut, vegetables and clover in winter. Also, area was cultivated with fruit trees such as grape, olive. The number of active burrows was counted during year by using the sand to close all burrows then count the opened ones at the next day during four consecutive days every month. The population of active burrows percentage in the area was estimated as follows.

$$\text{Population of active burrows \%} = \frac{\text{Number of active burrows}}{\text{Total burrows examined all over year}} \times 100$$

Food Consumption Method

The population density of rodents was estimated in the River Nile Bank by the food consumption method. The increase or decrease from the rodents population was estimated as percent from the initial food distributed as follows:

$$\text{Population density} = \frac{\text{Total food consumption (gm) during month}}{\text{Total food consumption (gm) allover the year}} \times 100$$

Colour Preference of Rodent Baits

Under Field Conditions

This study was carried out in poultry building at the Experiment Station of the Faculty of Agriculture, Assiut University. The slices of potatoes were dried and mixed by six colours (red, green, yellow, blue, brown and grey). Six wire box traps were used in each of the six coloured baited and distributed at random twice monthly for 6 months at 6 pm and collected at 7am. The captured rodents were classified and recorded for data processing.

Under Laboratory Conditions

Rodents were trapped and picked up to the laboratory. Healthy mature males and females of *R .r. frugivorus* (120-170gm), *R .r. alexandrinus* (90-150gm) and *A. niloticus* (120-150gm) were chosen for this experiment. Animals were singly caged and kept under ventilated laboratory conditions (temperature 25-35, R.H 60-70%) for two weeks and provided with enough bruised maize bait and water. Ten males and females were selected of each rodent species and baited with bruised maize mixed with colours (green, red, yellow, brown, blue and grey) and offered to each rodent species for one week. The daily coloured bait consumption per animal was recorded. The colored bait was replaced with colour free bait in new cage. Data analyzed by using Duncan's multiple range tests

Food Preference of Rodent Baits

This study was carried out in poultry building at the Experiment Station of the Faculty of Agriculture farm, Assiut University. The wire box traps were baited with four different baits (cucumber, bread, potato and tomato). Five traps were baited by one and distributed randomly, three times every week at 6 pm and collected at 7 am for two months. The captured rodents were classified and recorded.

Rodent Control

In this study three methods of controlling rodent were conducted as follows:

Mechanical Control

This method was carried out in two cultivated newly reclaimed lands. Each one was about Fadden. The Nile grass rat, *A. niloticus* was the dominant species considered. The rodent population was estimated in each site as active burrows for one year .The destroying of active burrows were used in one area to control rodent population. The decrease or increase in active burrows was monthly estimated as percent from the initial population.

Biological Control

This study was carried out in the seeds storages at the experimental station of the Faculty of Agriculture, Assiut University. In this study the cats, *Felis chaus nilotica* were used as Naturally Occurring Biological Control Agent (NOBA) to the rodents. The rodent population was estimated by the wire box traps before and after releasing the cats in the seed storages.

Chemical Control Method

The chemical control of rodents was carried out in the buildings and the River Nile Bank area.

In the Buildings

This study was carried out at two areas, poultry building in the Experiment Station of the Faculty of Agriculture, Assiut University and (ARC) building in Arab El-Awamer, Assiut governorate. Three units in each were chosen to conduct the feces method. The rodents were estimated in these areas by counting rodent feces before and after applying the rodenticides used in the present work were Zinc phosphide 3% and Supercaid 0.005%.The first area was treated with Zinc phosphide 3%, the second area was treated with 0.005% Supercaid. However the third area was served as control. Feces were recorded monthly. The reduction of feces was calculated and compared with control units.

In the River Nile Bank Area

Two sites in the River Nile bank were used chemical control by Zinc phosphide 3% and Supercaid 0.005%. The rodent population was estimated in these areas by amount the food consumption before and after applied the rodenticides. The first area was treated by Zinc phosphide 3% in November 2004. Also, the second area was treated by Zinc phosphide 3% in January and and supercaid 0.005% during July 2005.

RESULTS AND DISCUSSION

Species Composition of Rodents in Cultivated and Reclaimed Lands

Table 7.2 shows the species composition of rodents trapped from two different areas in Assiut Governorate during the period from June 2004 till May 2006. Species recorded were the white bellied rat, *Rattus rattus frugivorus*, the grey bellied rat, *Rattus rattus alexandrinus* and the Nile grass rat, *Arvicanthis niloticus*.

In the Faculty of agriculture Farm results *R. r. alexandrines* occupied the highest dominant percentage (52.21% and 43.56%) followed by *R. r. frugivorus* (24.63% and 34.16%), *A. niloticus* (23.16%) and (22.28%) during the first and second years.

In El-Ghorieb Farm *R.r.frugivorus* had the highest dominant percentage (62.67% and 49.18%) followed by *A. niloticus* (24.89% and 31.15%) and *R.r. alexandrines* (12.44% and 19.67%), during the first and second years.

Data in Table 7.2 and Figure 7.2 revealed that *R .r. frugivorus* was ranked high dominant percentage (28.30%) in El Ghorieb Farm rather than in the Faculty Farm (14.35%). This may be due to the presence of more prefer trees for nesting and feeding. Concerning, *R .r. alexandrinus* the highest dominant % was recorded in Faculty Farm (24.26%) rather than in El-Ghorieb Farm (7.84%).This may be attributed to the availability of food and shelter in Faculty Farm, which make them grow and reproduce faster than in other areas. The Nile grass rat, *A. niloticus* was more dominant (13.85%) in El-Ghorieb Farm than in the Faculty Farm (11.39%).This may be attributed to the availability of food in neighbored field crops and vegetables plantations in El-Ghorieb Farm.

Generally, Figure 7.2 illustrate that *R.r.alexandrinus* was more dominant species in Faculty Farm. However, *R.r.frugivorus* was the more dominant species in El-Ghorieb Farm. *R.r.alexandrinus* habitate the ecosystems in which poultry buildings established such as Faculty Farm. This finding is in agreement with sever authers included (Ali 1985 and Embarek, 1997).

Table 7.2: Total Number and Percentage of Rodent Species Captured from Study Areas at the Experiment Stations, Assiut University, June 2004 Till May 2006

Study Area	Years	Total	*A. niloticus*		*R.r. alexandrinus*		*R.r. frugivorus*	
			No.	%	No.	%	No.	%
Faculty Farm	1st	272	63	23.16	142	52.21	67	24.63
	2nd	202	45	22.28	88	43.56	69	34.16
	Total	474	108	22.78	230	48.53	136	28.69
	Average	237	54	11.39	115	24.26	68	14.35
El -Ghorieb Farm	1st	225	56	24.89	28	12.44	141	62.67
	2nd	183	57	31.15	36	19.67	90	49.18
	Total	408	113	27.70	64	15.69	231	56.61
	Average	204	56.50	13.85	32	7.84	115.50	28.30
Grand Total		*882	221	25.06	294	33.33	367	41.61

* Based on 5760 wire box traps

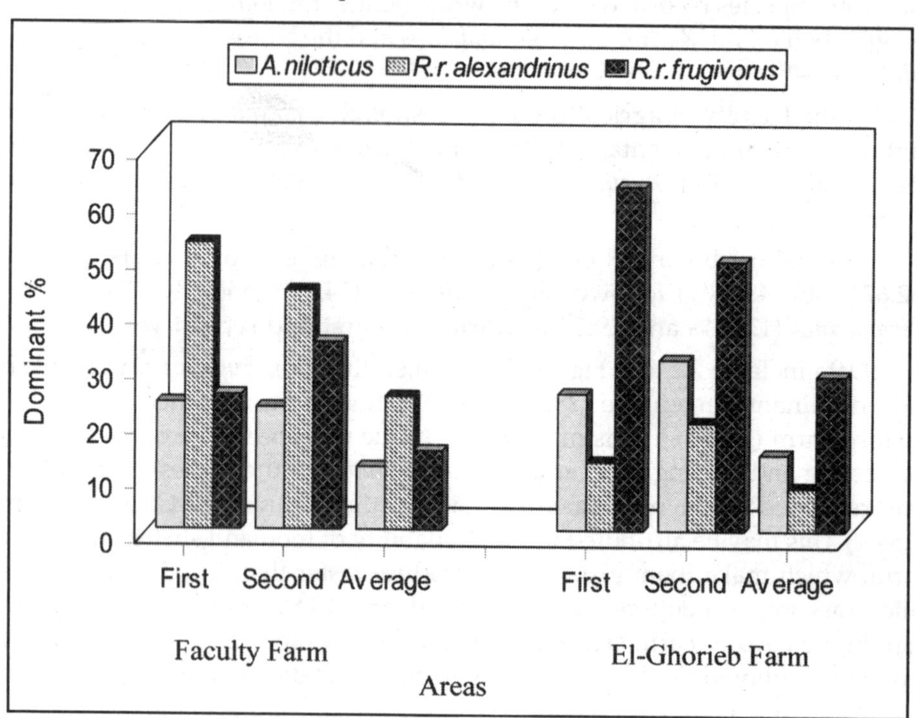

Fig. 7.2: Percentage of Rodent Species Captured from Study Areas at the Experiment Stations, Assiut University, June 2004 Till May 2006

Data in Table 7.3 and Figure 7.3 shows the distribution of rodents trapped from three areas in Assiut Governorate during the period from June 2004 till May 2005. Five species of rats and mice were recorded. The grey bellied rat, *R. r. alexandrinus* recorded the highest dominant percentage (33.33%) followed by the Nile grass rat, *A. niloticus* (32.46%), the Norway rat, *R. norvegicus* (24.56%), the house mouse *Mus musculus* (5.26%) and *Gerbillus gerbillus* (4.39%).

Table 7.3: Total Number and Percentage of Rodent Species Captured from the Study Areas, Assiut Governorate, 2004 till 2005

Study Areas	Total	*A. niloticus*		*R. norvegicus*		*R.r. alexandrinus*		*M. musculus*		*G. gerbillus*	
		No.	%	No.	%	No.	%	No.	%	No.	%
River Nile Bank	28	0	0.0	28	100	0	0.0	0	0.0	0	0.0
Arab El -Awamer	49	12	24.49	0	0.0	31	63.27	6	12.24	0	0.0
Newly reclaimed	37	25	67.57	0	0.0	7	18.92	0.0	0	5	13.51
Grand Total	*114	37	32.46	28	24.56	38	33.33	6	5.26	5	4.39

* Based on 1440 wire box traps.

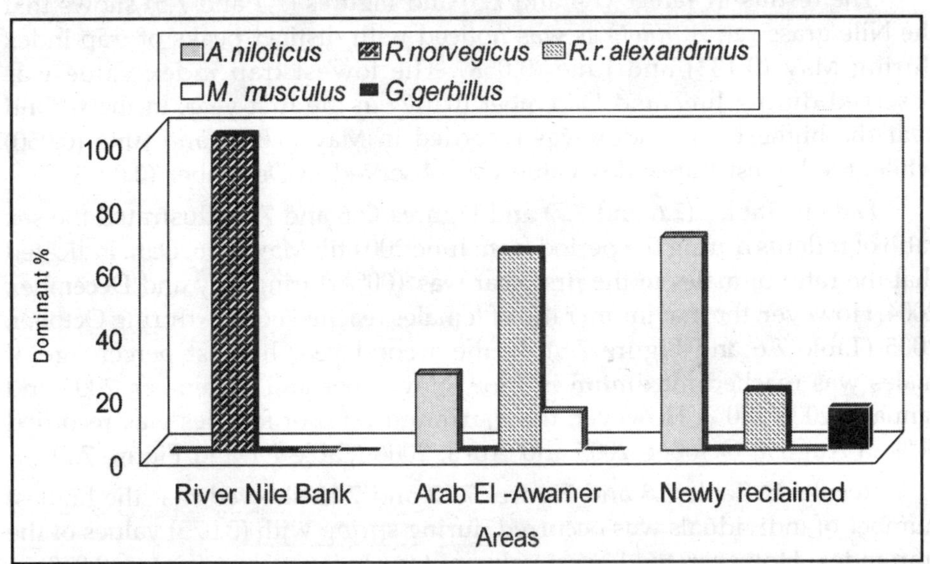

Fig. 7.3: Percentage of Rodent Species Captured from the Study Areas of Assiut Governorate, June 2004 Till May 2005

In the River Nile bank area *R. norvegicus* was ranked (100%), the other species were not captured by the traps.

In Arab El-Awamer *R .r. alexandrinus* was most dominant species (63.27%) followed by *A. niloticus* (24.49%) and *Mus musculus* (12.24%). However, *R.norvegicus* and *G. gerbillus* were not captured by the traps.

In newly reclamied area *A. niloticus* was the most dominant species (67.57%) followed by *R.r.alexandrinus* (18.92%) and *G. gerbillus* (13.51%).

Generally, the Norway rat, *R. norvegicus* was trapped from River Nile bank area only. This can be attributed to the extreme temperature and food prevailed in the area. On the other hand this may be due to the interspecific competation between this species and other species. *M.musculus* was trapped from Arab El-Awamer only this may be due to the presence of the buildings and factories in this area. *G. gerbillus* was recorded from newly reclaimed area.

This finding is in agreement with the results of Abdel-Gawad (1974), Abazaid (1990) and Abdel-Galil (2005). They reported that Egyptian gerbillus are strictly habitat the desert lands.

DETERMINATION OF THE POPULATION DENSITY OF RODENTS BY USING DIFFERENT METHODS

Trapping Method

Rodents in the Cultivated Area (Faculty Farm)

A. niloticus

The results in Tables (7.4 and 7.5) and Figures (7.4 and 7.5) shows that the Nile grass rat, *A. niloticus* was noticed with distinct peaks of trap index during May (0.133) and June (0.058). The lowest trap index value was observed during June and December (0.017) in the first year. In the second year the highest trap index was recorded in May (0.075) and June (0.050) while, the lowest trap index value was observed in December (0.0083).

Data in Tables (7.6 and 7.7) and Figures (7.6 and 7.7) illustrated the sex ratio of rodents during the period from June 2004 till May 2006. Data indicated that the ratio of males in the first year was 100% during July and December, 2004. However, the maximum ratio of females reached 66.67% during October, 2005 (Table 7.6 and Figure 7.6). In the second year highest percentage of males was reached maximum in June, November and December, 2005 and January, 2006 100%. However, the maximum ratio of females was recorded 50% in August, October, 2005 and April, 2006 (Table 7.7 and Figure 7.7).

Results in Table 7.8 and Figures 7.12 and 7.13 showed that the highest number of individuals was occurred during spring with (0.075) values of the trap index. However, the lowest value of trap index was in winter (0.028) in the first year. In the second year the highest value of trap index was (0.047) in spring and the lowest value of trap index was (0.017) in winter.

R.r. alexandrinus

Data in Tables 7.4 and 7.5 and Figures 7.4 and 7.5 revealed that the grey bellied rat, *R.r.alexandrinus* was noticed with distinct peaks of trap index value during September (0.20), June (0.150) and August (0.142).

Table 7.4: Number and Trap Index of Rodents Encountered in the Cultivated Area, Faculty Farm, Assiut University, June 2004 Till May 2005

	Species									Total Rodents		
	A. niloticus			*R.r. alexandrinus*			*R.r. frugivorus*					
Months	Number	%	Trap Index	Number	%	Trap Index	Number	%	Trap Index	Number	%	Trap Index
Junuary	7	23.33	0.058	18	60	0.15	5	16.67	0.041	30	40	0.25
July	2	13.33	0.017	11	73.34	0.092	2	13.33	0.017	15	20	0.13
August	5	16.67	0.042	17	56.67	0.142	8	26.67	0.067	30	40	0.25
Summer	14	18.67	0.039	46	67.33	0.128	15	20	0.042	75	100	0.208
September	6	16.22	0.050	24	64.86	0.20	7	18.92	0.058	37	58.73	0.31
October	3	27.27	0.025	5	45.46	0.042	3	27.27	0.025	11	17.46	0.09
November	3	20	0.025	9	60	0.075	3	20	0.025	15	23.81	0.13
Autumn	12	19.05	0.033	38	60.32	0.106	13	20.63	0.036	63	100	0.175
December	2	14.29	0.017	6	42.86	0.050	6	42.85	0.050	14	27.45	0.12
January	3	15	0.025	13	65	0.108	4	20	0.033	20	39.22	0.17
February	5	29.41	0.042	9	52.94	0.075	3	17.65	0.025	17	33.33	0.14
Winter	10	19.61	0.028	28	54.90	0.078	13	25.49	0.036	51	100	0.142
March	6	33.33	0.050	8	44.45	0.067	4	22.22	0.033	18	21.69	0.15
April	5	20.83	0.042	9	37.50	0.075	10	41.67	0.083	24	28.92	0.20
May	16	39.02	0.133	13	31.71	0.108	12	29.27	0.100	41	49.40	0.34
Spring	27	32.53	0.075	30	36.14	0.083	26	31.33	0.072	83	100	0.230
Grand Total	63	23.16	0.044	142	52.21	0.099	67	24.63	0.046	272	100	0.189

Table 7.5: Number and Trap Index of Rodents Encountered in the Cultivated Area, Faculty Farm, Assiut University, June 2005 Till May 2006

Months	Species									Total Rodents		
	A.niloticus			*R.r. alexandrinus*			*R.r. frugivorus*					
	Number	%	Trap Index	Number	%	Trap Index	Number	%	Trap Index	Number	%	Trap Index
Junuary	6	37.5	0.05	8	50	0.067	2	12.5	0.017	16	30.77	0.133
July	5	29.41	0.042	7	41.18	0.058	5	29.41	0.042	17	32.69	0.142
August	2	10	0.017	10	50	0.083	7	35	0.058	19	36.54	0.158
Summer	13	25	0.036	25	48.08	0.069	14	26.92	0.039	52	100	0.144
September	5	21.74	0.042	11	47.83	0.092	7	30.43	0.058	23	54.76	0.192
October	2	25	0.017	3	37.5	0.025	3	37.5	0.025	8	19.05	0.067
November	2	18.18	0.033	5	45.46	0.042	4	36.36	0.033	11	26.19	0.092
Autumn	9	21.43	0.025	19	45.24	0.053	14	33.33	0.039	42	100	0.117
December	1	8.33	0.0083	5	41.67	0.042	6	50	0.05	12	34.29	0.1
January	2	25	0.017	4	50	0.033	2	25	0.017	8	22.85	0.67
February	3	20	0.025	6	40	0.05	6	40	0.05	15	42.86	0.125
Winter	6	17.14	0.017	15	42.86	0.042	14	40	0.039	35	100	0.097
March	4	20	0.033	8	40	0.067	8	40	0.067	20	27.4	0.167
April	4	19.04	0.033	9	42.86	0.075	8	38.1	0.067	21	28.76	0.175
May	9	28.13	0.075	12	37.5	0.1	11	34.37	0.092	32	43.84	0.267
Spring	17	23.29	0.047	29	39.73	0.08	27	36.98	0.075	73	100	0.203
Grand Total	45	22.28	0.031	88	43.56	0.061	69	34.16	0.048	202	100	0.140

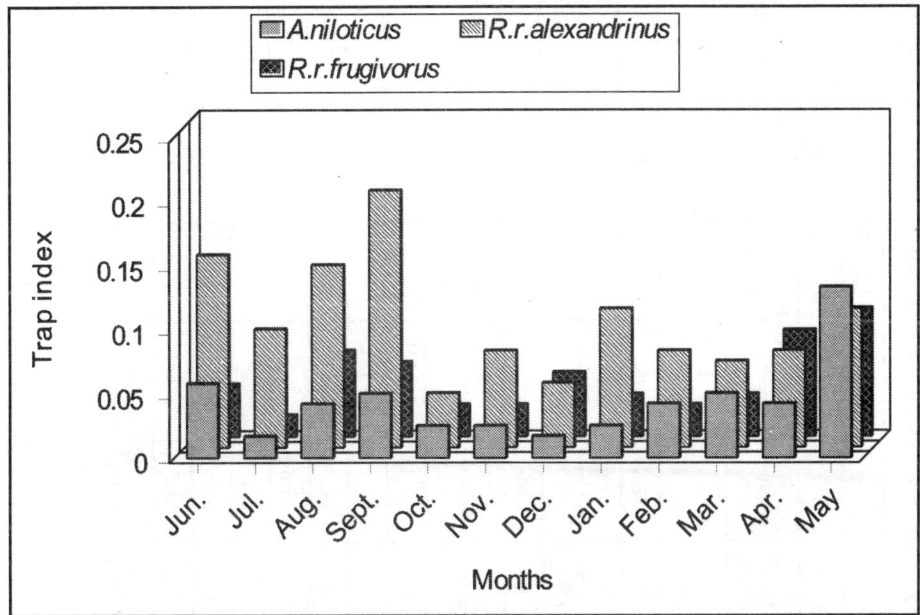

Fig. 7.4: Trap Index of Rodents Encountered in the Cultivated Area at Faculty Farm, Assiut University during June 2004 Till May 2005

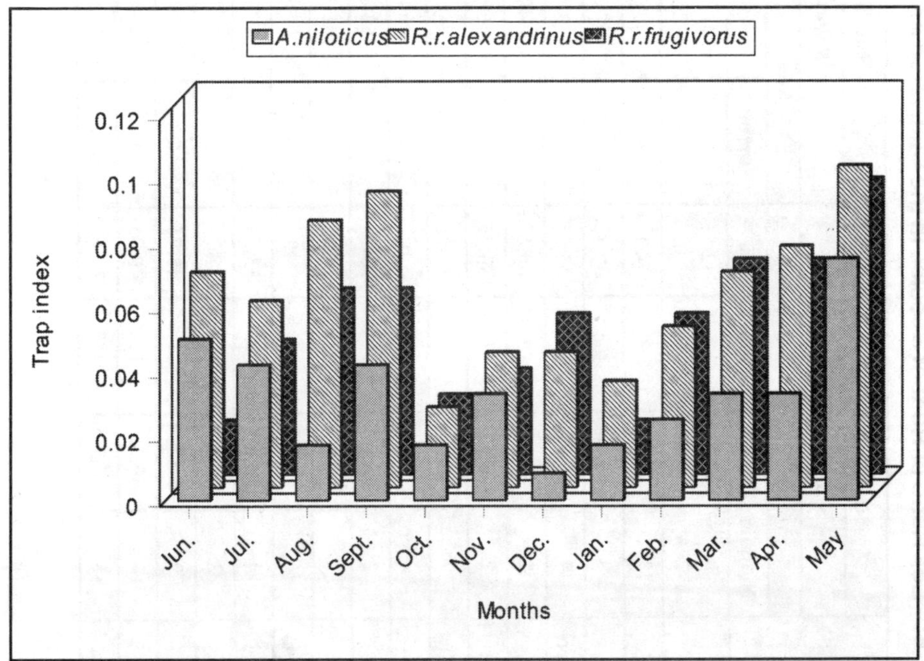

Fig. 7.5: Trap Index of Rodents Encountered in the Cultivated Area at Faculty Farm, Assiut University during June 2005 Till May 2006

Table 7.6: Sex Ratio of Rodent Species in the Cultivated Area, Faculty Farm, Assiut University, June 2004 Till May 2005

Months	Species											
	Arvicanthis niloticus				*Rattus.r. alexandrinus*				*Rattus.r. frugivorus*			
	Males		Females		Males		Females		Males		Females	
	Number	%	Number	%	Number	%	Number	%	Number	%	Number	%
June	4	57.14	3	42.86	8	44.45	10	55.55	3	60	2	40
July	2	100	0	0	8	72.73	3	27.27	1	50	1	50
August	3	60	2	40	8	47.06	9	52.94	4	50	4	50
Summer	9	64.28	5	35.72	24	52.18	22	47.82	8	53.33	7	46.67
September	4	66.67	2	33.33	9	37.50	15	62.50	4	57.15	3	42.85
October	1	33.33	2	66.67	2	40	3	60	2	66.67	1	33.33
November	2	66.67	1	33.33	6	66.67	3	33.33	2	66.67	1	33.33
Autumn	7	58.33	5	41.66	17	44.74	21	55.26	8	61.54	5	38.46
December	2	100	0	0	4	66.67	2	33.33	4	66.67	2	33.33
January	2	66.67	1	33.33	7	53.85	6	46.15	3	75	1	25
February	2	40	3	60	5	55.56	4	44.44	2	66.67	1	33.33
Winter	6	60	4	40	16	57.14	12	42.86	9	69.24	4	30.76
March	4	66.67	2	33.33	3	37.50	5	62.50	2	50	2	50
April	3	60	2	40	3	33.33	6	66.67	3	30	7	70
May	9	56.25	7	43.75	5	38.46	8	61.54	4	33.33	8	66.67
Spring	16	59.25	11	40.75	11	36.67	19	63.33	9	34.62	17	65.38
Grand Total	38	60.32	25	39.68	68	47.88	74	52.12	34	50.75	33	49.25

Table 7.7: Sex Ratio of Rodent Species in the Cultivated Area, Faculty Farm, Assiut University, June 2005 Till May 2006

Months	Species											
	Arvicanthis niloticus				*Rattus .r.alexandrinus*				*Rattus .r frugivorus*			
	Males		Females		Males		Females		Males		Females	
	Number	%	Number	%	Number	%	Number	%	Number.	%	Number	%
June	6	100	0	0	5	62.50	3	37.50	2	100	0	0
July	4	80	1	20	5	71.43	2	28.57	4	80	1	20
August	1	50	1	50	6	60	4	40	4	57.14	3	42.85
Summer	11	84.62	2	15.38	16	64	9	36	10	71.43	4	28.57
September	3	60	2	40	7	63.64	4	36.36	6	85.71	1	14.28
October	1	50	1	50	2	66.67	1	33.33	2	66.66	1	33.33
November	2	100	0	0	3	60	2	40	2	50	2	50
Autumn	6	66.67	3	33.33	12	63.15	7	36.85	10	71.43	4	28.57
December	1	100	0	0	4	80	1	20	5	83.33	1	16.66
January	2	100	0	0	3	75	1	25	2	100	0	0
February	2	66.67	1	33.33	5	83.33	1	16.67	3	50	3	50
Winter	5	83.34	1	16.66	12	80	3	20	10	71.43	4	28.57
March	3	75	1	25	6	75	2	25	5	62.5	3	37.5
April	2	50	2	50	6	66.67	3	33.33	5	62.50	3	37.5
May	7	77.78	2	22.22	8	66.67	4	33.33	5	45.45	6	54.55
Spring	12	70.59	5	2.41	20	68.96	9	31.04	15	55.56	12	44.44
Grand Total	34	77.27	10	22.73	60	68.18	28	31.82	45	65.22	24	34.78

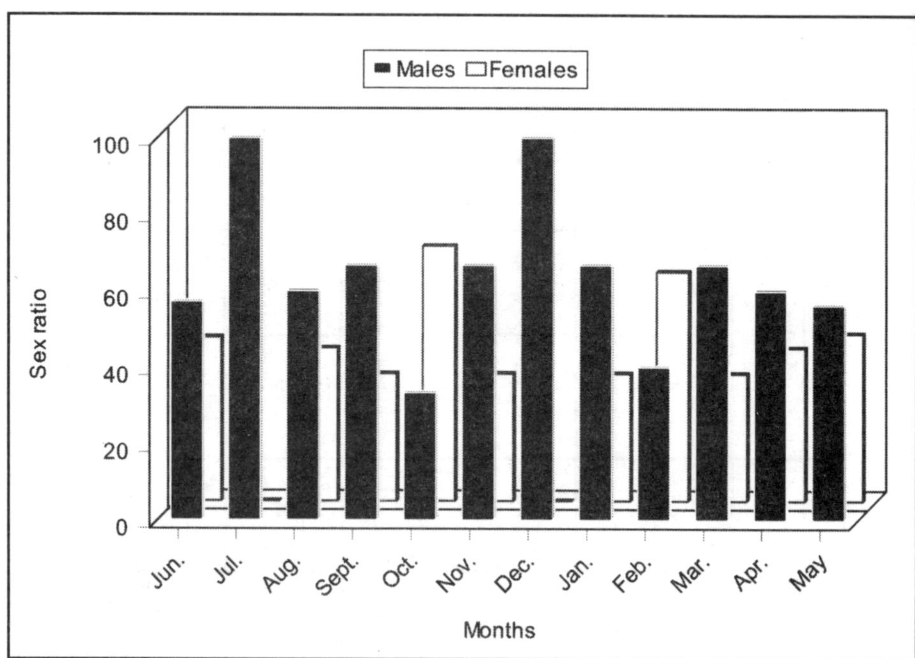

Fig. 7.6: Trap Index of *A.niloticus* Encountered in the Cultivated Area at Faculty Farm, Assiut University during June 2004 Till May 2005

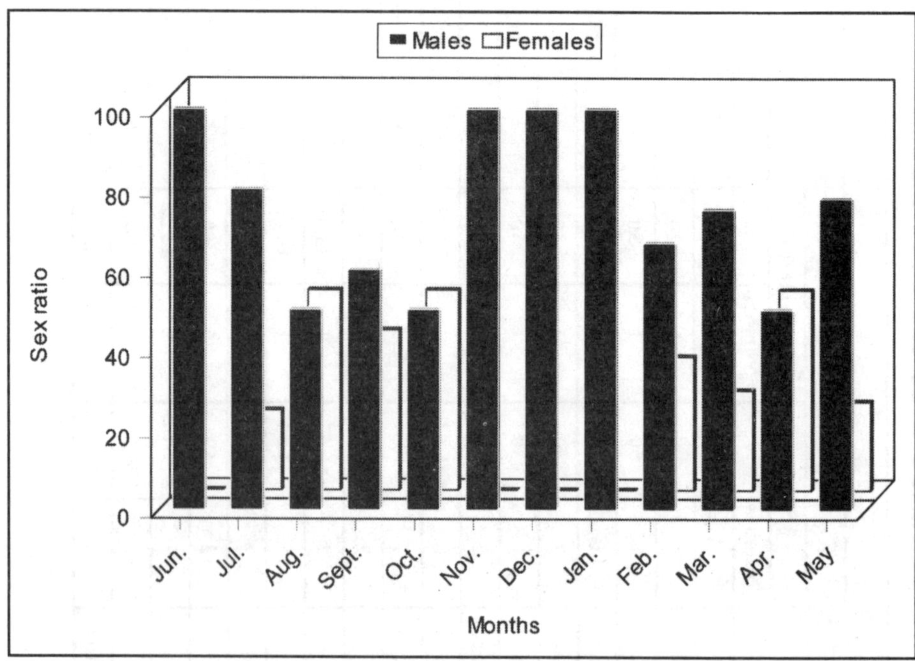

Fig. 7.7: Trap Index of *A. niloticus* Encountered in the Cultivated Area at Faculty Farm, Assiut University during June 2005 Till May 2006

Table 7.8: Seasonal Distribution and Trap Index of Certain Rodent Species in the Cultivated Area, Faculty Farm, Assiut University, June 2004 Till May 2006

Study Years	Season	*A. niloticus*			*R.r. alexandrinus*			*R.r. frugivorus*		
		Number	%	Trap Index	Number	%	Trap Index	Number	%	Trap Index
1st year	Summer	14	18.67	0.039	46	61.33	0.128	15	20	0.042
	Autumn	12	19.05	0.033	38	60.32	0.106	13	20.63	0.036
	Winter	10	19.61	0.028	28	54.90	0.078	13	25.49	0.036
	Spring	27	32.53	0.075	30	36.14	0.083	26	31.33	0.072
	Total	63	23.16	0.044	142	52.21	0.099	67	24.63	0.047
2nd year	Summer	13	25	0.036	25	48.08	0.069	14	26.92	0.039
	Autumn	9	21.43	0.025	19	45.24	0.053	14	33.33	0.039
	Winter	6	17.14	0.017	15	42.86	0.042	14	40	0.039
	Spring	17	23.29	0.047	29	39.73	0.081	27	36.99	0.075
	Total	45	22.28	0.031	88	43.56	0.061	69	34.16	0.048

The lowest trap index value was observed during October (0.042) and December (0.050) in 1st year. In 2nd year the highest trap index value was recorded during May (0.267) followed by September (0.192) and April (0.175). The lowest value of trap index was recorded during January (0.067).

Tables 7.6 and 7.7 and Figures 7.8 and 7.9 illustrated the sex ratio of rodents during the period from June 2004 till May 2006. Data indicated that the ratio of males in the first year was 72.73% during July. However, the maximum ratio of females reached 66.67% during April 2005 (Table 7.6 and Figure 7.11). In the second year the highest ratio of males was recorded in July (71.43%) while, the maximum ratio reached females recorded (37.50%) during June, 2006 (Table 7.7 and Figure 7.8).

Results in (Table 7.8) indicated that the highest number of individuals was occurred during summer with (0.128) value of the trap index followed by (0.106) in autumn and (0.083) in spring and (0.078) in winter in the first year. In the second year the highest value of trap index was (0.081) during spring and (0.069) in summer followed by (0.053) in autumn then (0.042) in winter.

R.r. frugivorus

Data in Tables (7.4 and 7.5) and Figures (7.4 and 7.5) showed that the white bellied rat, *R.r. frugivorus* was noticed with distinct peaks of trap index during May (0.100) and April (0.083). The lowest trap index value was observed during July (0.017) in the first year. In the second year the highest value of trap index was obtained during May (0.092). The lowest trap index value was recorded during January and June (0.017).

Results in Tables (7.6 and 7.7) and Figures (7.10 and 7.11) illustrated the sex ratio of rodents during the period from June 2004 till May 2006. Data indicated that the ratio of males in the first year was (75%) during January. However, the maximum ratio of females reached 70% during April, 2005 (Table 7.6 and Figure 7.10). In the second year the highest ratio of males was recorded during June and January (100%). The maximum ratio of females reached (54.56%) during May, 2006 (Table 7.7 and Figure 7.11). The results in (Table 7.8) represented that the white bellied rat *R.r. frugivorus* was the second species in abundance at the first and the second year in the cultivated area. The highest number of individuals was recorded during spring with trap index value (0.072). The lowest value of Trap index was recorded during winter and autumn (0.036) in the first year. In the second year the highest number of individuals was recorded during spring 0.075 followed by the summer, autumn and winter (0.039).

Data in Table (7.9) and Figures (7.14 and 7.15) showed that the highest ratio of males during winter 60.78% and summer 54.67%.The maximum ratio of females was recorded higher than the ratio of males during spring 56.63% in the first year. In the second year the maximum ratio of males were reached higher than ratio of females during all seasons.

Table 7.9: Seasonal Changes in Sex Ratio of Captured Rodent Species in the Cultivated Area, Faculty Farm, Assiut University, June 2004 Till May 2006

Study Years	Season	Males		Females	
		Number	%	Number	%
1st year	Summer	41	54.67	34	45.33
	Autumn	32	50.79	31	49.21
	Winter	31	60.78	20	39.22
	Spring	36	43.37	47	56.63
	Total	140	52.40	132	47.60
2nd year	Summer	37	71.15	15	28.85
	Autumn	28	66.67	14	33.33
	Winter	27	77.14	8	22.86
	Spring	47	64.38	26	35.62
	Total	139	69.83	63	30.17

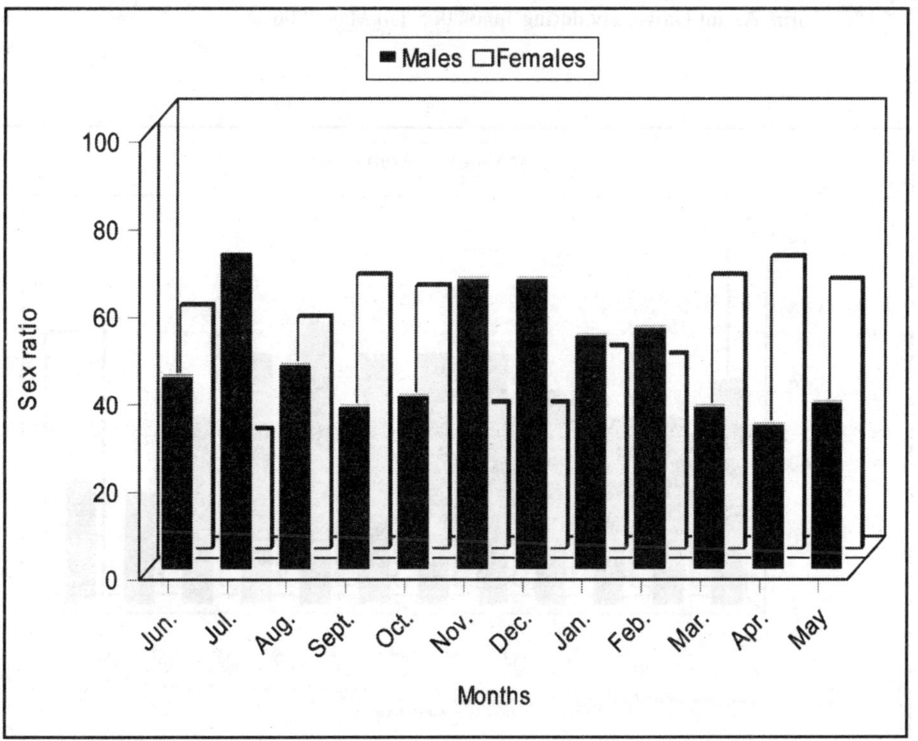

Fig. 7.8: Number and Trap Index of *R.r.alexandrinus* Encountered in the Cultivated Area at Faculty Farm, Assiut University during June 2004 Till May 2005

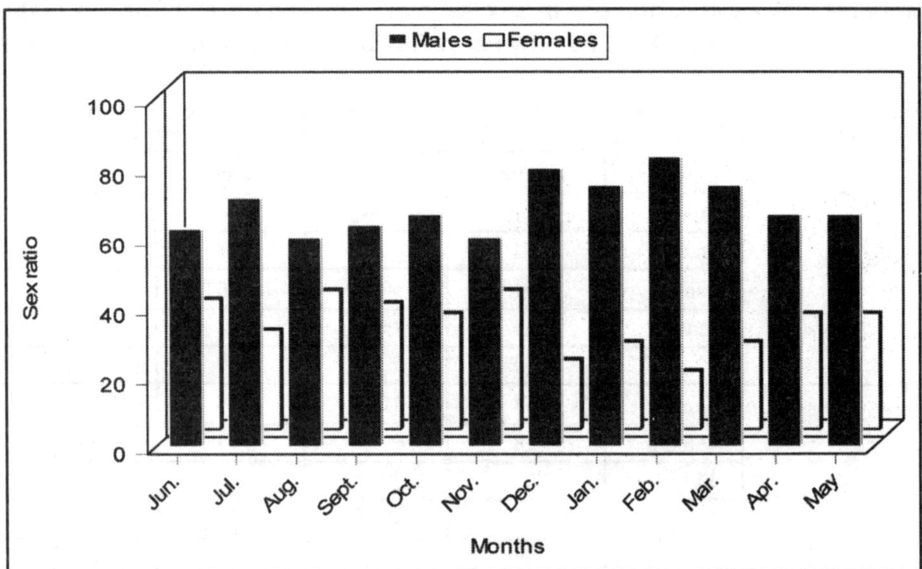

Fig. 7.9: Number and Trap Index of *R.r.alexandrinus* Encountered in the Cultivated Area at Faculty Farm, Assiut University during June 2005 Till May 2006

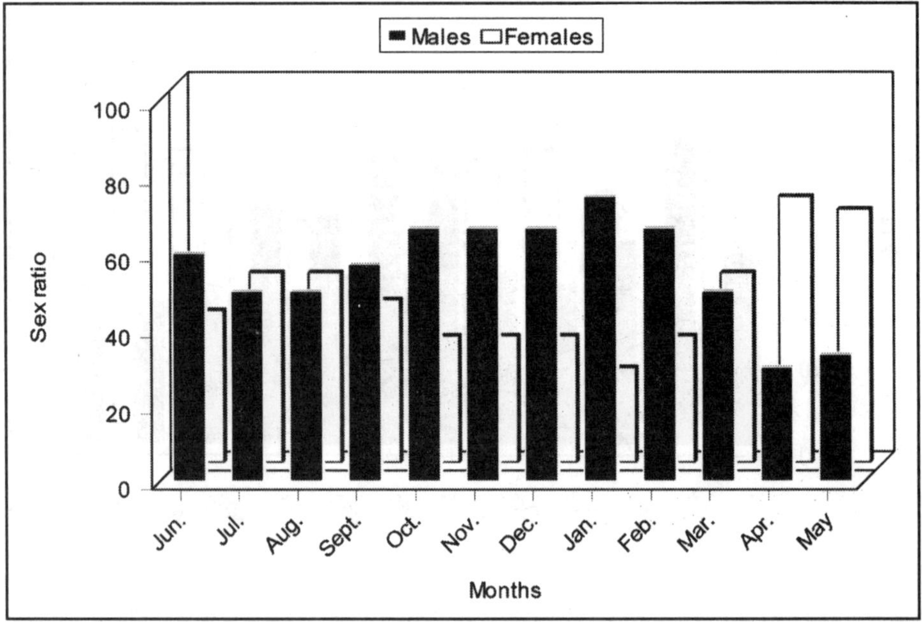

Fig. 7.10: Number and Trap Index of *R.r.frugivorus* Encountered in the Cultivated Area at Faculty Farm, Assiut University during June 2004 Till May 2005

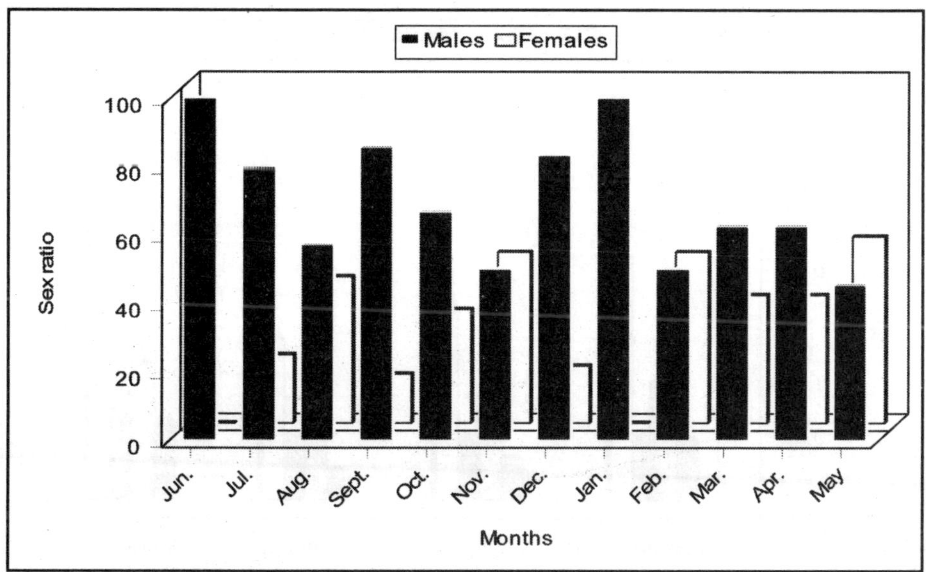

Fig. 7.11: Number and Trap Index of *R.r.frugivorus* Encountered in the Cultivated Area at Faculty Farm, Assiut University during June 2005 Till May 2006

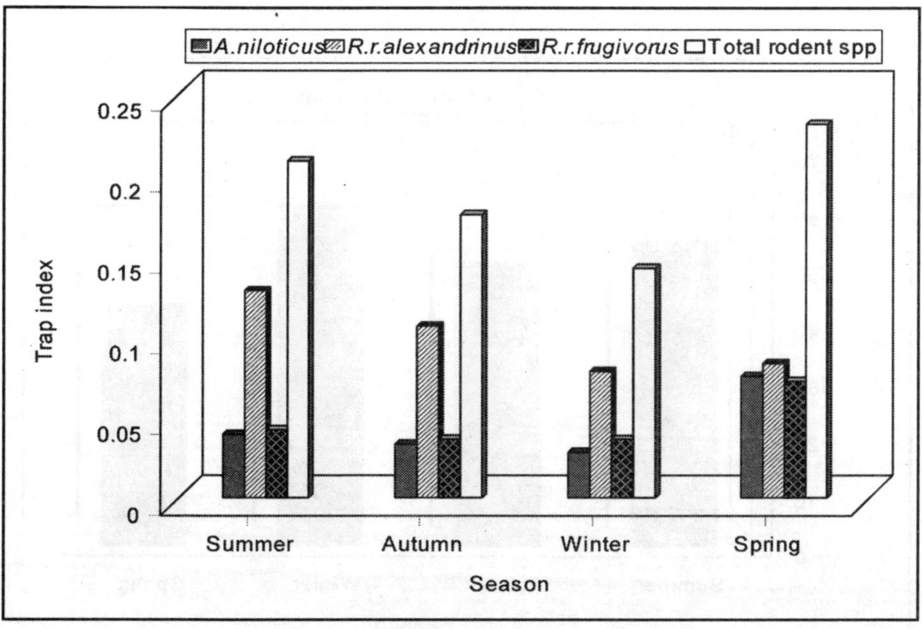

Fig. 7.12: Seasonal Distribution of Rodent Species in the Cultivated Area of Faculty Farm, Assiut University during June 2004 Till May 2005

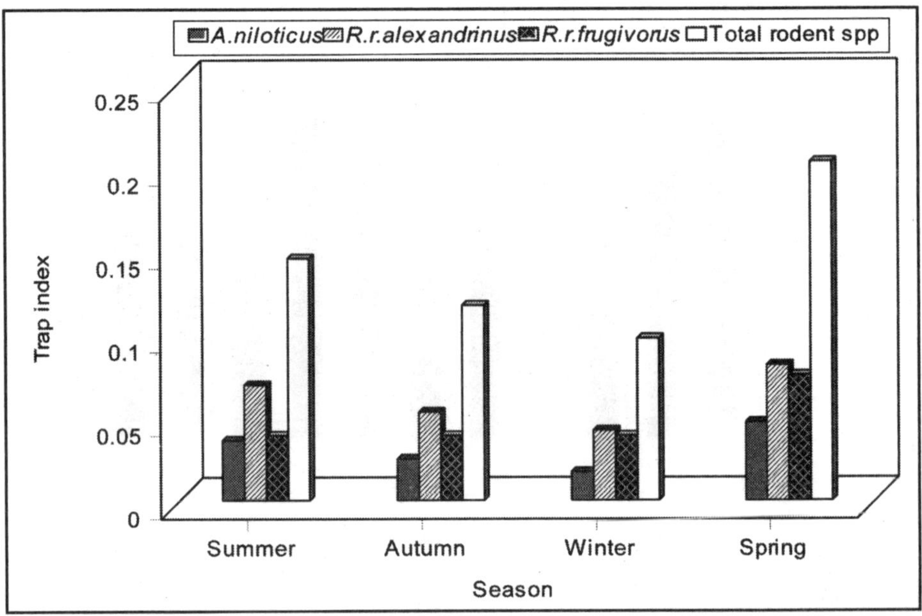

Fig. 7.13: Seasonal Distribution of Rodent Species in the Cultivated Area of Faculty Farm, Assiut University during June 2005 Till May 2006

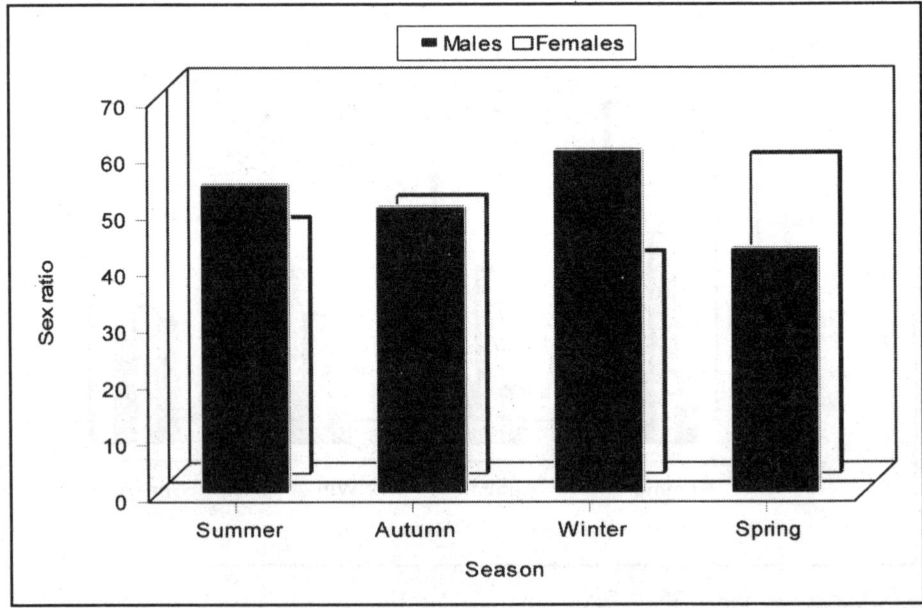

Fig. 7.14: Sex Ratio of Males and Females of Rodent Species in Faculty Farm at Assiut University during June 2004 Till May 2005

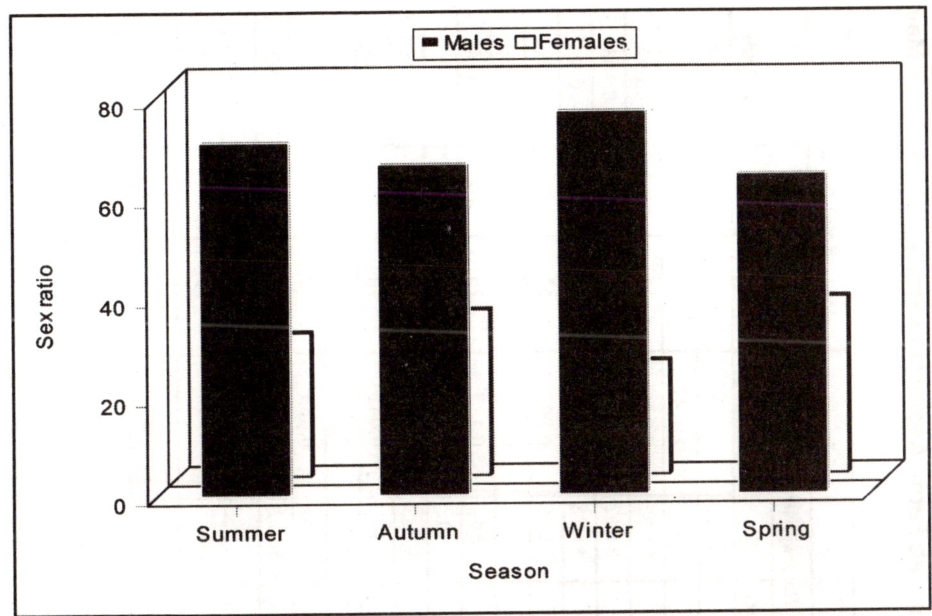

Fig. 7.15: Sex Ratio of Males and Females of Rodent Species in Faculty Farm at Assiut University during June 2005 Till May 2006

Generally, the above mentioned results indicated that *R.r. alexandrinus* the most abundant species in the first and second years. This may be due the availability of preferred food and shelter, the highest ratio of males was recorded in summer and winter to collected food while, the females tend in nests to take care of their young progeny and avoid extreme temperature. The highest trap index value was recorded in summer in the first year and in the spring during the second year may be due to increase in activity and fecundity. This agreement with of several authors such as Maher Ali *et al.*, (1974), Abdel-Gawad (1979), Abdel-Gawad *et al.*, (1982), Abazaid (1990) and Embarek (1997).

Rodents in the Reclaimed Area (El-Ghorieb Farm)

A. niloticus

Data in Tables (7.10 and 7.11) and Figures (7.16 and 7.17) showed that the Nile grass rat, *Arvicanthis niloticus* was noticed with distinct peaks of trap value index during October (0.083), September and march (0.067). The lowest trap index value was recorded during June (0.0083), August and November (0.017) in the first year (Table 7.10 and Figure 7.15). In the second year 2005-2006 the high value was recorded during October and may with an trap index values (0.083) while, the lowest value was obtained during February (0.0083) and August (0.017) (Table 7.11 and Figure 7.16).

Table 7.10: Number and Trap Index of Rodents Encountered at El-Ghorieb Farm, Assiut University, June 2004 till May 2005

Months	Species									Total Number		
	A. niloticus			*R r. alexandrinus*			*R.r. frugivorus*					
	Number	%	Trap Index	Number	%	Trap Index	Number	%	Trap Index	Total	%	Trap Index
June	1	12.50	0.0083	0	0	0	7	87.50	0.058	8	20.51	0.067
July	3	15	0.025	0	0	0	17	85	0.0142	20	51.28	0.167
August	2	18.18	0.017	0	0	0	9	81.82	0.075	11	28.21	0.092
Summer	6	15.38	0.017	0	0	0	33	84.62	0.092	39	100	0.108
September	8	20.51	0.067	8	20.51	0.067	20	51.28	0.167	36	51.43	0.3
October	10	47.62	0.083	0	0	0	11	52.38	0.092	21	30	0.172
November	2	15.38	0.017	0	0	0	11	84.62	0.092	13	18.57	0.108
Autumn	20	28.57	0.055	8	11.43	0.022	42	60	0.117	70	100	0.194
December	5	27.78	0.067	4	22.22	0.033	9	50	0.075	18	41.86	0.15
January	6	40	0.083	1	6.67	0.0083	8	53.33	0.067	15	34.88	0.125
February	0	0	0.017	5	50	0.042	5	50	0.042	10	23.26	0.083
Winter	11	25.58	0.092	10	23.26	0.083	22	51.16	0.183	43	100	0.119
March	8	36.35	0.067	4	18.18	0.033	10	45.45	0.083	22	30.14	0.183
April	4	17.39	0.033	6	26.09	0.05	13	56.52	0.108	23	31.50	0.192
May	7	25	0.058	0	0	0	21	75	0.175	28	38.36	0.233
Spring	19	26.03	0.053	10	1370	0.028	44	60.27	0.122	73	100	0.203
Grand Total	56	24.89	0.039	28	12.44	0.019	141	62.67	0.097	225		0.156

Table 7.11: Number and Trap Index of Rodents Encountered at El-Ghorieb Farm, Assiut University, June 2005 Till May 2006

	Species									Total Rodents		
	A. niloticus			*R.r. alexandrinus*			*R.r. frugivorus*					
Months	Number	%	Trap Index	Number	%	Trap Index	Number	%	Trap Index	Total	%	Trap Index
June	4	33.33	0.033	3	25	0.025	5	41.67	0.042	12	31.58	0.1
July	3	16.67	0.025	4	22.22	0.033	11	61.11	0.092	18	47.37	0.015
August	2	25	0.017	3	37.50	0.025	3	27.50	0.025	8	21.05	0.067
Summer	9	23.68	0.025	10	26.32	0.028	19	50	0.053	38	100	0.105
September	6	28.57	0.050	4	19.05	0.033	11	52.38	0.092	21	38.89	0.175
October	10	47.62	0.083	2	9.52	0.017	9	42.86	0.075	21	38.89	0.175
November	3	25	0.025	0	0	0	9	75	0.075	12	22.22	0.1
Autumn	19	35.19	0.053	6	11.11	0.017	29	53.70	0.081	54	100	0.15
December	3	25	0.025	2	16.67	0.017	7	58.33	0.058	12	36.37	0.1
January	3	30	0.025	1	10	0.0083	6	60	0.050	10	30.30	0.083
February	1	9.1	0.0083	5	45.45	0.042	5	45.45	0.042	11	33.33	0.092
Winter	7	21.21	0.019	8	24.24	0.022	18	54.55	0.050	33	100	0.092
March	8	40	0.067	5	25	0.042	7	35	0.058	20	34.48	0.167
April	4	22.22	0.033	5	27.78	0.042	9	50	0.075	18	31.04	0.15
May	10	50	0.083	2	10	0.017	8	40	0.067	20	34.48	0.167
Spring	22	37.93	0.061	12	20.69	0.033	24	41.38	0.067	58	100	0.161
Grand Total	57	31.15	0.039	36	19.67	0.025	90	49.18	0.063	183		0.127

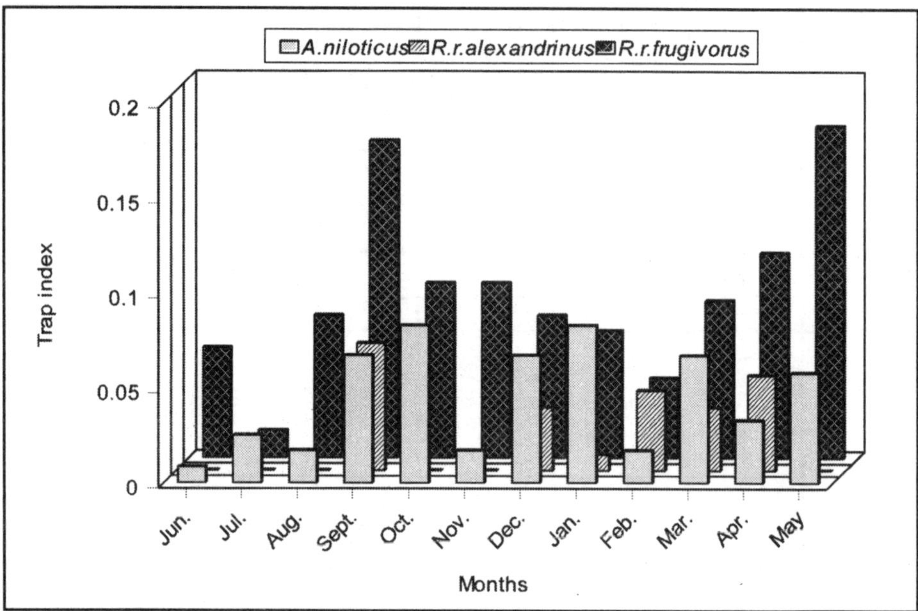

Fig. 7.16: Number and Trap Index of Rodents Encountered at EL-Ghorieb Farm, Assiut University during June 2004 Till May 2005

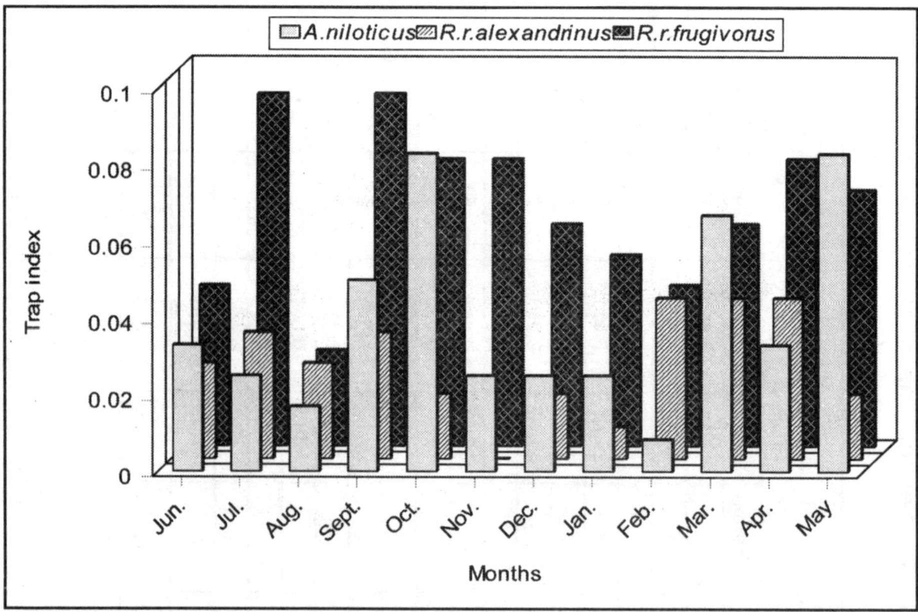

Fig. 7.17: Number and Trap Index of Rodents Encountered at EL-Ghorieb Farm, Assiut University during June 2005 Till May 2006

Data in Tables (7.12 and 7.13) and Figures (7.18 and 7.19) illustrated the sex ratio of rodents during the period from June 2004 till May 2006. Data indicated that the ratio of males in the first year was (100%) during June and August. However, the maximum ratio of females reached (57.14%) during May and (50%) during March, 2005 in the first year (Table 7.12 and figure 7.17). In the second year the highest ratio of males was recorded (100%) during June, February and March. Also, the highest ratio of females was obtained (50%) during August.

The results in (Table 7.14) and Figures (7.24 and 7.25) indicated that the highest number of individuals was recorded during autumn with a trap index value (0.056) while, the lowest value of trap index was (0.031) during winter in the first year. In the second year the highest value of trap index was (0.061) during spring while, the lowest value of trap index was (0.019) in winter and (0.025) during summer.

R.r. alexandrinus

Data in Tables (7.10 and 7.11) showed that the grey bellied rat, *R.r.alexandrinus* was noticed with distinct peaks of trap index value. In September it was (0.30) and May (0.233) while, the lowest trap index value was recorded during June (0.067) in the first year. However, in the second year the highest value of trap index was obtained during September and October (0.175), while the lowest trap index value was recorded during August (0.067).

Data in Tables (7.12 and 7.13) and Figures (7.20 and 7.21) illustrated that the sex ratio of rodents during the period from June 2004 till May 2006. Data indicated that the ratio of males in the first year (100%) during June. However, the maximum ratio of females reached (50%) during September, March and April (Table 7.12 and Figure 7.19). In the second year the highest ratio of males was recorded (100%) during June-August, December and January while, the highest ratio of females was observed (50%) in October.

Results in (Table 7.14) showed that the highest number of individuals was recorded during winter and spring with an trap index value (0.028) in the first year. In the second year the highest value of trap index was (0.033) during spring while, the lowest value of trap index was (0.017) during autumn.

R.r. frugivorus

Data in Tables (7.10 and 7.11) and Figures (7.16 and 7.17) showed that the white bellied rat, *R.r.frugivorus* was noticed with distinct peaks of trap index values during May (0.175) and September (0.067). The lowest trap index value was observed during February (0.042) in the first year (Table 7.10 and Figure 7.16). In the second year the highest peaks of trap index values were obtained during July and September (0.092) while, the lowest value was recorded during August (0.025).

Table 7.12: Sex Ratio of Rodent Species in El-Ghorieb Farm, Assiut University, June 2004 Till May 2005

Months	Species											
	A. niloticus				*Rattus.r.alexandrinus*				*Rattus.r.frugivorus*			
	Males		Females		Males		Females		Males		Females	
	Number	%	Number	%	Number	%	Number	%	Number	%	Number	%
June	1	100	0	0.0	0	0.0	0	0.0	4	57.14	3	42.86
July	2	66.67	1	33.33	0	0.0	0	0.0	9	52.94	8	47.06
August	2	100	0	0.0	0	0.0	0	0.0	8	88.89	1	11.11
Summer	5	83.33	1	16.67	0	0.0	0	0.0	21	63.64	12	36.36
September	5	62.50	3	37.50	4	50	4	50	10	50	10	50
Oct.	8	83.33	2	16.67	0	0.0	0	0.0	8	72.73	3	27.27
November	1	50	1	50	0	0.0	0	0.0	7	63.64	4	36.36
Autumn	14	70	6	30	4	50	4	50	25	59.52	17	40.48
December	4	80	1	20	3	75	1	25	6	66.67	3	33.33
January	4	66.67	2	33.33	1	100	0	0.0	4	50	4	50
February	0	0.0	0	0.0	3	60	2	40	5	100	0	0.0
Winter	8	72.73	3	27.27	7	70	3	30	15	68.18	7	31.82
March	4	50	4	50	2	50	2	50	7	70	3	30
April	3	75	1	25	3	50	3	50	6	46.15	7	53.85
May	3	42.86	4	57.14	0	0	0	0.0	10	47.62	11	52.38
Spring	10	52.63	9	47.37	5	100	5	100	23	52.27	21	47.73
Grand Total	37	66.07	19	33.93	16	57.14	12	42.86	84	59.57	57	40.43

Table 7.13: Sex Ratio of Rodent Species in El-Ghorieb Farm, Assiut University, June 2005 till May 2006

Months	Species											
	A. niloticus				*Rattus .r. alexandrinus*				*Rattus .r. frugivorus*			
	Males		Females		Males		Females		Males		Females	
	Number	%	Number	%	Number	%	Number	%	Number	%	Number	%
June	4	100	0	0.0	3	100	0	0.0	5	100	C	0.0
July	2	66.67	1	33.33	4	100	0	0.0	7	63.64	4	36.36
August	1	50	1	50	3	100	0	0.0	3	100	0	0.0
Summer	7	77.78	2	22.22	10	100	0	0.0	15	78.95	4	21.05
September	4	66.67	2	33.33	3	75	1	25	6	54.55	5	45.45
October	7	70	3	30	1	50	1	50	5	55.56	4	44.44
November	2	66.67	1	33.33	0	0.0	0	0.0	7	77.78	2	22.22
Autumn	13	68.42	6	31.58	4	66.67	2	33.33	18	62.07	11	37.93
December	3	100	0	0.0	2	100	0	0.0	6	85.71	1	14.29
January	2	66.67	1	33.33	1	100	0	0.0	5	83.33	1	16.67
February	1	100	0	0.0	4	80	1	20	2	40	3	60
Winter	6	85.71	1	14.29	7	87.50	1	12.50	13	72.22	5	27.28
March	5	62.50	3	37.50	3	60	2	40	4	57.14	3	42.86
April	4	100	0	0.0	4	80	1	20	6	66.67	3	33.33
May	6	60	4	40	2	100	0	0.0	5	62.50	3	37.50
Spring	15	68.18	7	31.82	9	75	3	25	15	62.50	9	37.50
Grand Total	41	71.93	16	28.07	30	83.33	6	16.66	61	67.78	29	32.22

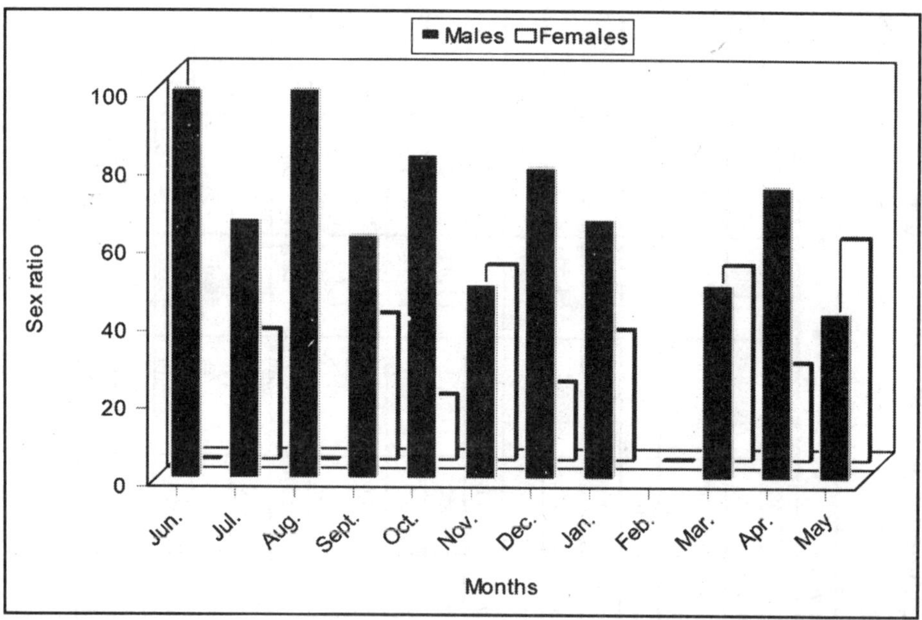

Fig. 7.18: Sex Ratio of *A.niloticus* in El-Ghorieb Farm at Assiut University during June 2004 Till May 2005

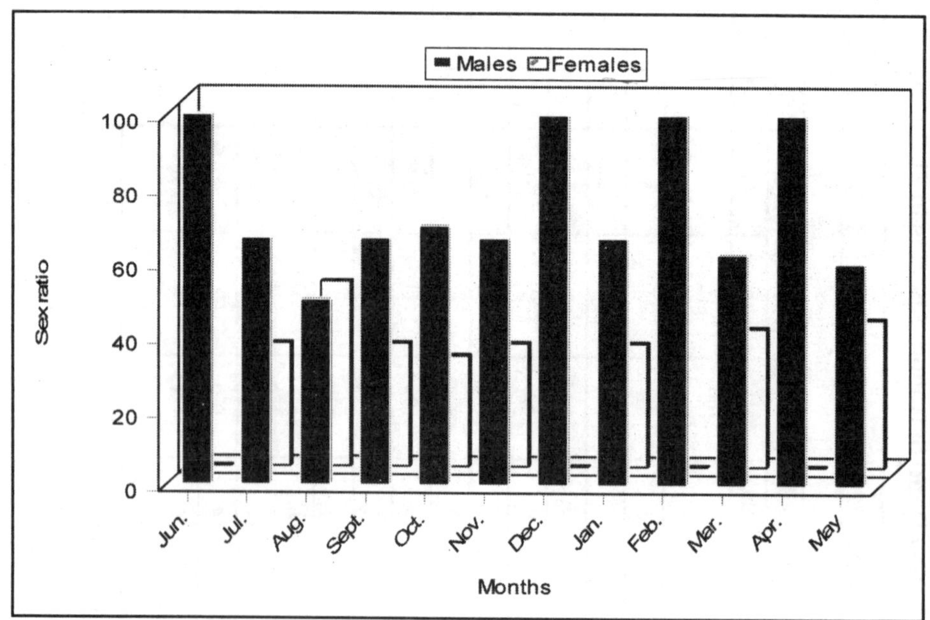

Fig. 7.19: Sex Ratio of *A.niloticus* in El-Ghorieb Farm at Assiut University during June 2005 Till May 2006

Table 7.14: Seasonal Distribution and Trap Index of Certain Rodent Species in El-Ghorieb Farm, Assiut University, June 2004 Till May 2006

		A.niloticus			*R .r. alexandrinus*			*R.r. frugivorus*		
Study Years	Season	Number	%	Trap Index	Number	%	Trap Index	Number	%	Trap Index
1st year	Summer	6	15.38	0.017	0	0.0	0	33	84.62	0.092
	Autumn	20	28.57	0.056	8	11.42	0.022	42	60	0.117
	Winter	11	25.58	0.031	10	23.26	0.028	22	51.16	0.061
	Spring	19	26.03	0.053	10	13.70	0.028	44	60.27	0.122
	Total	56	24.89	0.039	28	12.44	0.02	141	62.67	0.098
2nd year	Summer	9	23.68	0.025	10	26.32	0.028	19	50	0.053
	Autumn	19	35.19	0.053	6	11.11	0.017	29	53.70	0.081
	Winter	7	21.21	0.019	8	24.24	0.022	18	54.55	0.05
	Spring	22	37.93	0.061	12	20.69	0.033	24	41.38	0.067
	Total	57	31.15	0.04	36	19.67	0.025	90	49.18	0.063

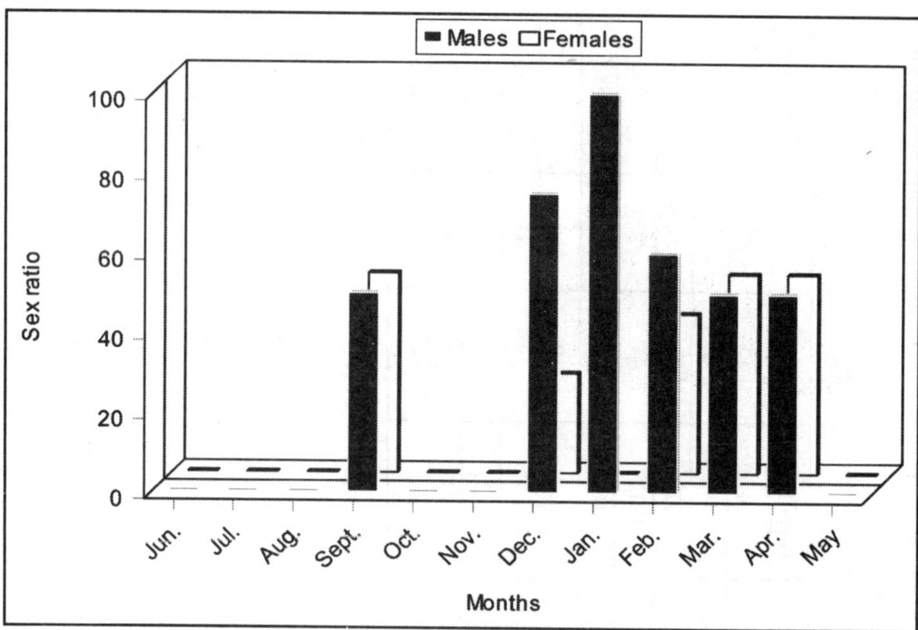

Fig. 7.20: Sex Ratio of *R.r.alexandrinus* in El-Ghorieb Farm at Assiut University during June 2004 Till May 2005

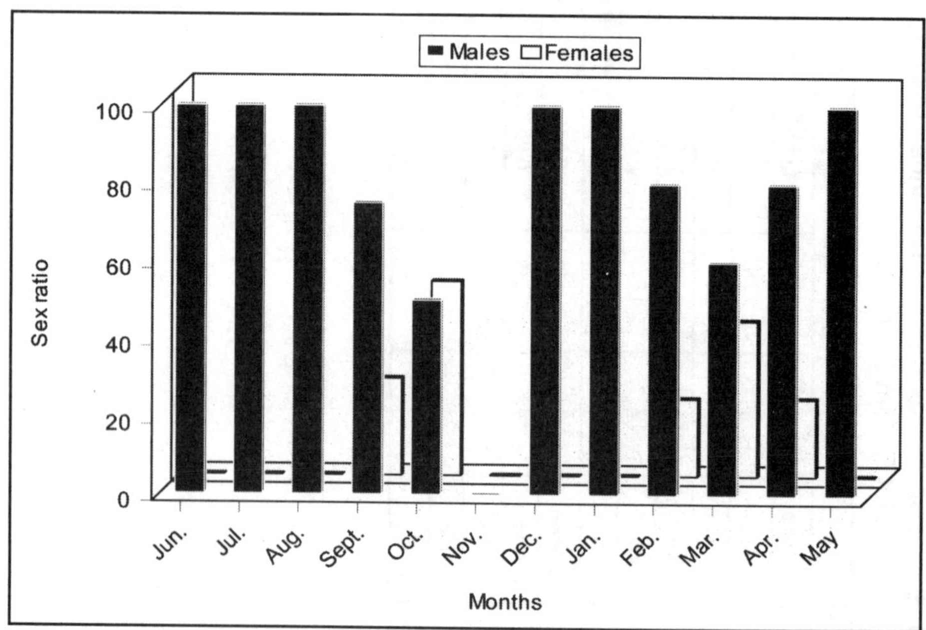

Fig. 7.21: Sex Ratio of *R.r.alexandrinus* in El-Ghorieb Farm at Assiut University during June 2005 Till May 2006

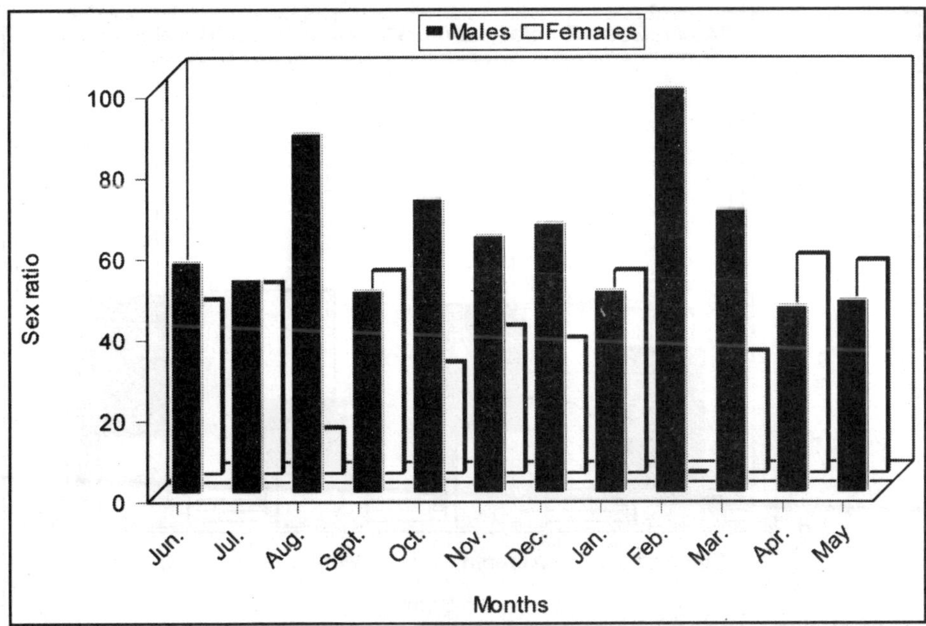

Fig. 7.22: Sex Ratio of *R.r.frugivorus* in El-Ghorieb Farm at Assiut University during June 2004 Till May 2005

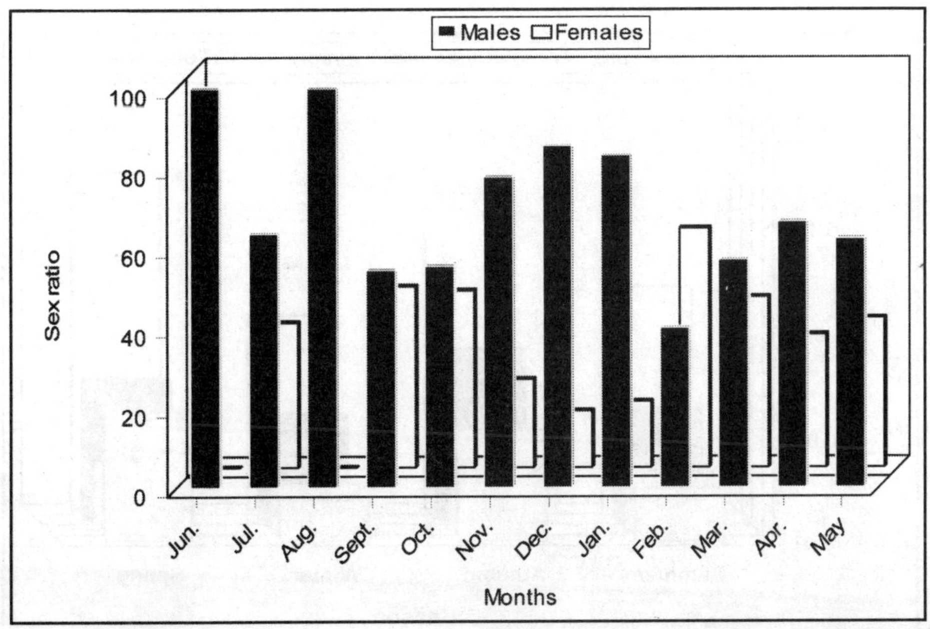

Fig. 7.23: Sex Ratio of *R.r.frugivorus* in El-Ghorieb Farm at Assiut University during June 2005 Till May 2006

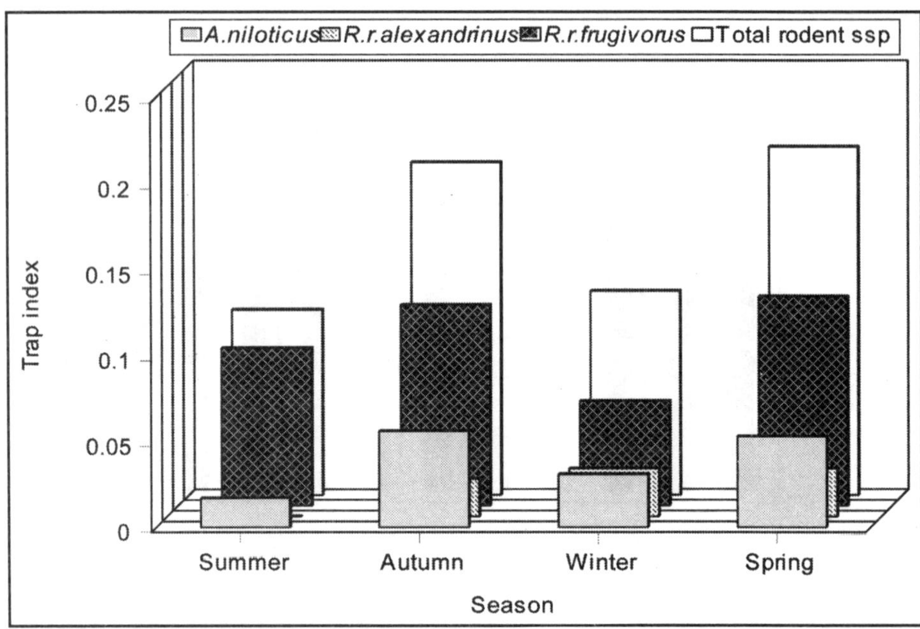

Fig. 7.24: Seasonal Distribution of Rodent Species in El-Ghorieb Farm during 2004-2005

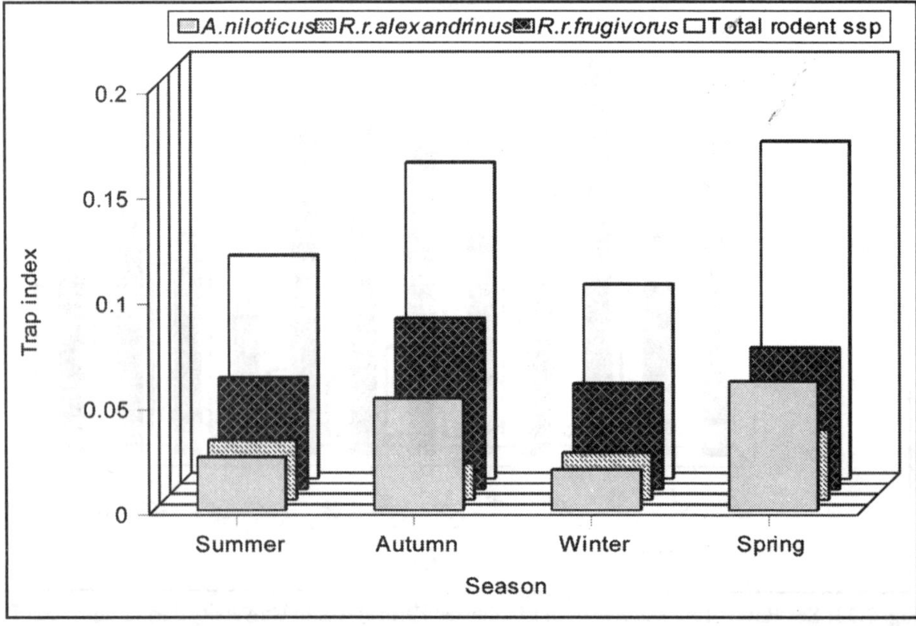

Fig. 7.25: Seasonal Distribution of Rodent Species in El-Ghorieb Farm during 2005-2006

The results in Tables (7.12 and 7.13) and Figures (7.22 and 7.23) illustrated the sex ratio of rodents during the period from June 2004 till May 2006. Data indicated that the ratio of males in the first year (100%) during February. However, the maximum ratio reached of females (53.85%) during April and (52.38) during May in the first year (Table 7.12 and Figure 7.21). In the second year highest ratio of males was recorded (100%) during June and August. However, the maximum ratio of females (60%) during February (Table 7.13 and Figure 7.22).

The highest number of individuals was occurred during spring with value of the trap index (0.122) and (0.117) in autumn followed by (0.092) during summer then (0.061) in winter in the first year. However in the second year the highest value of trap index was (0.081) during autumn and (0.067) during spring followed by (0.053) during summer then 0.050 in winter (Table 7.14) and Figures (7.24 and 7.25).

The sex ratio of rodent species were showed that males slightly out numbered females of rodent species (69.77%) during winter and (66.67%) in summer, while the females ratio was (47.95%) during spring in the first year. Also, the males ratio was higher than the females ratio during all seasons. It was in summer (84.21%), autumn (64.81%), winter (78.79%) and spring (67.24%) in the second year (Table 7.15) and figures (7.26 and 7.27).

Generally, the above mentioned results indicated that in El-Ghorieb Farm the white bellied rat *R. r. alexandrinus* was the most abundant species. This may be due to the great number of date palm trees in these area. Since, this species of rodents habitat trees as mentioned previously by several authors such as Abdel-Gawad *et al.*, (1982) and Embarek (1997). May be due to the increased activity and reproduction during some season. In addition to the rats move to the area after the harvesting of winter crops. the lowest density was observed during winter may be attributed to the high sensitivity of rodent species to the cold weather as pointed out by Salit (1972), Abdel-Gawad (1979) and Abdel-Gawad *et al.*, (1982).

Results in (Tables 7.16 and 7.17) and Figures (7.28 and 7.29) show that estimation of the sex ratio of males and females of rodent species at Faculty and El-Ghorieb Farms during June 2004 till May 2005. The ratio of males was recorded 62.48% in El-Ghorieb Farm rather than Faculty Farm 52.41% , while, the ratio of females was recorded 37.52% in El-Ghorieb Farm lowest than Faculty Farm 47.59%.While, results in (Table 7.17 and Figure 7.29) showed that the ratio of males was 73.76% in El-Ghorieb Farm highest than Faculty Farm 69.84%. However, the ratio of females was recorded 26.24% in El-Ghorieb Farm lowest than Faculty Farm 30.16%.

Generally, can say that the males ratio in El-Ghorieb Farm more than of the females ratio in Faculty Farm during the present study. This it may be due to disappear of females to care the young and the males go out of the burrows to discover and bring the food.

Table 7.15: Seasonal Changes in Sex Ratio of Rodent Species in El-Ghorieb Farm, Assiut University, June 2004 Till May 2006

Study Years	Season	Males		Females	
		Number	%	Number	%
1st year	Summer	26	66.67	13	33.33
	Autumn	43	61.43	27	38.57
	Winter	30	69.77	13	30.23
	Spring	38	52.05	35	47.95
	Total	137	62.48	88	37.52
2nd year	Summer	32	84.21	6	15.79
	Autumn	35	64.81	19	35.19
	Winter	26	78.79	7	21.21
	Spring	39	67.24	19	32.76
	Total	132	73.76	51	26.24

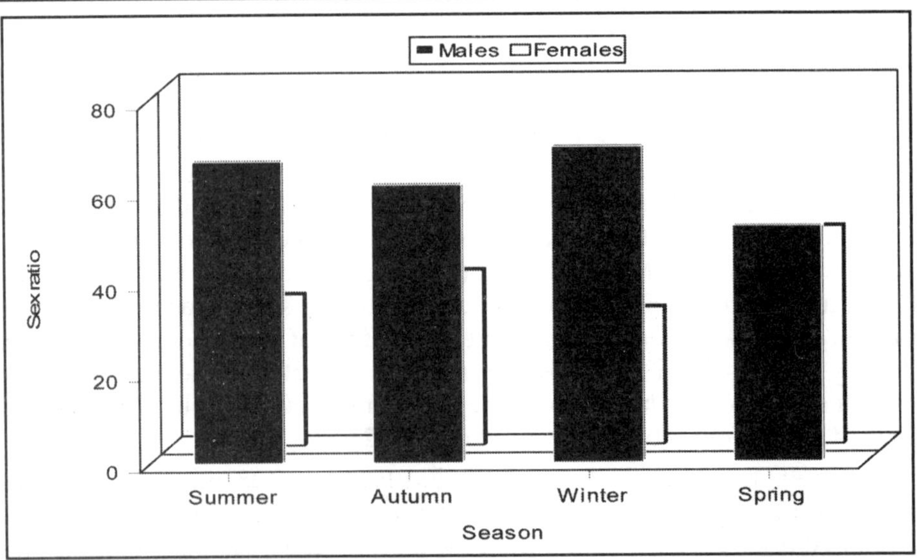

Fig. 7.26: Percentage of Males and Females Ratio of Rodent Species in El-Ghorieb Farm during 2004-2005

The results in (Table 7.18 and Figure 7.30) showed that the general population of rodent species in Faculty Farm was differ than in El-Ghorieb Farm during June 2004 till May 2005.The population was assessed by trap index was high in Faculty Farm (0.189), while in the El-Ghorieb Farm was recorded (0.156).This may be due to food obtained in Faculty Farm higher than El-Ghorieb Farm. The study of species distribution in Faculty Farm was showed that *R .r. alexandrinus* was ranked the first species 52.2% from total population followed by *R .r. frugivorus* 24.63% and *A. niloticus* 23.16%.While, in the El-Ghorieb Farm the first species was recorded *R.r.frugivorus* 62.67% followed by *A. niloticus* 24.89% and the last specie was *R.r. alexandrinus* 12.44%. This may be due to the mostly of fruit trees in El-Ghorieb Farm compared with Faculty Farm.

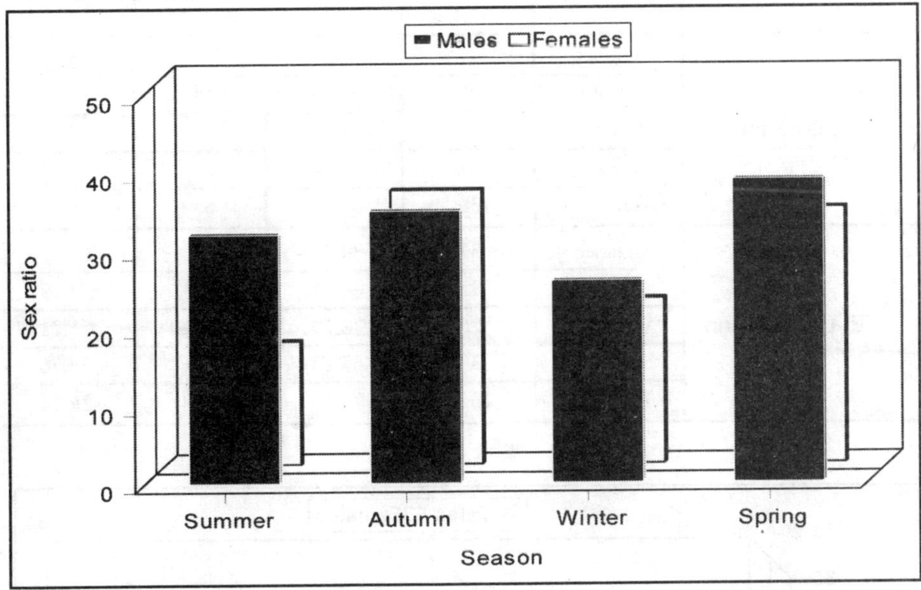

Fig. 7.27: Percentage of Males and Females Ratio to Rodent Species in El-Ghorieb Farm during 2005-2006

Table 7.16: Seasonal Changes in Sex Ratio of Rodent Species of Faculty and El-Ghorieb Farms, Assiut University, June 2004 Till May 2005

Area	Season	Males		Females	
		Number	%	Number	%
Faculty Farm	Summer	41	54.67	34	45.33
	Autumn	32	50.79	31	49.21
	Winter	31	60.78	20	39.22
	Spring	36	43.37	47	56.63
	Total	140	52.41	132	47.59
El-Ghorieb Farm	Summer	26	66.67	13	33.33
	Autumn	43	61.43	27	38.57
	Winter	30	69.77	13	30.23
	Spring	38	52.05	35	47.95
	Total	137	62.48	88	37.52

Table 7.17: Seasonal Changes in Sex Ratio of Rodent Species of Faculty and El-Ghorieb Farm, Assiut University, June 2005 Till May 2006

Area	Seasons	Males		Females	
		Number	%	Number	%
Faculty Farm	Summer	37	71.15	15	28.85
	Autumn	28	66.67	14	33.33
	Winter	27	77.14	8	22.86
	Spring	47	64.38	26	35.62
	Total	139	69.84	63	30.16
El-Ghorieb Farm	Summer	32	84.21	6	15.79
	Autumn	35	64.81	19	35.19
	Winter	26	78.79	7	21.21
	Spring	39	67.24	19	32.76
	Total	132	73.76	51	26.24

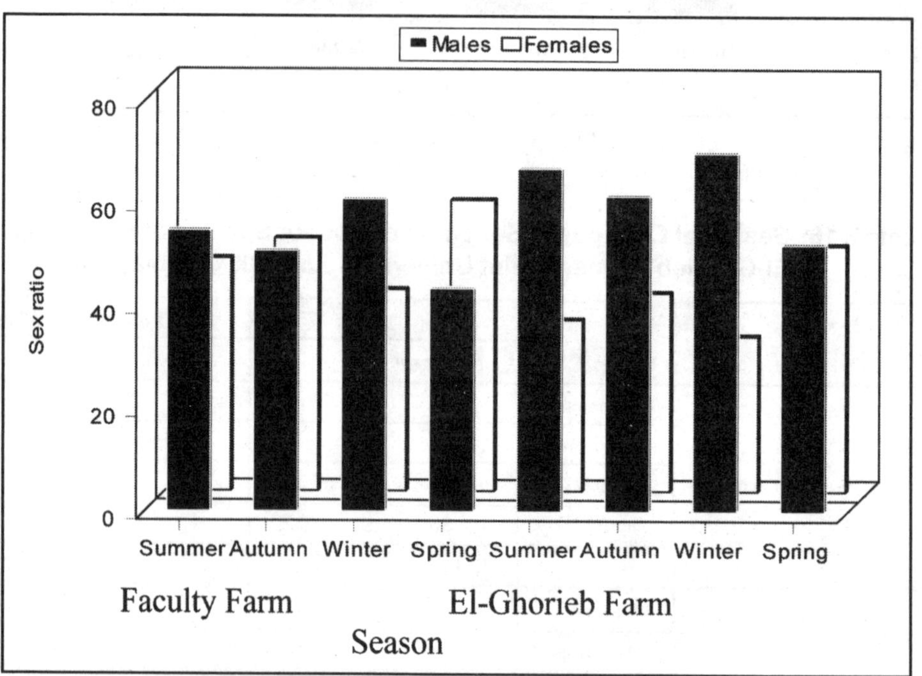

Fig. 7.28: Sex Ratio of Males and Females of Rodent Species in Faculty and El-Ghorieb Farms during 2004-2005

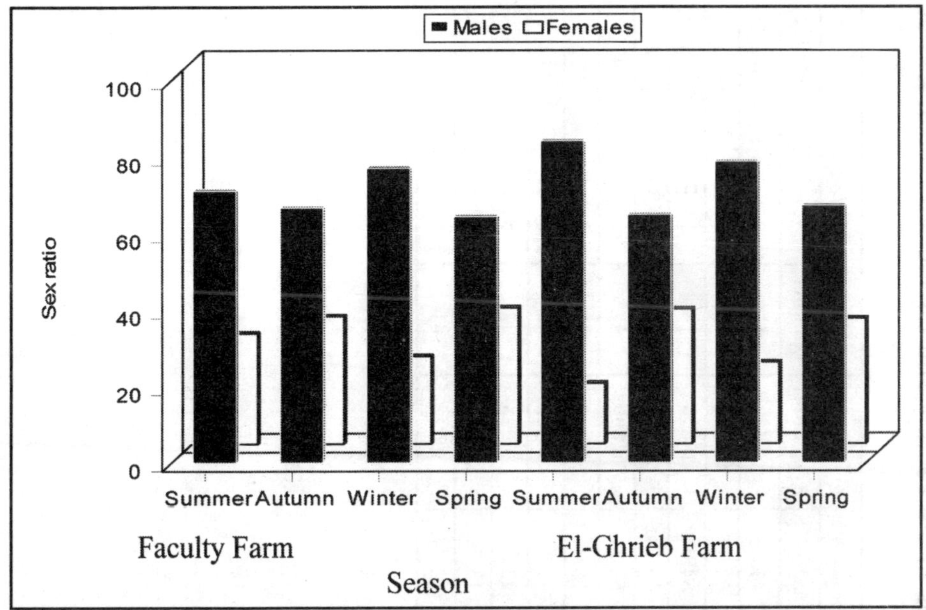

Fig. 7.29: Sex Ratio of Males and Females Ratio to Rodent Species in Faculty and El-Ghorieb Farms during 2005 Till 2006

In the Faculty Farm the highest population was recorded during spring (0.231) and summer with a trap index value (0.208) while, the lowest population was obtained during autumn (0.175) and winter. In El-Ghorieb Farm the highest population of rodent was recorded during spring (0.203) rat index values followed by autumn (0.194), the lowest was summer (0.108) and winter (0.119). This may be due to the difference either in the study areas or to difference of the land and covering plants.

Data in (Table 7.19 and Figure 7.31) indicated that the population of rodent species in Faculty Farm and El-Ghorieb Farm during June 2005 till May 2006 was decreased in both study areas compared with the first year 2004 till 2005.This may be due to the captured factor in the first year or to the food availability during this year.

The total populations in both areas assessed as trap index was high in Faculty Farm (0.140) while, in the El-Ghorieb Farm was recorded (0.127) trap index value. This may be due to the presence food which can be obtained in Faculty Farm higher than El-Ghorieb Farm.

The study of species distribution in Faculty Farm show that *R.r.alexandrinus* was ranked the first species 43.56% from total population followed by *R.r.frugivorus* 34.16% and *A.niloticus* 22.28%.While in the El-Ghorieb farm the first species was recorded *R.r. frugivorus* (49.18%) followed by *A.niloticus* (31.15%) and the last specie was *R.r.alexandrinus* (19.67%).This may be due to the mostly of fruit trees in El-Ghorieb Farm compared with Faculty Farm.

Table 7.18: Seasonal Distribution and Trap Index of Rodent Species in the Faculty and El-Ghorieb Farms, Assiut University, June 2004 Till May 2005

Location	Season	*A.niloticus*			*R.r. alexandrinus*			*R.r. frugivorus*		
		Number	%	Trap Index	Number	%	Trap Index	Number	%	Trap Index
Faculty Farm	Summer	14	18.67	0.039	46	61.33	0.128	15	20	0.042
	Autumn	12	19.05	0.033	38	60.32	0.106	13	20.63	0.036
	Winter	10	19.61	0.028	28	54.90	0.078	13	25.49	0.036
	Spring	27	32.53	0.075	30	36.14	0.083	26	31.33	0.072
	Total	63	23.16	0.044	142	52.21	0.099	67	24.63	0.047
El-Ghorieb Farm	Summer	6	15.38	0.017	0	0.0	0	33	84.62	0.092
	Autumn	20	28.57	0.056	8	11.42	0.022	42	60	0.117
	Winter	11	25.58	0.031	10	23.26	0.028	22	51.16	0.061
	Spring	19	26.03	0.053	10	13.70	0.028	44	60.27	0.122
	Total	56	24.89	0.039	28	12.44	0.02	141	62.67	0.098

Number of wire box trap = 360/season

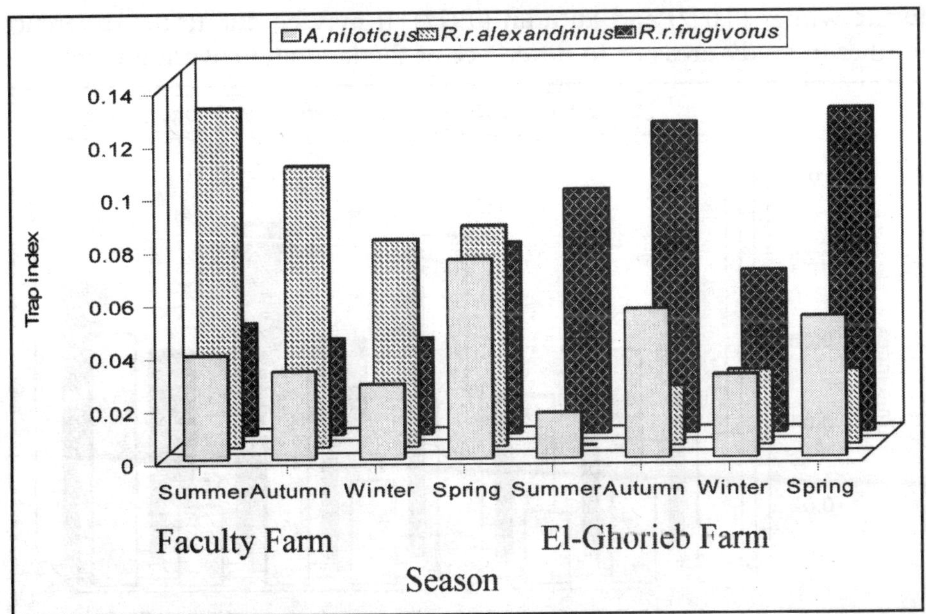

Fig. 7.30: Monthly Distribution of Rodent Species in Faculty and El-Ghorieb Farms during 2004-2005

Table 7.19: Seasonal Distribution and Trap Index of Rodent Species in the Faculty and El-Ghorieb Farms, Assiut University June 2005 Till May 2006

Location	Season	*A.niloticus*			*R.r.alexandrinus*			*R.r.frugivorus*		
		Number	%	Trap Index	Number	%	Trap Index	Number	%	Trap Index
Faculty Farm	Summer	13	25	0.036	25	48.08	0.069	14	26.92	0.039
	Autumn	9	21.43	0.025	19	45.24	0.053	14	33.33	0.039
	Winter	6	17.14	0.017	15	42.86	0.042	14	40	0.039
	Spring	17	23.29	0.047	29	39.73	0.081	27	36.99	0.075
	Total	45	22.28	0.031	88	43.56	0.061	69	34.16	0.048
El-Ghorieb Farm	Summer	9	23.68	0.025	10	26.32	0.028	19	50	0.053
	Autumn	19	35.19	0.053	6	11.11	0.017	29	53.70	0.081
	Winter	7	21.21	0.019	8	24.24	0.022	18	54.55	0.05
	Spring	22	37.93	0.061	12	20.69	0.033	24	41.38	0.067
	Total	57	31.15	0.04	36	19.67	0.025	90	49.18	0.063

In El-Ghorieb Farm the highest population of rodent was recorded during spring (0.160) rat index value followed by autumn (0.150). The lowest was trap index value was winter (0.092) and summer (0.106) rat index value. In Faculty Farm the highest population was recorded during spring (0.203) and summer (0.145) rat index value, while the lowest population was obtained during winter (0.097) and autumn (0.117). It may be due to the difference weather in study areas or to difference of the land and covering plants.

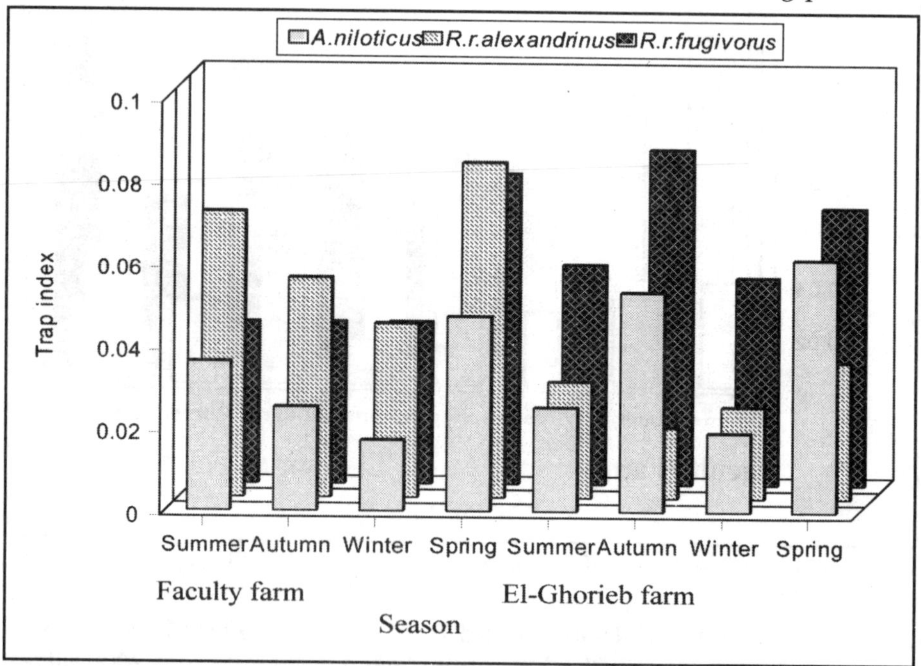

Fig. 7.31: Monthly Distribution of Rodent Species in Faculty and El-Ghorieb Farms during 2005-2006

Data in Tables (7.20 and 7.21) shows the population density of rodent species trapped over all total during both years 2004 till 2005 and 2005 till 2006. Results showed that the highest population of *A. niloticus* in field crops farm was recorded (10.86% and 8.57%) while, in El-Ghorieb Farm was recorded in vegetable plantations (7.85% and 10.13%) during 2004 till 2005 and 2005 till 2006 respectively. The percentage of grand total of this species in El-Ghorieb Farm was recorded lowest than Faculty Farm during the first year while, in the second year in El-Ghorieb Farm was recorded (14.81%) higher than Faculty Farm during the second year.Results showed that highest population of *R.r.alexandrinus* in poultry buildings was (27.16% and 21.56%) while, in El-Ghorieb Farm was in houses area (5.23% and 7.53%) during June 2004 till May 2005 and June 2005 till May 2006 respectively. The percentage of grand total of this species in Faculty Farm was recorded 28.57%, 22.86% higher than El-Ghorieb farm 5.63%, 9.35% during the first and second year.

Results showed that the highest population of *R.r.frugivorus* in poultry Farm was (9.26% and 11.17%) while, in El-Ghorieb Farm was in ornamental trees (12.68% and 12.21%) during 2004 till 2005 and 2005 till 2006 years respectively. The percentage of grand total of this species in El-Ghorieb Farm was (28.37% and 23.38%) higher than Faculty Farm (13.48% and 17.92%)

during the first and second year. In general the population density of rodent species in Faculty Farm was recorded 54.74% higher than El-Ghorieb Farm 45.27% in the first year while, in the second year the population density of rodent species in Faculty Farm was recorded 52.47% higher than El-Ghorieb Farm 47.53%. This may be due to the food abundance or suitable weather in Faculty Farm higher than El-Ghorieb Farm. This finding is agreement with those of other authors such as: Abdel-Gawad (1979).

Table 7.20: Numbers and Percentage of Certain Rodent Species Captured from Faculty and El-Ghorieb Farms of Assiut University from June 2004 Till May 2005

Location	Area	*A. niloticus*		*R.r.frugivorus*		*R.r.*alexandrinus		Total	
		Number	%	Number	%	Number	%	Number	%
Faculty Farm	Field Crops	54	10.86	5	1.01	5	1.01	64	12.88
	Poultry	3	0.60	46	9.26	135	27.16	184	37.02
	Fruit trees	6	1.21	16	3.22	2	0.40	24	4.83
	Total	63	12.68	67	13.48	142	28.57	272	54.74
El-Ghorieb Farm	Ornamental	10	2.01	63	12.68	1	0.20	74	14.89
	Vegetables	39	7.85	42	8.45	1	0.20	82	16.50
	Houses area	7	1.41	36	7.24	26	5.23	69	13.88
	Total	56	11.27	141	28.37	28	5.63	225	45.27
	Grand Total	119	23.95	208	41.85	170	34.20	497	100

Table 7.21: Numbers and Percentage of Certain Rodent Species Captured from Faculty and El-Ghorieb Farms of Assiut University from June 2005 till May 2006

Location	Area	*A. niloticus*		*R.r.frugivorus*		*R.r. alexandrinus*		Total	
		Number	%	Number	%	Number	%	Number	%
Faculty Farm	Field Crops	33	8.57	2	0.52	2	0.52	37	9.61
	Poultry	6	1.56	43	11.17	83	21.56	132	34.29
	Fruit trees	6	1.56	24	6.23	3	0.78	33	8.57
	Total	45	11.69	69	17.92	88	22.86	202	52.47
El-Ghorieb Farm	Ornamental	9	2.34	47	12.21	3	0.78	59	15.32
	Vegetables	39	10.13	25	6.49	4	1.04	68	17.66
	Houses area	9	2.34	18	4.68	29	7.53	56	14.55
	Total	57	14.81	90	23.38	36	9.35	183	47.53
	Grand Total	102	26.49	159	41.30	124	32.21	385	100

FECES METHOD

Data in Table 7.22 illustrate the number of rodent feces/m^2 in poultry buildings and Arab El-Awamer buildings. The results indicated that the number of rodent feces/m^2 in poultry farm recorded higher than in Arab EL-Awamer buildings. The highest population density in poultry farm was recorded (10.86%) in November and October (9.79%) while, the lowest percentage of rodent feces was in January (6.46%) followed by (7.57%) in March and May (7.92%).

Table 7.22: Number and Percentage of Rodent Feces/m^2 in Poultry Farm and Reclaimed Area by Using Feces Collecting Method in Assiut University

Months	Poultry Farm (Faculty Farm)		Arab El-Awamer (Reclaimed Area)	
	Number	%	Number	%
December 2004	219	8.37	120	9.85
January 2005	169	6.46	100	8.21
February	216	8.26	99	8.13
March	198	7.57	94	7.72
April	210	8.03	116	9.52
May	207	7.92	107	8.78
June	206	7.88	80	6.57
July	228	8.72	122	10.02
August	190	7.27	124	10.18
September	232	8.87	82	6.73
October	256	9.79	85	6.98
November	284	10.86	89	7.31
Total	2615	100.00	1218	100.00

In Arab El-Awamer buildings the highest percentage of rodent feces was recorded in August (10.18%) followed by (10.02%) in July and April (9.25%) while, the lowest was in June (6.57%), September (6.73%) and October (6.98%).

Data in Table 7.23 illustrated number and percentage of rodent species collected by various methods in different locations included the poultry area, newly reclaimed area and River Nile bank during 2004 till 2005.The results indicated that , in the poultry Farm in a two methods for estimation the population density of rodent species included firstly the wire-trap, the highest population was recorded in summer (28.18%). However, the lowest was in winter (21.55%). Secondly by using feces method , the highest population density was collected in autumn (26.32%) and the lowest was in winter (20.59%) and spring (20.97%).

Table 7.23: Number and Percentage of Rodents Collected by Various Methods in Different Locations in Assiut Governorate from September 2004 till August 2005

Area	Faculty Farm				Newly Reclaimed Area		River Nile Bank	
Method Months	Traped Rodents		Feces		Active Burrows		Food Consumption	
	Number	%	Number	%	Number	%	Weight (gm)	%
September 2004	29	16.02	232	8.87	129	15.62	1640	8.91
October	5	2.76	256	9.79	86	10.41	2100	11.40
November	12	6.63	284	10.86	112	13.56	1960	10.64
Autumn	46	25.41	772	29.52	327	39.59	5700	30.95
December	11	6.08	219	8.37	102	12.35	2080	11.30
January	16	8.84	169	6.46	75	9.08	2020	10.97
February	12	6.63	216	8.26	49	5.93	1520	8.25
Winter	39	21.55	604	23.10	226	27.36	5620	30.52
March	12	6.63	198	7.57	21	2.54	1130	6.14
April	19	10.50	210	8.03	17	2.06	1060	5.76
May	17	9.39	207	7.92	31	3.75	1010	5.48
Spring	45	24.86	615	23.52	69	8.35	3200	17.38
June	17	9.39	206	7.88	21	2.54	970	5.27
July	13	7.18	228	8.72	56	6.78	1345	7.30
August	21	11.60	190	7.27	127	15.38	1580	8.58
Summer	51	28.18	624	23.86	204	24.70	3895	21.15
Total	181	100.00	2615	100.00	826	100.00	18415	100.00

ACTIVE BURROWS METHOD

In newly reclaimed area active burrows method used to estimate the population density. The highest population was recorded in autumn (39.59%) and the lowest was in spring spring (8.35%) Table (7.23).

Generally speaking, high density of rodent active burrows was recorded in autumn after harvesting the summer crops and the rodents construct their burrows near the edges of the field. This agreement with Abdel-Gawad *et al.*, (1982) and Ali (1985).

FOOD CONSUMPTION METHOD

In River Nile bank the highest weight of food consumption was recorded in autumn (5700gm) while the lowest was obtained in spring (3200gm) table (7.23). This finding was in agreement with Abdel-Gawad *et al.*, (1982) and Ali (1985).

Generally, the above mentioned results indicated that the highest population of rodent feces may be due to the marked activity of rodents and food abundance in these months, while, the highest population of active burrows after harvesting the crops. Also, food consumption may be due to the increase of natural food during spring.

COLOUR PREFERENCE OF RODENT BAITS

Colour Preference Under Field Conditions

In this study used different colours in bait to study the preferred colour for collecting rodents. Data in Table (7.24) and Figure (7.32) showed that the green bait was the most preferable colour compared with the other colours such as red, yellow, blue, brown and grey baits.

Table 7.24: Number and Percentage of Rodent Species Collected by Coloured Bait Under Field Conditions at Assiut University Farm during 2004

Colours in Bait	*R.r. alexandrinus*		*R.r. frugivorus*		Grand Total
	Number	%	Number	%	
Red	6	15.79	4	16	10
Green	9	23.68	6	24	15
Yellow	6	15.79	2	8	8
Blue	5	13.16	4	16	9
Brown	7	18.42	2	8	9
Grey	5	13.16	7	28	12
Total	38	100	25	100	63
Grand percentage	60.32		39.68		

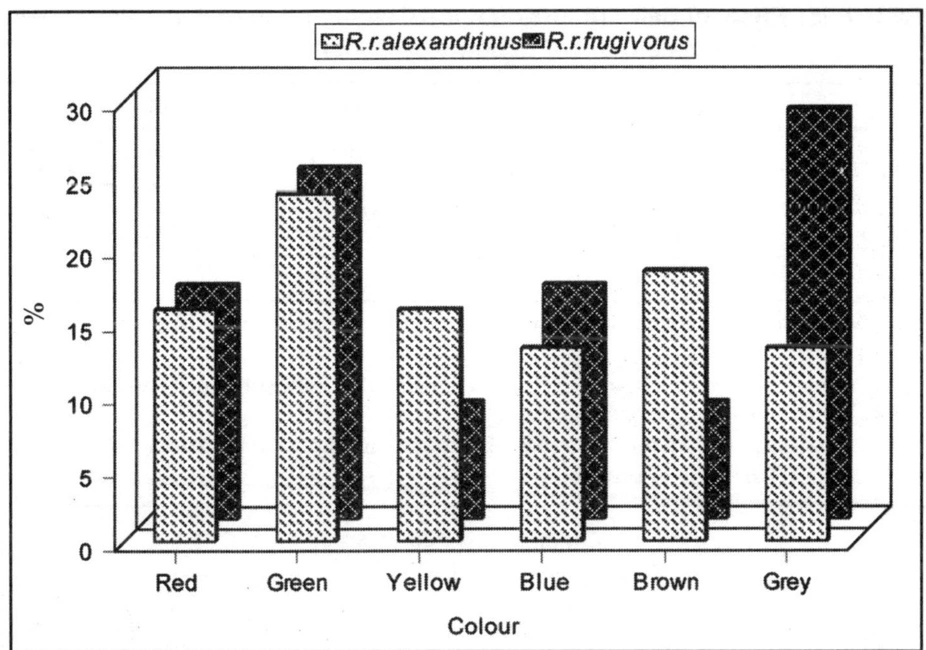

Fig. 7.32: Effect of bait colours on rodent attraction under field conditions, Assiut University during 2004.

The green bait attracted (23.81%) from and the second attraction bait Colour was grey (19.05%), the lowest one was the yellow bait with (12.69%) from the total captured rodent species.

The rodent species which captured from the study area were *R.r.alexandrinus* (60.32%) and *R.r.frugivorus* (39.68%).

Generally, can say that the rodent species preferred the colours bait in the traps specially the green colour, this data was in agreement with data reported by Ali (1985).

Colour Preference Under Laboratory Conditions

Data in Table (7.25) and Figure (7.33) illustrated the food consumption of rodent (*A. niloticus*) by gm of six colour bait (red, green, yellow, blue, brown, grey) under in laboratory conditions for 7 days. According to the mean consumption during seven days, it was observed that the consumption was high in grey bait (4.09 gm), green (3.43 gm) and red (3.21 gm). It was found that there was a significant difference in the animal consumption of the six colour baits tested for *A. niloticus*. Also, there was a significant difference in food consumed by males and females The average of food consumed by males was (3.72 gm) and by females was (2.62 gm).

Table 7.25: Effect of Bait Colours on Food Consumption of *A. niloticus* (Males and Females) Under Laboratory Conditions

	Food Consumption (gm) in Each Bait Colour						
Sex	Red	Green	Yellow	Blue	Brown	Grey	(2) Average
Male	(1)3.20 bc	3.86 ab	3.63 ab	3.91 ab	2.91 abc	4.83 a	(2)3.72 A
Female	3.23 bc	3.00 bc	2.05 cd	2.23 cd	1.86 d	3.34 bc	2.62 B
(3)Average	3.21 BC	3.43 AB	2.84 BC	3.07 BC	2.39 C	4.09 A	–

(1) Means followed by the same small letter(s), do not significantly differ at 0.05 level of probability.

(2) Means followed by the same capital letter, within the same column, do not significantly differ at 0.05 level of probability.

(3) Means followed by the same capital letter, within the same row, do not significantly differ at 0.05 level of probability.

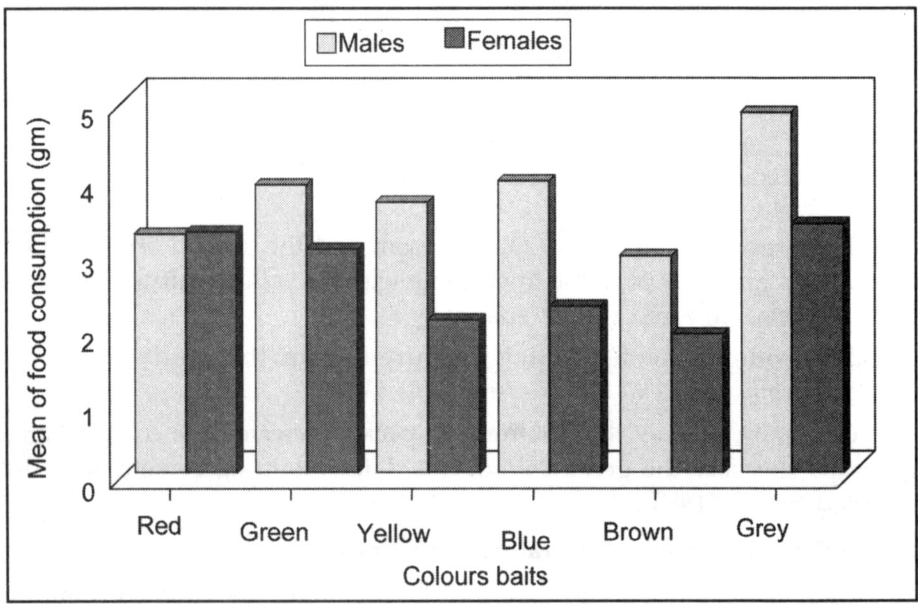

Fig. 7.33: Effect of Bait Colours on Food Consumption of *A. niloticus* (Males and Females) Under Laboratory Conditions

Data in Table (7.26) and Figure (7.34) summarize the consumption of rodent, *R.r.alexandrinus* by gm of six colours bait under laboratory conditions for 7 days. According to the mean consumption (in gm) during seven days, it was observed that the consumption was high in grey bait (3.20 gm), and red (3.11 gm). It was found that there was a significant difference in the animal consumption of the six colour baits tested for *R.r.alexandrinus*. Also, there was a significant difference between males and females consumption of the six colours bait tested. The average of food consumption males was (2.61 gm) and by females was (2.48 gm).

Table 7.26: Effect of Bait Colours on Food Consumption of *Rattus. r. alexandrinus* (Males and Females) Under Laboratory Conditions

	Food Consumption (gm) in Each Bait Colour						
Sex	Red	Green	Yellow	Blue	Brown	Grey	(2) Average
Male	(1)3.57 a	2.77a-d	1.83 e	2.40 cde	1.94 de	3.12 abc	2.61A
Female	2.66 b-e	1.94 de	2.20 de	2.66b-e	2.14 de	3.29 ab	2.48A
(3) Average	3.11 A	2.36 B	2.02 B	2.53 B	2.04 B	3.20 A	–

(1) Means followed by the same small letter(s), do not significantly differ at 0.05 level of probability.

(2) Means followed by the same capital letter, within the same column, do not significantly differ at 0.05 level of probability.

(3) Means followed by the same capital letter, within the same row, do not significantly differ at 0.05 level of probability.

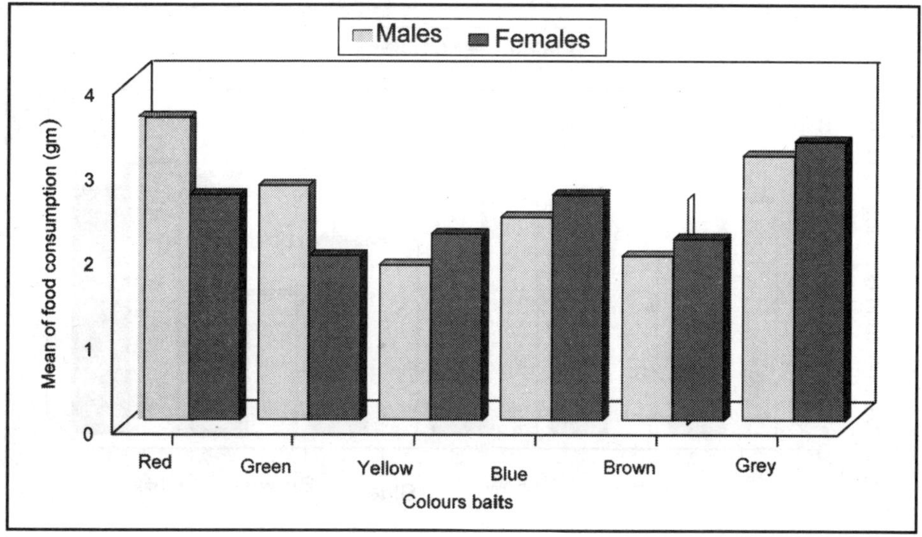

Fig. 7.34: Effect of Bait Colours on Food Consumption of *Rattus.r. alexandrinus* Males and Females Under Laboratory Conditions

Data in Table (7.27) and Figure (7.35) summarize the consumption of rodent, *R.r.frugivorus* by gm of six colours bait under laboratory conditions for 7 days. It was observed that the consumption was high in grey bait (4.76 gm), green (4.30 gm) and blue (3.55 gm) compared with the other colour bait. It was found that there was a significant difference in the animal consumption of the six colour baits tested for *R.r.frugivorus*. While found that there was a significant difference in males and females consumption of the six colour baits tested. The average of food consumption males was (3.99 gm) and by females was (3.04 gm).

Table 7.27: Effect of Bait Colours on Food Consumption of *Rattus. r. frugivorus* (Males and Females) Under Laboratory Conditions

Sex	Food Consumption (gm) in Each Bait Colour						
	Red	Green	Yellow	Blue	Brown	Grey	(2) Average
Male	(1)4.29 ab	4.31 ab	4.26 ab	3.54 bc	2.57cd	5.00a	3.99 A
Female	2.14 d	4.29 ab	2.14 d	3.57 bc	1.57 d	4.51ab	3.04 B
(3) Average	3.21C	4.30 AB	3.20 C	3.56B C	2.07 D	4.76 A	–

(1) Means followed by the same small letter(s), do not significantly differ at 0.05 level of probability.

(2) Means followed by the same capital letter, within the same column, do not significantly differ at 0.05 level of probability.

(3) Means followed by the same capital letter, within the same row, do not significantly differ at 0.05 level of probability.

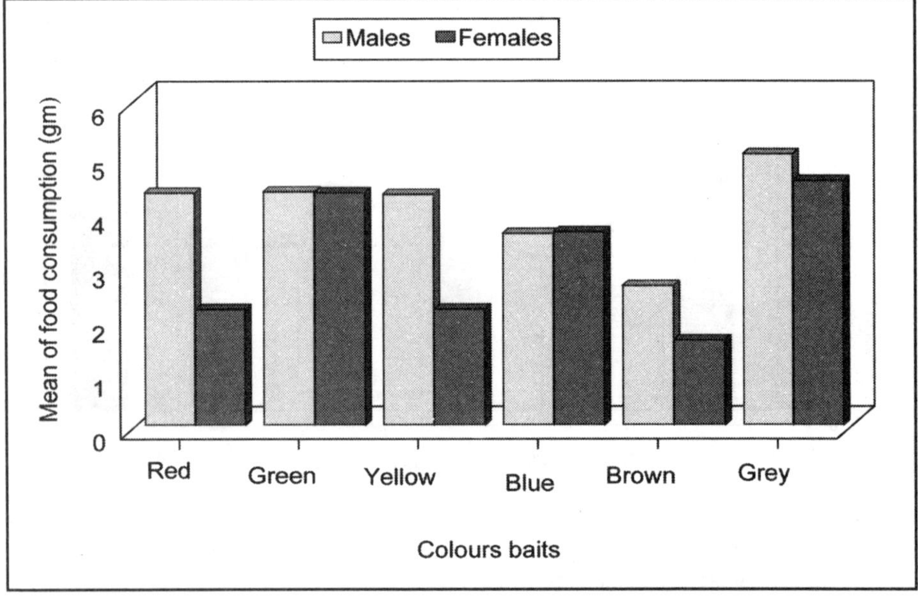

Fig. 7.35: Effect of Bait Colours on Food Consumption of *Rattus. r. frugivorus* (Males and Females) Under Laboratory Conditions

Generally, the above mentioned results emphasized the significant effect of colour in bait of rodents. These results may be useful in preparation of rodenticides baits used in rodent control.

FOOD PREFERENCE OF RODENT BAITS

This study was carried out under the field conditions in the Faculty Farm (grain storages) to reveal the preference of the trap baits. In this study we used some vegetables and food materials such as cucumber, tomato, bread, potato.

Data in Table (7.28) and Figure (7.36) show that cucumbers bait was the most attractive to rodents species. This bait attracted about (37.04%) from total captured males, tomato (25.93%), while the lowest was potato bait (16.66%). The highest captured females were recorded in cucumber bait (37.50%) from total captured females, (tomato 25%) and the lowest was potato bait (12.50%). The average percentage of baits in general was highest in cucumber (37.27%) and the lowest was obtained in potato bait (14.58%).The results showed that the males were (62.79%) more attractive to the trap baits than females (27.21%).This may be due to the females preferred to stay in the burrows to care these young.

Table 7.28: Effect of Food Types on Rodent Attraction to Baits Under Field Conditions at Assiut University during 2004

Sex Ratio Bait Type	No. Trapped Rodents				
	Males		Females		Total
	Number	%	Number	%	
Cucumber	20	37.04	12	37.50	32
Tomato	14	25.93	8	25	22
Bread	11	20.37	8	25	19
Potato	9	16.66	4	12.50	13
Total	54	100	32	100	86

Generally, the rodent species preferred the vegetable baits in the traps. These may be useful in preparation of rodenticides baits in rodent control, or to capture rodents for use in the experimental studies.

Baits preference tests should be done periodically to find out the proper bait for rodenticides formulation and to overcome the shyness of rodent baits.

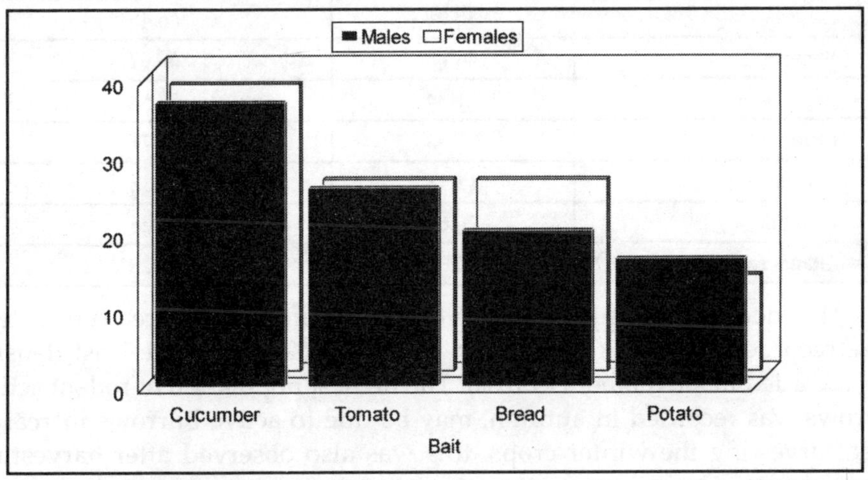

Fig. 7.36: Effect of Baits Types on Attraction of Rodents Males and Females Under Field Conditions at Assiut University during 2004

RODENT CONTROL

Mechanical Control

Data in Table (7.29) and Figure (7.37) show that the fluctuation in number of rodent active burrows in two newly reclaimed area (first area untreated, second area) treated by hand destroying of active burrows. The Nile grass rat, *Arvicanthis niloticus* was the predominant most in this area.

Table 7.29: Percentage of Reduction Between Active Burrows of Rodent in Treated Area by Handling Destroying and Untreated Area to Control of Rodents in Newly Reclaimed Area, Assiut Governorate, 2004 Till 2005

Months	Untreated Area (I)	Treated (Hand Destroying) Area (II)
	Reduction %	Reduction %
December	47.15	66.52
January	44.85	64.34
February	53.77	73.66
Winter	48.05	67.17
March	52.27	64.52
April	56.42	65.38
May	50	79.17
Spring	52.41	71.43
June	61.82	41.38
July	57.25	65.91
August	30.98	66.46
Summer	44.86	63.67
September	21.34	57.58
October	27.73	35.71
November	13.18	53.33
Autumn	20.63	49.25
Grand Total	39.35	63.25

The increased of reduction active burrows in the first area (untreated) were recorded in June (61.82%) and July (57.25%), while the least density was recorded in November (13.18%). The highest population of rodent active burrows was recorded in autumn, may be due to active burrows increased after harvesting the winter crops, this was also observed after harvesting summer crops.

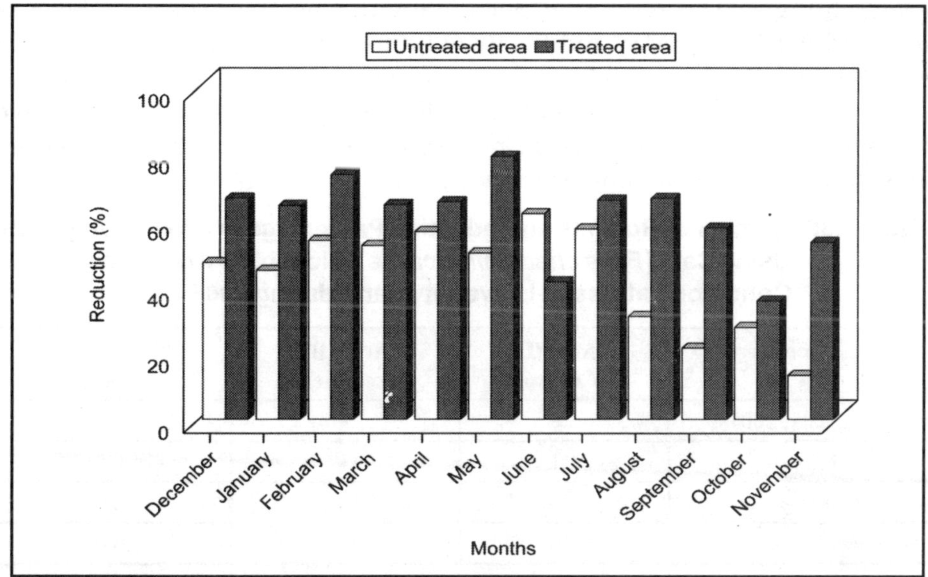

Fig. 7.37: Percentage of Reduction Between Active Burrows of Rodent in Treated Area by Handling Destroying and Untreated Area to Control of Rodents in Newly Reclaimed Area, Assiut Governorate from December 2004 Till November 2005

In the second area (treated), the increased of reduction to active burrows was recorded in May 79.17% and February (73.66%), while the least reduction was recorded in October 35.71% and June (41.38%) .The high population of rodent active burrows was recorded in autumn and summer, while the least population of active burrows in spring . The reduction percentage of rodent active burrows at the end of experiments was 39.35% in untreated and 633.25% in treated.

Generally speaking, the high reduction of rodent active burrows in the untreated area was recorded in spring (52.41%) the lowest in autumn 20.63%. In treated area the high reduction of rodent active burrows was recorded in spring 71.43%. The lowest in autumn 49.20%, the percentage of reduction in untreated area (41.49%), while in treated area (62.88%). Mechanical control have profound effects on rodent population under field conditions, these results are in agreement with data obtained by table (7.29).

The above mentioned results proved that mechanical control method achieved great success in rodent control under field conditions without environmental pollution. This finding is in agreement with these finding of Abdel-Gawad (2001).

Biological Control of Rodent

Data in Table (7.30) and Figure (7.38) show the number of rodents before and after release cats (*Felis chaus nilotica*) to control rodents biologically in grain storages. The reduction percentage during the experimental was recorded (90.91%) in May and fluctuated during period (June 88.89%), (July 85.71%). Results showed the efficiency of cats against the rodents presented in grain storages. in early months after the experiment. After four and five months there was a decreased in percentage of reduction (40%). However, after sex and seven months treatment the reduction (33.33%).

Table 7.30: Number of Rodents an Reduction Percentage in Grain Storages by Using Cats (*Felis chaus nilotica*) as Abiocontrol Agent Under Field Conditions at Assiut University Farm during 2005

Months	Area (I) Control	Area (II) Treatment	Reduction %
January, 2005	6	9	0.0
February	11	11	0.0
March	13	13	0.0
April	10	12	0.0
May	11	1	90.91
June	9	1	88.89
July	7	1	85.71
August	9	2	77.78
September	5	3	40.0
October	5	3	40.0
November	6	4	33.33
December	6	4	33.33

Cats released a May, 1st 2005

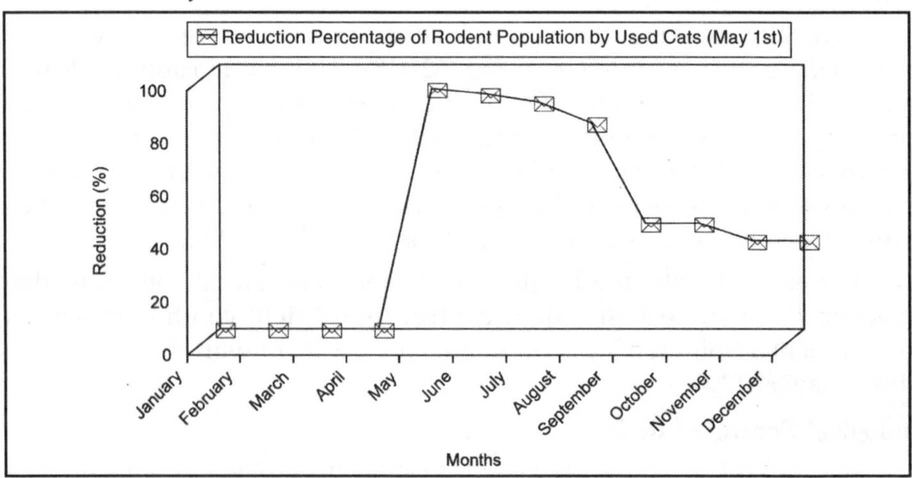

Fig. 7.38: Percentage of Reduction in Rodent Population Before and After Releasing Cats in Storages at Assiut University from January Till December 2005

In general the release of predator (cats) in grain storages against the rodents and damage in grains storages.

Finally the efficiency of the present predator (cats) against rodents in the tested area may be due to of the predators feed on a variety of prey species and switch their attention for one to the other according to relative abundance. This switching behavior has two important effects, it allows the predator to survive when a particular prey species is low in numbers and it helps to keep in check it. Keshta (2003).

Chemical Control

Evaluation of the efficacy of two rodenticides, Supercaid (0.005% bromadilone) and 3% zinc phosphide against rodents using single feeding under field conditions in Faculty farm and Arab El-Awamer

Data in Tables (7.31 and 7.32) and Figures (7.39 and 7.40). In area treated with Zinc phosphide the high reduction in population density of feces was recorded in (July 85.60% and 82%), August (89.20%) and (74.80%) in Faculty Farm August (78.71%, 90.24%), September (91.13%, 88.47%) in Arab El-Awamer area.

Table 7.31: Efficiency of Two Rodenticides Applied Once on Rodent Population Density (as Number of Feces), Under Field Conditions, Faculty Farm, Assiut University during 2005

	Months	Zinc Phosphide		Supercaid		Control	
Before	January 15/2005	104		95		81	
	30	100		85		88	
	February15	118		106		104	
	28	132		108		112	
	March 15	167		124		104	
	30	207		133		94	
	April 15	193		156		96	
	30	90		121		114	
	Mean	138.88	(0.0) reduction%	116	(0.0) reduction%	99.13	(0.0) reduction%
After	May, 15	60	56.80	119	+2.59	101	+1.89
	30	44	68.32	115	0.86	106	+6.93
	June 15	50	64.00	94	18.97	112	+12.98
	30	36	74.08	79	31.90	94	5.18
	July 15	20	85.60	91	21.55	108	+8.95
	30	25	82.00	76	34.48	120	+21.05
	August 15	15	89.20	88	24.14	105	+5.92
	30	35	74.80	73	37.07	85	14.25

(Table Contd...)

After	September 15	44	68.32	72	37.93	111	+11.97
	30	58	58.24	75	35.34	121	+22.06
	October 15	67	51.76	72	37.93	125	+26.10
	30	79	43.12	58	50.00	131	+32.15
	November 15	93	33.04	64	44.83	142	+43.25
	30	104	25.12	47	59.48	142	+43.25
	December 15	117	15.75	46	60.34	118	+19.04
	30	123	11.43	58	50.00	101	+1.89
	Mean	60.63	56.35	76.69	34.21	113.88	17.30

Table 7.32: Efficiency of Two Rodenticides Applied Once on Rodent Population Density (as number of feces), Under Field Conditions, Arab El-Awamer, Assiut Governorate, 2004 Till 2005

	Months	ZincPhosphide		Supercaid		Control	
Before	December 15, 2004	62		50		61	
	30	131		72		59	
	January 15, 2005	158		90		52	
	30	100		60		48	
	Mean	112.75	(0.0) reduction %	68	(0.0) reduction %	55	(0.0) reduction%
After	February 15	53	52.99	33	51.47	46	16.36
	28	56	50.33	28	58.82	53	3.64
	March 15	38	66.30	24	64.71	41	25.45
	30	18	84.04	18	73.53	53	3.64
	April 15	18	84.04	22	67.65	53	3.64
	30	18	84.04	25	63.24	63	+14.55
	May 15	28	75.17	42	38.24	77	+40.00
	30	36	68.07	27	60.29	30	45.45
	January 15	35	68.96	27	60.29	38	30.91
	30	31	72.51	27	60.29	42	23.64
	July 15	38	66.30	34	50.00	44	20.00
	30	31	72.51	30	55.88	78	+41.82
	August 15	24	78.71	22	67.65	69	+25.45
	30	11	90.24	15	77.94	55	–
	September 15	10	91.13	13	80.88	37	32.73
	30	13	88.47	20	70.59	45	18.18
	October 15	18	84.04	23	66.18	42	23.64
	30	35	68.96	41	39.71	43	21.82
	November 15, 2005	43	61.86	52	23.53	45	18.18
	30	52	53.88	60	11.76	44	20.00
	Mean	30.3	73.13	29.15	57.13	49.9	21.46

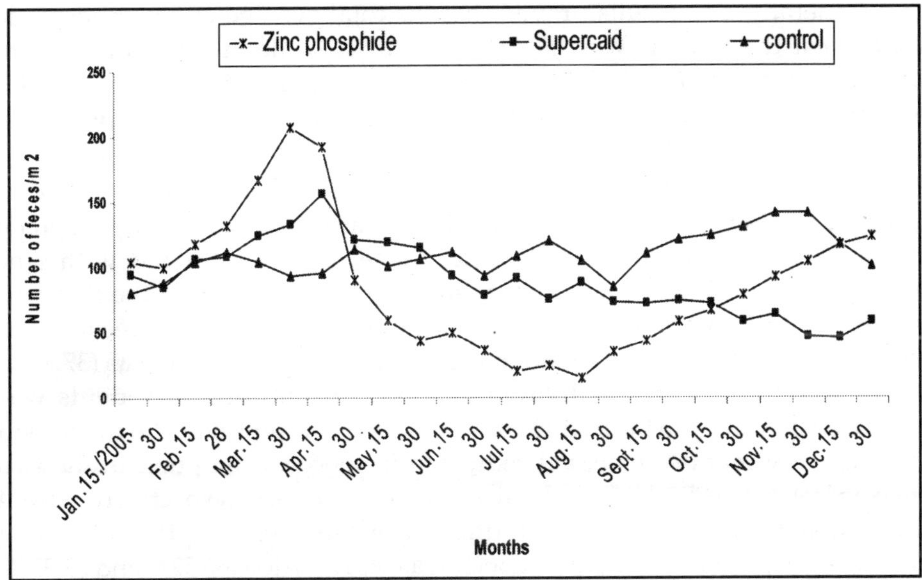

Fig. 7.39: Efficiency of Two Rodenticides Applied Once on Rodents Population Density (as number of feces) Under Field Conditions, Faculty Farm at Assiut University during 2005

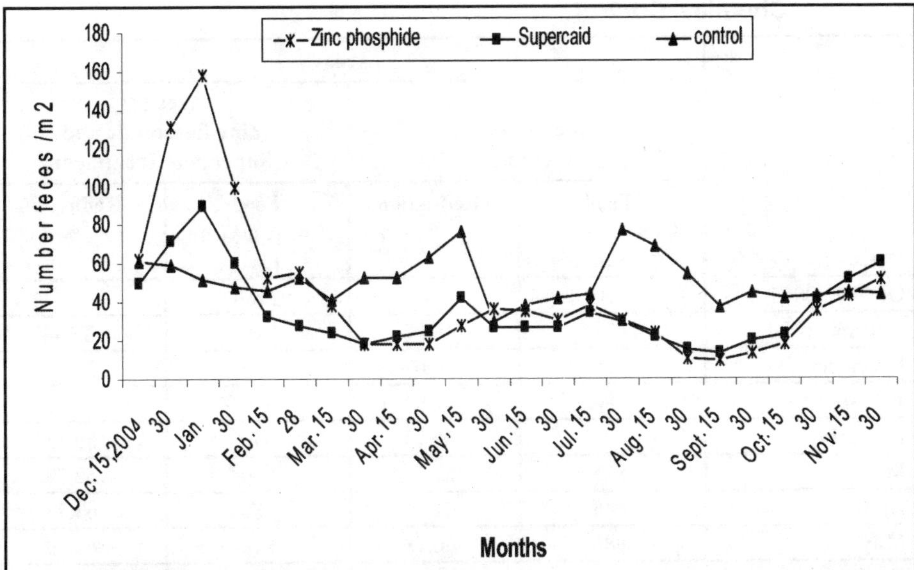

Fig. 7.40: Efficiency of Two Rodenticides Applied Once on Rodent Population Density (as number of feces) Under Field Conditions, Arab El-Awamer at Assiut Governorate during 2004 Till 2005

In the second area treated by supercaid the reduction in population density of feces was recorded in November (44.83% and 59.48%), October (60.34% and 50%) in Faculty Farm and November (44.83%, 59.48%), October (60.34, 50%) followed by control.

Generally, The results proved that the total average of zinc phosphide 3% against the rodents was (56.35%), (73.13%) while in treated area with supercaid was recorded (34.21%), (57.13)%.in faculty farm and Arab El-Awamer, respectively. The present data proved that zinc phosphide 3% concentration gave efficiency higher than supercaid against rodents.

Data in Table (7.33) show that high population density of food consumption before and after treated. The first area treated by zinc phosphide 3% in November during 2004, while the second area treated with zinc phosphide 3% in January and supercaid 0.005% during July. In the first area the reduction in amount of food consumption by rodents was recorded in (November, 48.87%), while found that the reduction percentage was (37.44%) in the second area. The reduction of food consumption of rodents was decreased gradually in the two areas. While used zinc phosphide in the second area (January month) increased reduction in food consumption in the two areas (52.94 % and 55.35%) in the first and second areas respectively. Also it was found that the increase in reduction of food consumption of rodent after using supercaid July in the second area was recorded (66.52% and 62.33%) in the first and second areas respectively.

Table 7.33: Monthly Reduction of Food Consumption Before and After Using Chemical Control

Months	Areas			
	Area (1) Zinc Phosphide Treatment		Area (2) Zinc Phosphide and Supercaid Treatment	
	Food Consumption (gm)	Reduction %	Food Consumption (gm)	Reduction %
October, 2004	2210	–	2150	–
November	1130 *	48.87	1345	37.44
December	1245	43.67	1400	34.88
January	1040	52.94	960 *	55.35
February	890	59.73	870	59.53
March	855	61.31	800	62.79
April	845	61.76	780	63.72
May	880	60.18	810	62.33
June	840	61.99	880	59.07
July	740	66.52	810 **	62.33
August	675	69.46	735	65.81
September	530	76.02	685	68.14

* Zinc phosphide 3%

** Supercaid 0.005%

In conclusion, the recommended procedure for rodent control applying zinc phosphide followed by anticoagulants twice annually, seems to be satisfactory being applied within areas holding different culture i.e. farms, buildings, open areas. However, It is rather important to give all possible attention to environmental sanitation. At the same time, type of applied anticoagulant should be changed upon appearance sings of resistance of rodents under control to such product.

SUMMARY

The development of an effective strategy for implementation of rodent pest management programmes in cultivated and newly reclaimed agro ecosystems in Egypt is of great importance.

So, the present work was carried out on rodents during the period from June 2004 till May 2006. Five areas in Assiut Governorate were chosen to determine the species composition of rodents, the population density by several methods, colour and food preference in rodent baits and control of rodents. Results can be summarized as follows:

Species Composition of Rodents in Cultivated and Reclaimed Lands

Species composition of rodents in Faculty and El-Ghorieb Farms revealed the presence of three species of rats included the Nile grass rat, *Arvicanthis niloticus* (Desm.), the grey bellied rat, *Rattus rattus alexandrinus* (Linn.) and the white bellied rat, *Rattus rattus frugivorus* (Linn.). The *R.r. alexandrinus* recorded an average dominant percentage (24.26% and 7.84%) in Faculty and El-Ghorieb Farms, respectively. However, the average dominant% for *R.r.frugivorus* was (14.35% and 28.30%) and for *A. niloticus* (11.39% and 13.85%) in Faculty and El-Ghorieb Farms, respectively.

The Norway rat, *Rattus norvegicus* was the only rodent encountered in the River Nile Bank. Also, survey of rodents in Arab-El-Awamer and a newly reclaimed area revealed the presence of four species of rats included *A. niloticus, R.r.alexandrinus,* the house mouse, *Mus musculus* and lesser gerbia, *Gerbillus gerbillus*. The dominant percentage values of *R .r. alexandrinus* was (63.27% and 18.92%), *A. niloticus* (24.49% and 67.57%), *M. musculus* (12.24% and 0.0) and *G. gerbillus* (0.0 and 13.51%) in Arab El-Awamer and the newly reclaimed area, respectively. The presence of *Mus musculus* may be due to the establishment of building or the husbandry beside the study areas.

Determination of the Population Density of Rodents by Using Different Methods

Trapping Method

Generally, the number of rodents trapped recorded from the Faculty and El-Ghorieb Farms from June 2005 till May 2006 was decreased (385 individuals) compared with this number which trapped from the same area

(497 individuals) through June 2004 till May 2005. The decreased of the density may be due to the trapping during the last year or due to the decreased of the food in this area through this year.

In the Faculty and El-Ghorieb Farms the highest seasonal trap index values was recorded in spring while, the lowest values in winter. In general, males outnumbered females.

Feces Method

In poultry farm, the highest population was observed during in November (10.86%). The lowest population was during January (6.46%) and March (7.57%).

In Arab El-Awamer the highest population was recorded in August (10.18%) and July (10.02%). The lowest was (6.57%) in June and September (6.73%). This may be due to the marked activity of rodents and food abundance in these months.

Active Burrows Method

In newly reclaimed area, the highest population density of rodents determined by using active burrows method was recorded in autumn (39.59%). The lowest was (8.35%) in spring. This may be due to increase in active burrow after harvesting the crops.

Food Consumption Method

In River Nile bank, the highest amount of food consumed was recorded during the autumn season (5700gm). The lowest was observed during spring (3200gm).This may be due to the increase of natural food during spring.

Colours Preference of Rodent Bait

Colour Preference Under Field Conditions

Six colored baits were tested. The results indicated that rodents preferred the green, grey and red baits rather than the yellow, brown and blue baits. We can say that the rodent species preferred the coloured baits in the traps especially the green colour.

Colour Preference Under Laboratory Conditions

In this study six colored baits were tested. Results revealed that rodents preferred the grey, green and red baits more than the yellow, blue and brown baits. This finding may be useful in preparation of rodent baits for rodent control.

Food Preference of Rodents Baits

Four rodent baits were used included cucumber, tomato, bread and potato. Results indicated that cucumber and tomato baits attracted the highest number of rodent species followed by the other baits. This may be useful to the preparation of rodent baits in rodent control, or to capture rodent for use as an experimental animal. Baits preference tests should be done periodically to find out the proper bait for rodenticide formulation and to overcome the shyness of rodent baits.

Rodents Control

Mechanical Control

The highest reduction of rodent active burrows in the untreated area was recorded in spring (52.21%), while the lowest was (20.63%) in autumn. In treated area high reduction of rodent active burrows was recorded in spring (71.43%) the lowest was (49.20%) in autumn.

Mechanical control of rodents by using the destruction of rodent active burrows achieved great success in rodent control under field conditions without environmental pollution and not costly.

Biological Control

Cats (*Felis chaus nilotica*) as Naturally Occurring Biological Control Agent (NOBCA) were used in grain storages. The percentage of reduction during the presence was recorded as 90.91%. After 6 months the reduction % of the predator was 33.33%.

The decreased in the efficiency of cats in reduction rodents population after six or seven months may be due to the predation prey efficiency of cats. Also, the feeding habits of the cats to prey upon variety of preys and switch their attention for one to other prey species according to the relative abundance. This switching behavior has two important effects, it allows the predator to survive when a particular prey species is low in numbers and it helps to keep it in check.

Chemical Control

Two rodenticides zinc phosphide 3% and supercaid (bromadilone 0.005%) were tested against rodents by using single feeding under field conditions.

Generally speaking, the recorded results proved that the total average of zinc phosphide 3% was effective against the rodents with a reduction percentage (56.35% and 73.13%), while in treated area with supercaid was (34.21% and 57.13%).In the Faculty Farm and Arab El-Awamer, respectively.

The reduction in the population density of rodents determined by rodent feces proved that zinc phosphide 3% concentration gave efficiency higher than supercaid against rodents.

In the River Nile bank area zinc phosphide 3% during (November) during 2004 was used in the first area and the second area was treated with zinc phosphide 3% in (January) and supercaid 0.005% in (July) .The reduction in food consumption was recorded in the first area during November 48.87%

and 37.44% in the second area. However, used zinc phosphide 3 % in the second area (January, 2005) showed that increased reduction in amount food consumption in the two area were recorded (52.94% and 55.35% respectively). Also, results proved an increase in reduction of food consumption of rodent after using supercaid (July) in the second area was 66.52% and 62.33% in the first and second areas, respectively.

In conclusion, the recommended procedure for rodent control is applying zinc phosphide followed by anticoagulants twice annually seems to be satisfactory being applied within areas holding different habitats such as farms, buildings, open areas. However, it is rather important to give all possible attention to environmental sanitation. At the same time, type of applied anticoagulant should be changed upon appearance signs of resistance of rodents under control to such product.

CONCLUSION

The strategies adopted for Managing Rodent Pests (MRP) varies from agro ecosystems to the other such as desert and semi-desert ecosystems. However, the present work was initiated to through a beam of light on the Management Strategies of Rodents (MSR) within different Ecosystems. The conclusion that has been achieved from the conducted experiments could be summarized in the following points:

1. The differences in species composition of rodents depending on locality, habitat type and preferred food.
2. High population density of rodents occurred in spring was increased activity. However, the lowest density was during winter season.
3. It is of interest to point herein that grey and green colour of rodent baits can be used effectively in preparation of rodenticides baits.
4. The rodent species preferred the vegetable baits in the traps. This can be useful to prepare rodent baits to capture rodents.
5. The control of rodents depends upon the locality, neighboring and available food.
6. Mechanical, biological and chemical control methods can be used effectively in an Integrated Pest Management Approach (IPMA) for the regulation of the rodents population density.

REFERENCES

Abazaid, A.A. (1990). Efficiency of Some Common and Used Rodenticides and Some New Alternative Against Rodents in Qena Governorate. M.Sc. Thesis, Fac. Agric., Assiut Univ.

Abazaid, A.A. (1997). Ecological and Toxicological Studies in Rodents in Qena Governorate, "Upper Egypt". Ph.D. Thesis, Fac. Agric., Assiut Univ.

Abdel-Galil, Y.M.A. (1997). Food Preference on Some Rodent Species Infesting Agriculture Crops. M.Sc. Thesis Fac. Agric., (Zoology) Al-Azhar Univ.

Abdel-Galil, Y.M.A. (2005). Comparative Studies on Rodenticides Against Some Rodents. Ph.D., Thesis Fac. Agric., Al-Azhar Univ.

Abdel-Gawad, K.H. (1974). Ecological and Toxicological Studies on Commensal and House Hold Rodents in Assiut Area. M.Sc. Thesis, Fac. Agric., Assiut Univ.

Abdel-Gawad, K.H. (1979). Studies on the Inter-relation Between Rodents and Their Ectoparasites in the Cultivated and Semi-arid Zones. Ph.D. Thesis, Fac. Agric., Assiut Univ.

Abdel-Gawad, K.H. (1987). Seasonal Distribution of Rodent Species and Their Associated Ectoparasites in New Cultivated Lands. Assiut J. Agric. Sc., 18 (3): 343-352.

Abdel-Gawad, K.H. (2001a). Evaluation of Some Chemical and Mechanical Methods to Reduce Rodent Population in Maize Fields. 1st. Int. Conf., Safe Alternatives of Pesticides for Pest Management Assiut Univ., Egypt. 421-429.

Abdel-Gawad, K.H. (2001b). Rodent Control in the Student Buildings at Assiut. 1st. Int. Conf. Safe Alternative of Pesticides for Pest Management Assiut Univ., Egypt: 413-420.

Abdel-Gawad, K.H. and Maher Ali, A. (1982a). The Active Burrows as Parameter for the Detection of Population Density of Rodents during Rat Control Campaigns. Assiut J. Agric. Sc., 13 (2): 115-120.

Abdel-Gawad, K.H. and Maher Ali, A. (1982b). Food Preference and Food Consumption of Various Rodent Species. Assiut J. Agric. Sci., 13 (2): 13-18.

Abdel-Gawad, K.H. and A.I. Farghal (1982). Levels of Egypt Rodents Sensitivity to Warfarin. Assiut J. Agric. Sc., 13 (2): 145-152.

Abdel-Gawad, K.H.; A.M. Salit and Maher Ali, A. (1982). Population Density of Rodent Species in Agricultural and Semi-arid Area. Assiut J. Agric. Sc., 13 (2): 27-37.

Abdel-Karim, S.M. (1991). Studies on Rodent in Sharkia Governorate. Ph.D. Thesis, Fac. Agric., Zagazig Univ., Egypt.

Abd El-Rahman, A.; A. Metwally and M.E. El-Naggar (1991). Rat Acceptance of Non-toxic Baits in Ryan Qatar State. Egypt J. Agric. Res., 69 (1): 257-261.

Ahmed, M.Y.M. (2001). Studies on the Field Rats. M.Sc. Thesis Fac. Agric. AL-Azhar Univ.

Ahmed, H.S.K .(2006). Studies on Damage Caused by Rodents on Some Field Crops and its Control in Upper Egypt (Assiut Area). M.Sc. Thesis Agric., Al-Azhar Univ.

Al-Gendy, A.A.R. (2004). Laboratory and Field Studies on Some Rodent in Egypt. Ph.D. Thesis Fac. Agric., Al-Azhar Univ. Egypt.

Ali, M.K. (1985). Studies on Rodents and Their Ectoparasites in Sohag Governorate. M.Sc. Thesis Fac. Agric., Assiut Univ.

Ali, M.K. (1991). Recent Trends in Rodent Control and Efficacy of its Chemical Agents. Ph.D. Sc. Thesis Fac. Agric., Assiut Univ.

Asran, A.A. (1994). Population Dynamics and Reproduction Aspects of the Nile Rat, *Arvicanthis niloticus*. Egypt. J. Agric., Res., 69 (1): 273-279.

Asran, A.A.; H.I. El-Deeb and M.A. El-Halfawy (1992). Field Trials on Certain Anticoagulant Rodenticides Against the Field Rat *Arvicanthis niloticus*. Egypt, J. Agric. Res., 70 (2): 461-467.

Asran, A.A.; H.I.El-Deeb; G.Kuehnert and M.A. El-Halfawy (1985). Population Density of Rodent in Different Locations in Fayoum Governorate, J. Agric. Sc., Mansoura Univ.,10 (4): 1527-1528.

Baghdadi, S.A.S. (2006). Ecological Studies on Rodent Species on Al-Azhar University Farm in Assiut and its Control. M.Sc. Thesis Fac. Agric., Al-Azhar Univ., Egypt.

Blackwell, G.L.; M.A. Potter; E.O. Minot (2001). Rodent and Predator Population Dynamics in an Eruptive System. Ecol. Modelling, 25: 227-245.

Castillo, E.; J. Priotto; A.M. Ambrosio; M.C. Provensal; N. Pini; M.A. Morales; A. Steinmann and J.J. Polop (2003). Commensal and Wild Rodents in an Urban Area of Argentina. Int. Biodeterioration, 52: 135-141.

Cavia, R.; I.G. Villafane; E.A. Cattadino; D.N. Bilenca; M.H. Mino and M. Busch (2005). Effects of Cereal Harvest on Abundance and Spatial Distribution of the Rodent Akodon Azarae in Central Argentina. Agric. Ecosys., and Environ., 107: 95-99.

Chander-sheikher; S.D. Jain and C. Sheiker (1996). Mode of Application and Performance of Rodenticides in Vegetable Crops. Indian J. Agric. Sc .66 (7): 437-440.

Dielenberg, R.A.; J.C. Arnold and I.S. Mcgregor (1999). Low-dose Midazolam Attenuates Predatory Odor Avoidance in Rats. Pharmacology Biochemistry and Behaviour, 62 (2): 197-201.

Dolbeer, R.A. (1999). Overview and Management of Vertebrate Pests. In: Ruberson, J.R.(Ed.), Handbook of Pest Management. Marcel Dekker, New York: 663-691.

Dowing, J.E. and E.C. Murphy (1994). Ecology of Ship Rats (*Rattus rattus*) in Akauri (Agathis australis) Forest in North Land. New Zealand. J. Ecol., 18: 19-27.

Ebaid, N.M.; Z.H. Zidan; H.I. El-Deeb and A.A. Mourad (1999). Certain Biological Aspects Assosiated with *Gerbillus gerbillus* and *Meriones shawi* Rodents at Selected Reclaimed Areas of Egypt. Ann., Agric., Sc. Ain Shams Univ., Egypt, 44 (2): 791-797.

Eisemann, J.D.; B.E. Petersen and K.A. Fagerstone (2003). Efficacy of Zinc Phosphide for Controlling Norway Rat, Roof Rat, House Mise, *Peromyscus spp*, Prairie Dogs and Squirrels. Proceedings of the 10th Wildlif., Damage Manage. Conf. Literature Review. 335-349.

El-Bahrawy, A.A.F. (1986). Studies on Ecology and Control of Some Rodent Species in Ismailia Governorate. Ph.D. Thesis, Fac. Agric., Suez Univ., Egypt.

El-Deeb, H.I.; Lokma, H.E. and El-Fishawi, A.A. (1992). Fields Studies on Population Dynamics and Reproductive Biology of the Nile Rat, *A. niloticus*. Zagazig J. Agric. Res., 9 (3): 1431-1435.

El-Deeb, H.I.; A.A. Asran; G. Kuehnert and M.A. El-Halafawy (1985). Bait Preference and Bait Consumption of the Nile Rat, *Arvicanthis niloticus*. Zagazig J. Agric. Res., 12 (1): 515-522.

El-Deeb, H.I.; A. Metwally; N.El-Hwashy and I.Q. Ibrahim (1996). Survey and Population Density of Domestic Rodent Species in Different Habitats of Some Governorates in Egypt. Al-Azhar, J. Res., 23: 233-248.

El-Deeb, H.I.; Z.H. Zidan; N. El-Hawshy and A.A. Mourad (1999). Survey Studies on Rodent Fauna the New Reclaimed Area and Their Role on Crop Damage in Egypt. Ann., Agric. Sci., Ain Shams., Egypt, 44 (2): 775-790.

El-Eraky, S.A.; K.H. Abdel-Gawad; A.I. Farghal and A.A. Abazied (2000). Evaluation of Some Mechanical Control Measures to Reduce Rodent Population in Upper Egypt. The 2nd Scientific Conference of Agricultural Sciences, Assiut, 519-522.

El-Fekey, M.A. (1990). Studies on Small Rodents and Their Fleas Species of Public Health Importance in Sabahiya Experimental Station with Special Reference to Their Control. M.Sc. Thesis, Fac. Agric., Alex., Univ., Egypt.

El-Nashar, M.A. (1998). Ecological and Toxicological Studies on Some Egyptian Rodents in Certain Traditional Cultivated Areas in Some Governorates in Egypt. M.Sc. Thesis Fac. Agric., Al-Azhar Univ., Egypt.

El-Sherbiny, A.H, (1987). Cyclic Fluctuations in Rodent Populations: Review of Current Researches. Egypt.J. Wildl. and Nat. Resoures, Vol. 9. pp. 17.

Embarak, M.Z. (1997). Ecological and Control Studies on Rodents and Their Ectoparasites in Cultivated and Newly-Reclaimed Areas. M. Sc. Thesis Fac. Agric., Assiut Univ.

Farghal, A.I.; S.A. El-Eraky; K.H. Abdel-Gawad and A.A. Abazied (2000). Laboratory and Field Evaluation of Some Rodenticides Against Rodent Species in Upper Egypt. The 2nd Sci. Conf. Agric. Sci., Assiut, 531-536.

Feliciano, B.R.; F.A.S. Fernandes; D. Frettas and M.S.L. Figueiredo (2002). Population Dynamics of Small Rodents in a Grassland Between Fragments of Atlantic Forest in South Eastern Brazil. Mammalian Biology, 67: 304 -314.

Fitzgerald, B.A. (1991). The Diet of Feral Cats (*Felis catus*) on Raoul Island, Kermadec Group. New Zeland Journal of Ecology, 15, 123-129.

Gill, J.E. (1992). Laboratory Evaluation of the Toxicity of Flocoumafen as a Single-feed Rodenticide to Seven Rodent Species. Int. Biodeterioration.30: (1): 65-76.

Girard, B.; V. Paul; J.D. Tyler (1999). The Status of *Rattus rattus* and *Rattus norvegicus* in Southwestern Oklahma. Proc. Okla. Acad. Sci., 70: 43-44.

Greaves, J.H. (1989). Rodent Pests and Their Control in the Near East. FAO Plant Production and Protection Tech. Paper No. 95, Rome.

Helal, T.Y. and M. Zedan (1982). Efficiency of Ratak in Rodent Control in Hospital in Assiut Region. Assiut J. Agric. Sci., 13 (2): 137-143.

Hussain, I. and E.Ahmad (1990). Traditional and Non-chemical Methods of Rodent Control. Training Manual on Vertebrate Pest Management, 63-66.

Hussin, S.S.M. (1991). Ecological Studies and Control of Certain Rodents in Beni-suef Governorate. M.Sc. Thesis Fac. Agric., Cairo Univ., Egypt.

Hygnstrom, S.E.; K.C.V. Cauteren; R.A. Hines and C.W. Mansfield (2000). Efficacy of in-furrow Zinc Phosphide Pellets for Controlling Rodent Damage in on-till Corn. Int. Biodeterioration, 43: 215-222.

Ibrahim, I.K. (1995). Studies on the Toxicity Effect of Some Substances on Rodents in Egypt. M.Sc. Thesis, Fac. Agric., Al-Azhar Univ., Egypt.

Jackson, W.B. (2001). Current Rodenticide Strategies. International Biodeterioration 48: 127-136.

Johnston, J.J.; D.L. Nolte; B.A. Kimball; K.R. Perry and J.C. Hurley (2005). Increasing Acceptance and Efficacy of Zinc Phosphide Rodenticides Baits via Modification of the Carbohydrate Profile. Crop Protection, 24: 381-385.

Kaur, H. and V.R. Parshad (2005). Laboratory and Field Evaluation of Three Odorant Compounds for Improving Attraction of the Lesser Bandicoot Rat, *Bandicota bengalensis* (Gray) to 0.0375% Coumatetraly Bait, Int. Biodeterioration 56: 135-142.

Keshta, T.M.S. (2003). Studies on Some Biological Rodent Control Factors. Ph.D. Thesis Fac. Agric., Al-Azhar Univ.

Khan, A.A.; S. Munir; A.R. Shakoor (1998). Development of Under-ground Baiting Technique for Control of Rats in Rice Fields in Pakistan. Int. Biodeterioation. 42: 129-134 .

King, C.M. (1984). Immigrant Killer: Introduced Predators and the Conservation of Birds in New Zealand. Oxford University Press, Auckland, NZ.

Kitahara, E. (1981). Comparative Studies on the Application of the Zinc Phosphide Rodenticide Against the Japanese Field Vole, *Microtus montebelli* (Milne-Edwarda). Forest Products Research Institute No. 314.

Maclennan, D.; J. Ferguson and N. Buxton (2000). *Rattus rattus* on the Shiant Islands a Study of Distribution and Abundance. Hebridean Naturalist, 13, 7-17.

Maher Ali, A. (1972). Planning for Rodent Control Field Experiment. 1st Symposium of Rodent and Their Control in Egypt. 241.

Maher Ali, A. and Abdel-Gawad, K.H. (1982). On Some Practical Methods to Control the Nile Grass Rat , *A.niloticus* (Desm.) . 2nd Symposium on Rodent Control in Egypt. Assiut J. Agric. Sc., 13: 81-84.

Maher Ali, A,; M.A. Salit; I. Sheta and M.G. Mourad (1974). Ectoparasites on Rodent in the Nile Valley, Upper Egypt. J. Egypt Pupl. Hlih.59 (1): 3-19.

Meehan, A.P. (1984). Rats and Mice: Their Biology and Control. Rentokil, East Grinstead, Sussex, UK.

Mikhail, G.H. (1988). Chemical Control of *Rattus sp.* in Certain Egyptian Regions. M.Sc. Thesis Fac. Agric., Ain Shams Univ., Egypt.

Miller, C.J. and T.K. Miller (1995). Population Dynamics and Diet of Rodents on Rangitoto Island, New Zealand, Including the Effect of A 1080 Poison Operation. New Zealand J. Ecol., 19 (1): 19-27.

Moran, S. (1999). Rejection of Dyed Field Rodent Baits by Feral Pigeons and Chukar Partridges. Phytoparasitica 27 (1): 9-17.

Moran, S. (2003). Toxicity of Cholecalciferol Wheat Bait to the Field Rodents *Microtus guentheri* and *Meriones tristrami.* Crop Protection, 22. 341-345.

Mourad, A.A.M. (1997). Ecological, Biological and Toxicological Studies on Rodents Species at the Newly Reclaimed Lands. M.Sc. Thesis Fac. Agric., Ain Shams Univ., Egypt.

Oconnor, C.E.; L.H. Booth (2001). Palatability of Rodent Baits to Wild House Mice. Sc., Conservation.

Parshad, V.R.; and C.S. Malhi (1995). Comparative Efficacy of Two Methods of Delivering an Anticoagulant Rodenticide to Three Species of South Asian Rodents. Int. Biodeterioration, 36 (1-2): 89-102.

Parshad, V.R.; N. Ahmad and G. Chopra (1987). Deterioration of Poultry Farm Environment by Commensal Rodents and Their Control. Int. Biodeterioration, 23 (1): 29-46.

Saied, A.A.M. (1985). Integrated Control of Rodents. Ph.D. Thesis Fac. Agric., Al-Azhar Univ., Egypt.

Salit, A.M. (1972). Ecological Studies on Wild and Domestic Rodents in Desert Area of Egypt.1st. Sc. Symp of Rodent and Their Control in Egypt: 61-70.

Shafi, M.M.; S.M. Ahmed ; A. Pervez and S. Ahmad (1992) . Enhancement of Poison Bait Acceptance Through Taste Additives in *Rattusnorvegicus*. Journal of Stored Products Research.28, (4): 239-243.

Shehab, A.; F. Samara and A. Daoud (2000). The Effectiveness of Different Bait Bases of Zinc Phosphide in Controlling Social Voles *Microtus socialis* in the Middle of Syria. The 2nd Scientific Conference of Agricultural Sciences, Assiut, Oct.

Sherwin, C.M. and E.F. Glen (2003). Cage Colour Preference and Effects of Home Cage Colour on Anxiety in Laboratory Mice. Anim. Behav., 66: 1085-1092.

ShriPrakash; S. Kumar; V. Veer; N.G. Purnanand; K.S. Pandeyc and K.M. Rao (2003). Laboratory Evaluation of Four Rodenticides Admixed in a Cereal-based Bait Against Commensal Rat, *Rattus rattus* (L.) (Rodentia: Muridae: Murinae). J. of Stored Products Research, 39. 141-147.

Singleton, G.R. and P, R. Brown (1999). Management of Mouse Plagues in Australia, Integeration of Population Ecology, Biocontrol and Best Farm Praticein Cown, P.D., Feare, C.J. Advances in Vertebrate Pest Management. Filander Verlage Furt. 189-204.

Tabeni, S. and R.A. Ojeda (2005). Ecology of the Monte Desert Small Mammals in Disturbed and Undisturbed Habitats. Journal of Arid Environment 63: 244-255.

Twigg, L.E.; G.R. Martin and T.S. Stevens (2002). Effect of Lengthy Storage on the Palatability and Efficacy of Zinc Phosphide Wheat Bait Used for Controlling House Mice. Wildlife-Research. 29 (2): 141-149.

Vaziri, A.S. and A. Farid (1995). The Comparative Efficacy of Two Rodenticides Against *Rattus norvegicus* Barkenhout and *Nesokia indica* Gray. Appl. Entomol. and Phytopathology 62) 1-2: (96-105).

Welhong, J.I.; C.R. Veitch and J. Craig (1999). An Evaluation of the Efficiency of Rodent Trapping Methods the Effect of Trap Arrangement, Cover Type and Bait. New Zealand J. Ecol., 23 (1): 45-51.

Yaghoobi-Ershadi, M.R.; A.A. Akhavan; A.R.Z. Ramazani; E. Javadian and M. M. Emami (2000). Field Trial for the Control of Zoonotic Cutaneous Leishmaniosis in Badrood, Iran. Ann., Saudi Medicine., 382-392

Yossef, A. E. (1996). Ecological, Biological and Toxicological Studies on Rats in Stores and Shoguns, Ph.D. Thesis, Fac. Agric., Menofia Univ., Egypt.

Yunker, C.E. and Guirqirs, S. (1969). Studies of Rodent Burrows and Their Ectoparasites in the Egyptian Desert. J.Egypt.Publ. Health Assoc., 44 (5): 498-542.

Zaghloul, T.M. and M. Zakaria (1986). Laboratory Evaluation of Certain Biocides Against the House Mouse, *Mus musculus* in Kuwait. Proc. 2nd. Symposium on Recent Advances in Rodent Control, Kuwait: 19.

Pages: 168-178

NATURAL ECOSYSTEM AND CLIMATE CHANGE
Edited by: **Dr. Pawan Kumar 'Bharti'; Dr. Khwairakpam Gajananda**
ISBN: 978-93-5056-745-6
Edition: 2015
Published by: **Discovery Publishing House Pvt. Ltd., New Delhi (India)**

CHAPTER - 8

Climate Change
An Overview

Shobhit Rawat

INTRODUCTION

Climate is e average weather condition of a large area over a long period of time may be 30 or 35 years. The climate of a place is permanent in nature and does not change like weather. The climate change is long period change in the information of the weather. The change is measured.

The change is measured by measuring the elements of the climate. These elements of climate are temperature, pressure, wind pattern, humidity. To understand the climate change takes some examples:

1. The duration of summer increase whereas duration of winter decreases this happens due to the climate change.
2. The level of the sea rise continuous due to climate change.

CAUSES OF CLIMATE CHANGE

Green House Gases

We can say that green house gases are responsible for climate change and Global warming. The green house gases are that gas which keeps the

Student of Mechanical Engineering, Department of Applied Science and Humanities, Dronacharya Group of Institutions, Greater Noida - 201 308, India.

atmosphere warm and maintain the average temperature of the planet. Green house gases include Carbon Dioxide (CO_2), Methane, Nitrous, and Water Vapour. Greenhouse gas emissions by world (see figure 8.1)

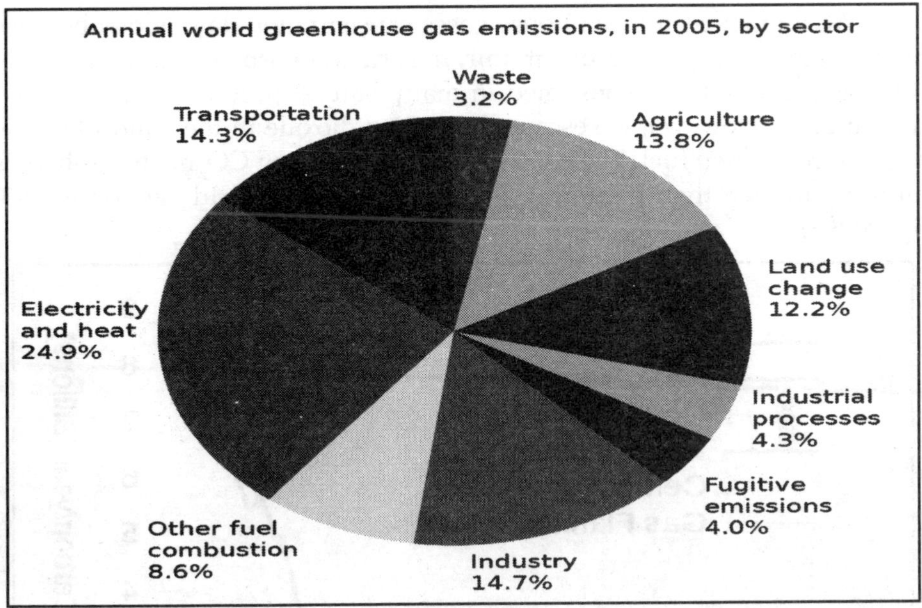

Fig. 8.1: GHGs from Various Sources

Source: http://commons.wikimedia.org/wiki/File:Annual_world_greenhouse_gas_emissions,_in_2005,_by_sector.png)

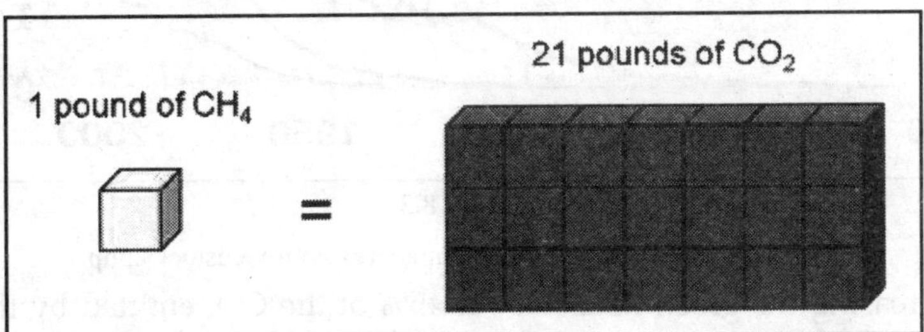

Fig. 8.2: A Single Molecules of Methane has About 25 Times of Warming Power of a Single Carbon Dioxide CO_2) Molecules

Source: http://epa.gov/climatechange/ghgemissions/gases/ch4.html

The green house gases act as the "Sanjivani Booti" for supporting the life on earth. The green house gases act as the layer, which help to keep the planet warm and maintain the planet average temperature.

In the absence of green house gases, this heat release into space and the average temperature of the planet would be below the freezing point but in that the temperature not life supported temperature.

If the green house gases present in the atmosphere in limit it support. whereas if the concentration green house gases increase it is responsible for creating many problems and this happens in today's world.

We influence on green house gases concentration day by day because many green house gases occur naturally in Earth's atmosphere. Carbon dioxide (CO_2) is produced and consumed in many natural processes that is called carbon cycle. However, we escape the carbon dioxide in the atmosphere by burning coal, fossil fuel. The concentration of releasing CO_2 in atmosphere is more by human than natural. Carbon emission by world (see figure 8.3, figure 8.4).

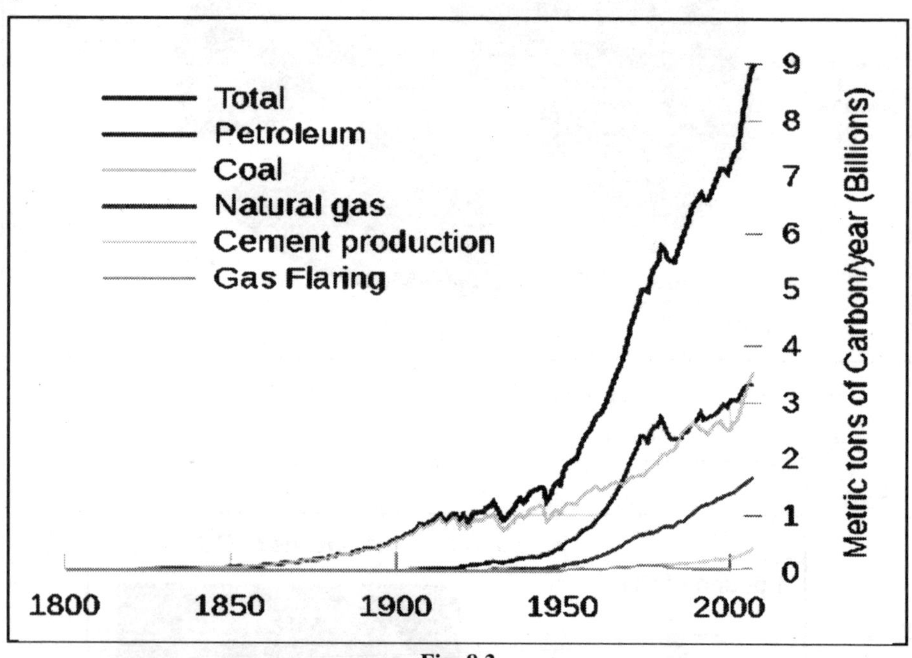

Fig. 8.3

Source: https://www.greatpointenergy.com/feedstocks.php

Increasing the green house about 45% of the CO_2 emitted by the human activities increasing the concentration of green house gases in atmosphere tends to increase the average temperature of the atmosphere. We all know about the ozone layer. The ozone layer is defected by human activities; 20 to 15 years ago we use CFC gases in A.C. and refrigerator. CFC leads to the depletion of the ozone layer and U.V. rays fall on the earth directly. CFC is present in atmosphere for long time because it is not a natural green house gas.

Today, atmosphere CO_2 concentration exceed 390 parts per million, nearly 40% higher than pre-industrial level.

Human activities have also increased other important green house gases like methane. Methane is produced by burning of fossil fuel, raising of livestock, decay of landfill waste and other activities increase sharply through 1980's before starting level off at about two-and-a half oxide has increased by roughly 15% since 1750.

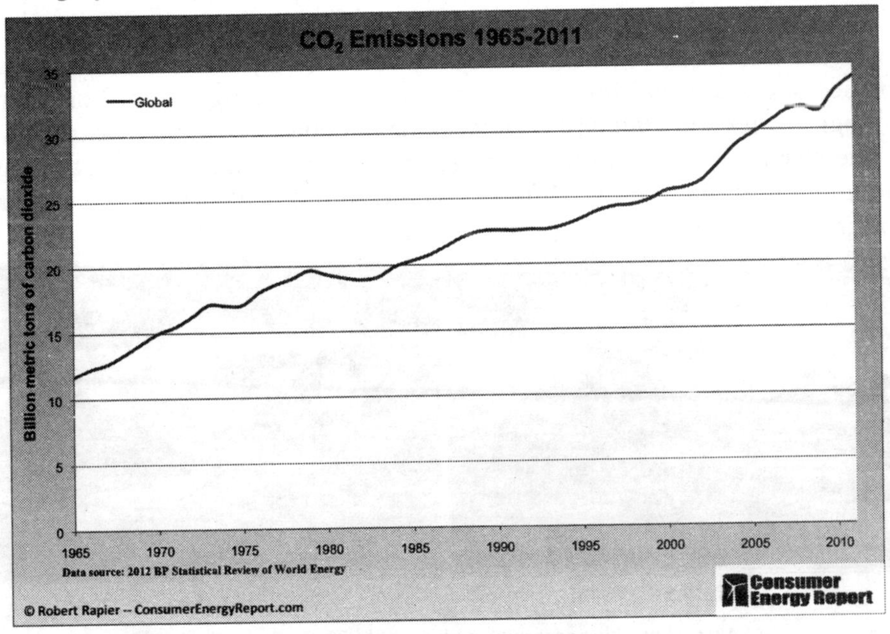

Fig. 8.4: CO_2 Emmission

Source: http://www.energytrendsinsider.com/2012/07/02/global-carbon-dioxide-emissions-facts-and-figures/)

Green house gases are referred to as forcing negotiator because of their ability to change the planets energy balance.

Green house gases regulate the earth atmosphere temperature up and down.

Carbon dioxide (CO_2) presents in the atmosphere more quantity than methane and for much longer time. A forcing negotiator. As I told that human activities are responsible for climate change. Deforestation is responsible for climate change. Deforestation is responsible for 10% to 20% excess of carbon dioxide emitted to the atmosphere each year.

Rising temperature due to the concentration of green house gases increases in atmosphere, have produce distinct pattern of warming earth surface. We see significant seasonal disappearance is observed in arctic due to stronger warming.

For example: the second half of the both century saw intense winter warming season parts of Canada, Alaska and Northern Europe and Asia, while summer warming was particularly and some other places, including parts of the US west.

Global warming is also significant on snow and ice, especially in response to the strong warming across the Arctic sea ice has dropped by roughly 10% per decade since satellite monitoring began in 1978.

This melting has especially strange in late summer expect large part of the Arctic Ocean ice free for the weeds at a time. Many of the world's glaciers and ice sheet are melting in response to the warming trend. Long term average winter snowfall and snowpack have debases in many regions, such as the sierra Neruda mountain range in western United States, Himalaya Mountain in India. See two different pictures of same Glaciers. You can find that in figure (8.5) have more ice than figure (8.6).

Fig. 8.5

Fig. 8.6

Source: http://disappearingice.blogspot.in/2012/12/glaciers.html

The excess heat caused by human emitted green house gases has warmed the world.

Water expand due to melting of glacier, ice sheet and ice caps contribute to increase the level of sea, and rivers measurement made by tide gauge and augmented by satellites show that since 1870, Global average sea level then risen by 8 inches(0.2 meter)

In India the corresponding sea level rise at the end of 21st century relative to the end of 20 century ranges. Ongoing sea level rises have already submerged several low lying islands in Sundarban displacing thousands of people.

POLLUTION

Air Pollution

Nowadays the automobile industries being growth in manufacturing the all type vehicle in all sector such as government private and public sector to make the comfortable life to people, they use these vehicle. These vehicles release the carbon mono oxide & carbon dioxide in the atmosphere. Other industries also involved to spread air pollution by electricity generation through big grantors to supply the electricity to the industry these grantors also involved in air pollution by release of gases and chemical into the atmosphere. Common gaseous pollutants include carbon monoxide, sulphur dioxide, chlorofluorocarbons (CFCs) and nitrogen oxides produced by various manmade activities.

Noise Pollution

Pollution creates by high-intensity noise which can we produced by Airplane, Jet, Traffic and Industrial noise, as well as high-intensity sonar.

Water Pollution

The pollution instinctive with the discharge of wastewater from commercial and industrial waste (intentionally or through spills) into surface water discharges of untreated domestic sewage, and chemical contaminants, such as chlorine, from treated sewage; release of waste and contaminants into surface runoff flowing to surface waters (including urban runoff and agricultural runoff, which may contain chemical fertilizers and pesticides); waste disposal and leaching into groundwater littering.

POPULATION

I think that human population give significant contribution in climate change on global warming. If human population increase rapidly, that is happened nowadays.

Then, that is not so far when we face many criticise problems regarding floods, Trench water fossil fuels etc.

If population increases they demand land for live, they demand works (factory), to fulfil the demands of people. We have to convert our agricultural lands forest land into concrete land. Otherwise violence is happened for food, work property etc.

We know if we don't have agricultural land, where our farmers grow crop, we also know without food we cannot survive. See the table (8.1) of world population and table (8.2) of growth rate in India.

The lifestyle and population are equally important. In 2008 the New York Times state that the inhabitants of developed nations of world consumer resource like oil and metals at a rate almost 32 times greater than those developing world, who make up the majority of the human population.

Some problems related with over population of human and over consumption are:

1. Inadequate fresh water and sewage treatment and affluent discharge some countries like Saudi Arabia use expensive desalination to solve the problem of water shortages.
2. Deficit of natural resources, fossil fuels. Data of fossil fuels consumed by India. See the Figure (8.7)

3. Increasing levels of air pollution, water pollution, soil contamination and noise pollution.
4. Deforestation and loss of ecosystem that valuably contribute to global atmospheric oxygen and CO_2 balance.

"It is bad to hear that about eight million hectares of forest are lost each year."

5. Mass extinction from reduced habitat in tropical forest due to slash and burnt techniques that sometimes are practiced by shifting cultivation, especially in country with rapidly expanding rural population present extinction rates may be as high as 1, 40,000 spectres lost per year. As February 2011, the IUCIU red list a total of 801 animal spectres having gone extinct during human history.
6. Unhygienic living condition for many based upon water resources depletion discharge of raw sewage and solid waste disposal. See the data of solid waste composition in world. See the Figure (6.8).

Table 8.1: Population of Major Countries

Rank	Country (or Dependent Territory)	Population	Date	% of World Population	Source
1.	China	1,367,140,000	October 6, 2014	19%	Official population clock
2.	India	1,260,550,000	October 6, 2014	17.5%	Population clock
3.	United States	318,861,000	October 6, 2014	4.43%	Official population clock
4.	Indonesia	252,164,800	July 1, 2014	3.51%	Official estimate
5.	Brazil	203,250,000	October 6, 2014	2.83%	Official population clock
6.	Pakistan	188,020,000	July 1, 2014	2.61%	Official annual projection
7.	Nigeria	178,517,000	July 1, 2014	2.48%	UN projection
8.	Bangladesh	157,092,000	October 6, 2014	2.18%	Official population clock
9.	Russia[9]	146,149,200	August 1, 2014	2.03%	Official estimate
10.	Japan	127,040,000	September 1, 2014	1.77%	Monthly official estimate

Source: http://en.wikipedia.org/wiki/Population

Table 8.2: Population Growth Rate (%) in India

Country	2000	2001	2002	2003	2004	2005	2006	2007	2008	2009	2010	2011	2012
India	1.58	1.55	1.51	1.47	1.44	1.4	1.38	1.61	1.58	1.55	1.38	1.34	1.31

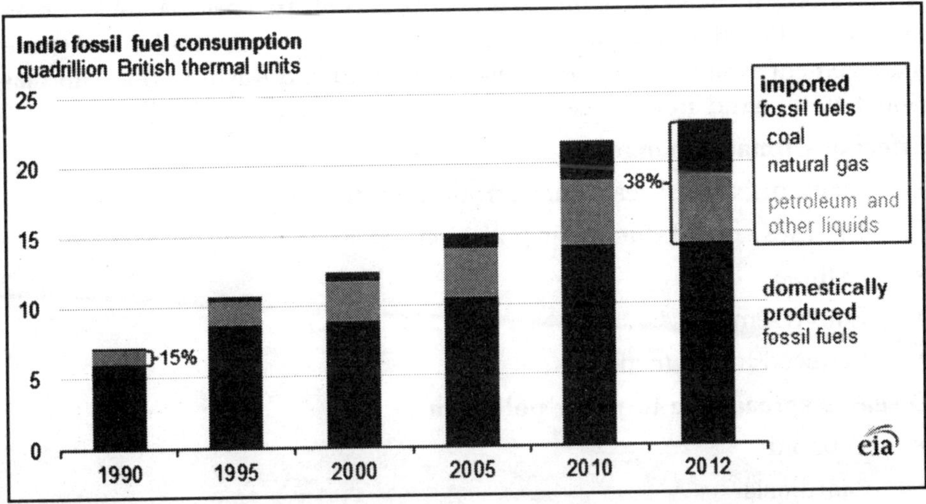

Fig. 8.7: Fossil Fuel Consumption in India

Source: http://www.eia.gov/todayinenergy/detail.cfm?id=17551

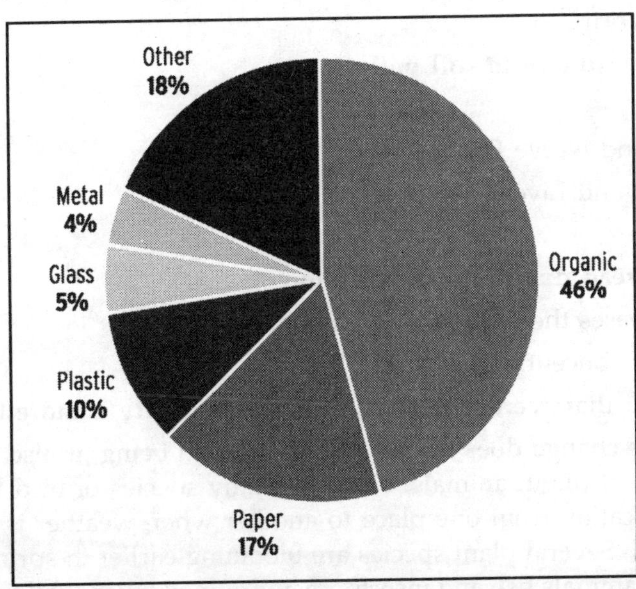

Fig. 6.8: Solid Waste Composition in World

Source: http://www.truth-out.org/news/item/15432-garbage-in-garbage-out-struggling-haiti-signs-costly-private-garbage-disposal-deal?tmpl=component)

The fraction of total precipitation (Continuous condensation of water vapour in the air result in the formation of minute droplets of water.

When these droplets join together, they form bigger drops, which became become too heavy to float and start falling down) falling in the heaviest 1% of rain storm increase by about 20% over past century. This changed increase the risk of flooding and put additional stress on sewage and storm water management system. It may be causes of Jammu and Kashmir flood and last year Uttarakhand flood.

Effect of Climate Change

1. Many diseases spread our surrounding due to pollution

   Diseases spread due to air pollution

- Asthma
- Emphysema
- Reduced lung function

Diseases spread due to water pollution

- Typhoid
- Giardiasis
- Amoebiasis
- Ascariasis
- Hookworm

Diseases spread due to soil pollution

- Censer
- Brain and Nerve Damage
- Kidney and Liver Diseases
- Malaria

Diseases spread due to noise pollution

- It decreases the efficiency of a man
- Lack of concentration

It is shocked that average percent of diseases in city is more than village.

2. Climate change does not affect only human being ,it also effect many. Species of plant, animals, bird etc .Many species of bird have shifted their location from one place to another when weather is not suitable for bird. Several plant species are blooming earlier in spring and some bird, mammals,fish and insects are migrating earlier, while other species are altering their seasonal breeding pattern. Many species extinct from their original habitat due to improper climate conditions.

3. It also affected our agriculture and food production is also effected by the climate change. As we see in this year monsoon is very week in our country due to which farmer is not able to grow crop and also not able to irrigate the field.
4. In summer we see that temperature increase up to 40 to 50. This leads to more evaporation and make the land unfertile land.
5. Sea water become more acidic because CO_2 reacts in seawater to form carbonic acid, the acidification of the world's oceans is an- other certain outcome of elevated CO_2 concentrations in the atmosphere. It is estimated that the oceans have absorbed between one-quarter and one-third of the excess CO_2 from human activities, becoming nearly 30% more acidic than during preindustrial times.

Step to minimise effect of climate change and global warming

As above discussion we see that green house gases play significant role in climate change than population.

To minimise the effect of green houses gases we have to adopted eco-friendly technology. Such as:

1. We can use solar energy, hydropower and wind energy to full fill the demand of electricity.
2. We can use CNG (Compressed Natural Gas) in vehicle.
3. We can use public transport.
4. We can improve our engines and machines to minimise the emission of Co_2 gas.
5. We have to put emphasis on plantation.
6. We have to adopted sustainable type of development our environment.

If we want to save to humanity from the crises of food that we should adopted terrace farming.

Use more efficient method for insulating, heating, cooling and lighting.

Buildings, upgrade industrial equipment and process to be more efficient and encourage the purchase of efficient home appliance and vehicles.

CONCLUSION

As we discussed in our article, what is climate change? Effect of climate change, causes of climate change now time to think how we can minimise the effect of climate change from our atmosphere.

To minimise or to stop global warming first of all we have to change our thinking regarding climate or atmosphere and we need to aware the people about climate change.

REFERENCES

Pawan K.B. *Climate Change and Agriculture* (First ed). Delhi: Discovery Publishing House, 2012.

Pawan K.B. Environment Monitoring and Assessment in Antarctica PK Bharti - Emerging Trends in Biotechnological Research, 2012.

Graf, H.F.; Feichter, J.; Langmann, B. "Volcanic Sulphur Emissions: Estiamtes of Source Strength and its Contribution to the Global Sulphate Distribution" (pdf). Journal of Geophysical Research: Atmospheres 102: 10727-10738. doi:10.1029/96JD03265. 1997.

"IPCC Fourth Assessment Report: Climate Change 2007". http://www.ipcc.ch/index.htm. Retrieved 31 July, 2014.

"Volcanic Gases and Their Effects". U.S. Department of the Interior. 2006-01-10. Retrieved 21 January, 2008.

Index

A

A. niloticus, 106, 123
Acacia catechu, 7
Acacia mangium, 7
Acacia nilotica, 8
Agriculture Research Review, 88
Agroforestry for climate change mitigation and livelihood security, 1-20
  agroforestry for
    adaptation to climate change, 13-14
    fuelwood production, 9
    mitigating climate change, 14-16
  alley cropping, 7-8
  apiculture with trees, 12
  aquaforestry, 12-13
  benefits from
    agroforestry, 3
    alley cropping, 8
    shelterbelts, 10-11
  constraints in agroforestry technology adoption, 17-19
  crop combinations with plantation crops, 9
  decreasing land resources, 4
  definitions of agroforestry, 2-3
  depletion of forest, 5-6
  different agroforestry systems in India, 7
  economic benefits, 4
  environmental benefits, 3-4
  fuel wood crisis, 5
  homegardens, 12
  introduction, 2
  limiting carrying capacity of the land, 4-5
  multipurpose trees and shrubs on field bunds, 8-9
  multispecies tree gardens, 7
  mushroom in mixed tree species, 13
  need of agroforestry, 4
  overexploitation of land resource, 5
  overgrazing, 5
  protein bank, 11
  role of agroforestry in adapting and mitigating climate change, 13
  scope of agroforestry in India, 6-7
  shelterbelts, 10
  social benefits, 4
  soil erosion, 5
  trees and shrubs on pasture, 11
Akpa Martins, O., 71
Aloe vera, 9
Ani Augustine, O., 71
Arctic Ocean, 172
Arctic sea, 172
Artocarpus spp., 7
Arvicanthis niloticus, 92
Arya, Garima, 21
Aspergillus, 25
Assiut Governorte of Egypt, 102
Assiut University, 106
Azadirachta indica, 8

B

Bambusa, 10

Bhakra Dam, 33

Bombax malabaricum, 11

Bonaventure, C., 57

Boopphiuls microplus, 77

Brassica rapa, 66

C

Cassia siamea, 9

Catchment Area Treatment plan (CAT), 37

Catla, 12

CFC, 54, 170, 173

Chand, Kesar, 31

Climate change, 168-178

causes of

climate change, 168-172

atmosphere CO_2 concentration exceed 390 parts per million, 170-172

green house gases, 168-170

effect of climate change, 176-177

introduction, 168

pollution, 172-173

air pollution, 172-173

noise pollution, 173

water pollution, 173

population, 173-177

Clostridium thermoacetium, 26

CNG (Compressed Natural Gas), 177

Cordial dichtotoma, 11

Cumulative Impact Assessment (CIA), 47

D

Dalbergia sissoo, 13

Dalbergia, 10

Desoky, Abd El-Aleem Saad Soliman, 87

E

E., Oyeagu Chika, 71

Echezona, 57

Ecosystem and Environment, 88

Effect of climate change on pesticide use, 57-70

adaptation strategies, 67

benefits and problems of using pesticides, 60-61

improved productivity, 60

other areas, 61

protect crop losses/yield reductions, 60

quality of food, 61

vector disease control, 60-61

classification of pesticides, 59

climate change, 58

definition of terms, 58

effects of climate change on pesticide usage, 62-64

fungal diseases, 64-65

how to mitigate the problems, 66-67

implication of climate change for pest and diseases, 64

insect pests, 64

insect populations, 65

insect-borne diseases, 65

introduction, 57-58

pest outbreak, 66

pesticide, 58

problems of pesticides usage, 61-62

weeds, 65-66

EIA, 47

El-Ghorieb Farm, 135, 136, 139

Environmental impacts of hydropower projects, 31-50

chemical properties of the soil, 41

effectiveness of environmental impact assessment studies, 37

estimation of major soil nutrients, 35-36

hydropower potential in river satluj basin, 36-37

introduction, 32

ionic components and trace metals of water, 45

measurement of soil moisture, 34-35
methodology, 33-36
soil analysis method, 34
soil moisture constants, 34
nitrogen, 41-42
pH, EC and TDS, 41
phosphorus, 42
potassium, 42
results and discussion, 36-45
soil and water analysis adjoining area of hydro power projects in satluj basin, 37-39
soil color, 39
soil moisture, 39-41
soil pH and electrical conductivity, 35
soil quality of under construction projects in upper satluj river basin, 43-44
soil texture, 39
status of water quality at adjacent areas of HEPs in satluj basin, 44-45
study area, 32-33
water analysis, 36
Escherichia coli, 26

F

Faculty Farm, 137, 139
Felis chaus nilotica, 153
Food and Agricultural Organization, 58
Fusarium, 25

G

Gerbillus gerbillus, 89, 92
GHG, 58, 63
Glaciers, 172
Global warming and microorganisms, 21-30
introduction, 22
its consequences, 24-25
microorganism reduce the global warming, 25-28
why and how it happened, 22-24
Global warming, 22
Gmelina arborea, 7
Green House Effect (GHE), 22

H

HEPs, 32
Himachal Pradesh State Electricity Board, 46

I

ICRAF, 3
Indian Himalayan Region (IHR), 32
Integrated Pest Management Approach (IPMA), 162
Intergovernmental Panel on Climate Change (IPCC), 24
International Biodeterioration, 88

K

Kaushik, Purshotam, 21
Khanna, Monika, 51
Khanna, Roma, 51
Kuniyal, Jagdish Chandra, 31

L

Livelihood security, 1-20

M

M. musculus, 110
Mammalian Biology, 88
Management strategies for rodents within different ecosystems, 87-167
active burrows method, 94, 146
biological control, 97-98
of rodent, 153-155
chemical control, 98-102, 155-159
colour preference of rodent baits, 94-95, 105-106, 146-150
colour preference under
field conditions, 146-147
laboratory conditions, 147-150
of rodent bait, 160
determination of the population density of rodents by using different methods, 89, 104-105, 110-143, 159-160
feces method, 93, 144-145

food consumption method, 94
food preference of rodent baits, 95-96, 106
food consumption method, 146
food preference of rodent baits, 150-151, 160-161
introduction, 87-88
materials and methods, 103-107
mechanical control, 96-97, 152-153
review of literature, 88-89
results and discussion, 107-110
rodent control, 96, 106-107, 152-159, 161-162
species composition of rodents, 89
species composition of rodents in cultivated and reclaimed lands, 103-104, 107-110, 159
trapping method, 89-93, 110-143
Management Strategies of Rodents (MSR), 162
Managing Rodent Pests (MRP), 162
Mangifera indica, 7
Mangifera, 10
Mansarover lake, 32
MFCs, 28
Microtus socialis, 94
Millennium Development Goals, 62
Mrigal, 12
Mus musculus, 89

N

National Hydroelectric Power Corporation, 46
National Thermal Power Corporation (NTPC), 46
National Wasteland Development Board, 6
Naturally Occurring Biological Control Agent, 161
New York Times, 173
NOBÁ, 97, 106
Nocardia Streptomyces, 25

O

Ogechi, Vivian, 57
Osadebe, 57

P

Participatory Technology Development (PTD), 17
Patra, Alok Kumar, 1
Pesticides, 57-70
Phoenix dactifera, 7
Phoma, 25
Pinus, 10

R

R.r. alexandrines, 127
Raksa Taal, 32
Rattus rattus frugivorus, 89, 107, 118, 127
Rawat, Shobhit, 168
Rhusradicans L., 66
River Longcchen Khabab, 32
River Sutlej, 32
Rohu, 12
Role of human being in changing global environment and its impact on human health, 51-56
introduction, 51-53
impact of environmental change on human health, 54-55
role of human being in changing environment, 53-54
Ruminant animals to climate change and its mitigation strategies, 71-86
benefits of reducing enteric methane emissions, 81
fats and oilseeds, 79
feeding higher grain diets, 78
grain type, 78-79
immunization, 80
introduction, 72-73
ionophores, 80
methane, 73
methanogenic archaea, 75

mitigation strategies of methane production by ruminants, 78-81

probiotics, 80

reducing CH_4 by increasing

animal productivity, 81

feed conversion efficiency, 81

relationship between greenhouse gases, greenhouse effects, global warming and climate change, 74

rumen microbiology, 75

ruminant animal and methane production, 76

ruminant physiology, 74

use of corn silage and small grain silages, 79-80

use of legumes, 79

vulnerability of livestock sector to climate change, 77-78

S

Saccharomyces cerevisiae, 80

Sanjivani Booti, 169

Satluj basin, 31-50

Sharma, Dev Dutt, 31

Strategic Environment Assessment (SEA), 47

Syzygium, 10

T

Transfer of Technology (ToT), 17

Tricoderma, 25

U

United Nations Framework, 58

USEPA, 58

V

Vulpes vulpes, 98